Memory Thinking for C & C++ Linux Diagnostics

Slides with Descriptions and Source Code Illustrations

Second Edition

Dmitry Vostokov
Software Diagnostics Services

OpenTask

Memory Thinking for C & C++ Linux Diagnostics: Slides with Descriptions and Source Code Illustrations, Second Edition

Published by OpenTask, Republic of Ireland

OpenTask books are available through booksellers and distributors worldwide. For further information or comments, send requests to press@opentask.com.

Product and company names mentioned in this book may be trademarks of their owners.

A CIP catalog record for this book is available from the British Library.

ISBN-13: 978-1912636563 (Paperback)

Revision 2.03 (May 2025)

Table of Contents

Preface

This full-color reference book is a part of the Accelerated C & C++ for Linux Diagnostics training course organized by Software Diagnostics Services (www.patterndiagnostics.com). The text contains slides, brief notes highlighting particular points, and illustrative source code fragments. The second edition added 45 Visual Studio Code projects with more than 5,500 lines of code. The book's detailed Table of Contents makes the usual Index redundant. We hope this reference is helpful for the following audiences:

- C and C++ developers who want to deepen their knowledge;
- Software engineers developing and maintaining products on Linux platforms;
- Technical support, escalation, DevSecOps, cloud and site reliability engineers dealing with complex software issues;
- Quality assurance engineers who test software on Linux platforms;
- Security and vulnerability researchers, reverse engineers, malware and memory forensics analysts.

If you encounter any error, please use the contact form on the Software Diagnostics Services web site or, alternatively, via Twitter @DumpAnalysis.

Facebook group:

http://www.facebook.com/groups/dumpanalysis

LinkedIn page and group:

https://www.linkedin.com/company/software-diagnostics-institute/
https://www.linkedin.com/groups/8473045/

About the Author

Dmitry Vostokov is an internationally recognized expert, speaker, educator, scientist, inventor, and author. He founded the pattern-oriented software diagnostics, forensics, and prognostics discipline (Systematic Software Diagnostics) and Software Diagnostics Institute (DA+TA: DumpAnalysis.org + TraceAnalysis.org). Vostokov has also authored over 50 books on software diagnostics, anomaly detection and analysis, software and memory forensics, root cause analysis and problem solving, memory dump analysis, debugging, software trace and log analysis, reverse engineering, and malware analysis. He has over 30 years of experience in software architecture, design, development, and maintenance in various industries, including leadership, technical, and people management roles. Dmitry founded OpenTask Iterative and Incremental Publishing (OpenTask.com) and Software Diagnostics Technology and Services (former Memory Dump Analysis Services) PatternDiagnostics.com. In his spare time, he explores Software Narratology and Quantum Software Diagnostics. His interest areas are theoretical software diagnostics and its mathematical and computer science foundations, application of formal logic, semiotics, artificial intelligence, machine learning, and data mining to diagnostics and anomaly detection, software diagnostics engineering and diagnostics-driven development, diagnostics workflow and interaction. Recent interest areas also include functional programming, cloud native computing, monitoring, observability, visualization, security, automation, applications of category theory to software diagnostics, development and big data, and diagnostics of artificial intelligence.

Introduction

Original Training Course Name

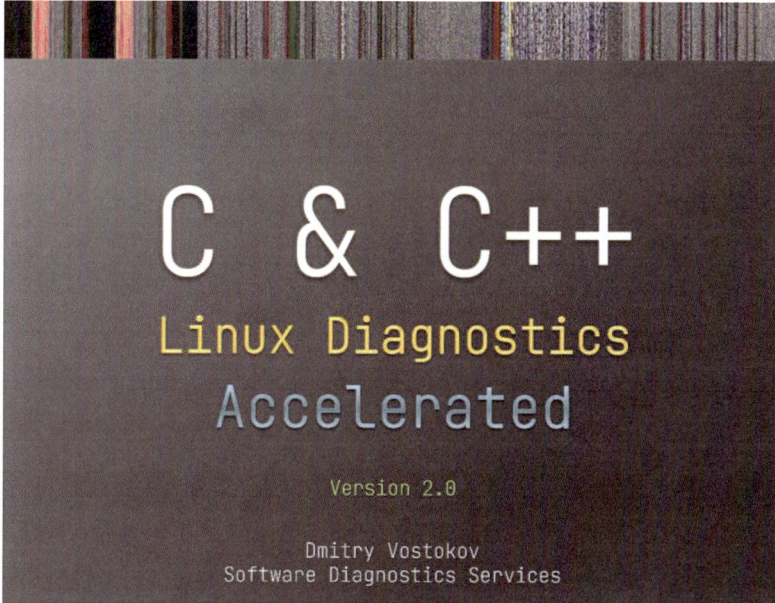

Prerequisites

To get most of this training, you are expected to have basic development experience in a programming language other than C or C++ and optional basic memory dump analysis experience. I also included the necessary x64 and A64 disassembly reviews for some topics.

Training Goals

Training Goals

- Review common fundamentals of C and C++

- Review C++ specifics

- Use GDB for learning C and C++ internals

- See how C and C++ knowledge is used during diagnostics and debugging

© 2024 Software Diagnostics Services

Our primary goal is to learn C and C++ and its internals in an accelerated fashion. First, we review common C and C++ fundamentals necessary for software diagnostics. Then, we learn various C and C++ features focusing on memory and internals. We also see examples of how the knowledge of C and C++ helps in diagnostics and debugging.

Training Principles

Training Principles

- Talk only about what I can show

- Lots of pictures

- Lots of examples

- Original content and examples

© 2024 Software Diagnostics Services

There were many training formats to consider, and I decided that the best way is to concentrate on slides and code examples you can verify.

Schedule

Schedule

◉ std::vector<Session> sessions;

◉ assert(sessions.size() == 12);

◉ assert(sessions.capacity() > 12);

© 2024 Software Diagnostics Services

I plan the training to have only 12 one-hour sessions, but I may extend it to more sessions if necessary to fit all material in sufficient detail.

Training Idea

Training Idea

◉ Similar course for Windows

◉ Core dump analysis training

◉ Reversing training

◉ Linux API training

© 2024 Software Diagnostics Services

After I created a similar Windows-based training, it was natural to port it to Linux. Also, attendees of core dump analysis and reversing training courses asked questions related to C and C++, and I realized that they would have also benefitted if they had this training. This training may also fill some gaps between these courses. Finally, I recently developed the **Accelerated Linux API** training course (see the References section at the end of the book), where solid knowledge of classic C and C++ is assumed, and the current C and C++ course may provide such knowledge.

Version 2.0 Idea

Unfortunately, the first version didn't include some important topics and source code projects were not included too. After I developed the **Memory Thinking for Rust** training with extensive source code support, I realized that a similar project structure would bene-fit C and C++ training.

General C & C++ Aspects

The general C and C++ aspects that we discuss in this course:

- Philosophy of pointers
- Structures, classes, and objects
- Promotions and conversions
- Macros, types, and synonyms
- Source code organization, PImpl
- Pointer dereference walkthrough
- Functions and function pointers
- Inheritance
- Operators, function objects
- Destructors, virtual destructors
- Local stack variables and values
- Memory operators and expressions

- Alignment
- Slicing
- Iterators as pointers
- Lambdas and their internals
- Threads and synchronization
- Memory and pointers
- Basic types
- Memory and structures
- Uniform initialization
- Memory storage
- References (lvalues and rvalues)
- Values, lvalues, rvalues
- Constant values and expressions
- Namespaces
- Constructors, copy, move, assignment
- Virtual functions, pure methods
- VTBL and VPTR
- Access levels
- Overloading, overriding
- Templates
- Memory ownership, RAII
- Smart pointers
- Deleted and default members
- Unions
- Conversion constructors
- Variadic functions and templates
- Enumerations

Highlighted topics are new to this edition.

What We Do Not Cover

There are some remaining C++ topics that we did not include in the first edition but promised to include in the second edition:

- Legacy C
- Concepts
- Coroutines
- Modules
- Tasks
- Ranges
- Container and algorithm semantics and pragmatics
- Container allocators
- Polymorphic allocators

We promise to include these topics in the third edition of this course.

Linux C & C++ Aspects

In addition, we also discuss related Linux aspects, including:

- Linux-specific type aliases and macros
- LP64
- Necessary x64 and A64 disassembly
- Parameter passing
- Implicit parameter

Why C & C++?

Why C & C++?

- ◉ Interfacing
- ◉ Malware analysis
- ◉ Vulnerability analysis and exploitation
- ◉ Reversing
- ◉ Diagnostics
- ◉ Low-level debugging
- ◉ OS Monitoring
- ◉ Memory forensics
- ◉ Crash and hang analysis
- ◉ Secure coding
- ◉ Static code analysis
- ◉ Trace and log analysis

© 2024 Software Diagnostics Services

First, why did we create this course? Even if you don't develop in C and C++, the knowledge of C and C++ and their internals is necessary for many software construction and post-construction activities:

- Interfacing
- Malware analysis
- Vulnerability analysis and exploitation
- Reversing
- **Diagnostics**
- Low-level debugging
- **OS Monitoring**
- Memory forensics
- **Crash and hang analysis**
- Secure coding
- Static code analysis
- **Trace and log analysis**

In this training, we mostly look at C and C++ from a software diagnostics perspective. This perspective includes memory dump analysis and, partially, trace and log analysis. The knowledge of C and C++ is tacitly assumed in my other courses, where most abnormal software behavior modeling exercises are written in C and C++. Of course, there is an intersection of what we learn with other areas.

Which C & C++?

Which C and C++? We look at a unified presentation approach combining all C and C++ variants. Since this course is about diagnostics and not designing and implementing code, we generally do not make distinctions in slides. It is not possible to cover all the differences in the short time that we have. We also describe things as they are in Linux programming, not as they ought to be from the latest C++ standards. However, in the second edition, we provide separate source code projects for separate categories: plain C (we choose C11 in makefiles), C++ as a better C (modifications needed to make C code compile as C++), classic C++ (before C++11), and modern C++ (mostly C++17) with some illustrated features from C++20 and C++23.

My History of C & C++

This history slide is only about C and C++ languages. Despite many years, it is still easy to recall when I started learning C. It was shortly after I started my university education. And although my first programming language was FORTRAN, I read the classic K&R book in a library. C++ is harder to recall, but most likely, it was in 1989, at least according to my old CV, which is the source of truth. I definitely started using C++ in commercial projects around 1991 but used it as a better C, and there was no standard template library (STL) at that time. I recall some fascinating C++ GUI frameworks for MS-DOS, like Zinc. In

1994-1995, I designed a word processor, and in the process, I implicitly used many design patterns I later discovered in the GOF book in 2000. The authors also use a word processor for illustration. I mainly understood C++ as C++ in 2000 when I read a book about CORBA distributed object technology that used C++. I continued learning C++ by reading many books of that time and learned the merits of using STL and also how to use it effectively. In 2001, I joined a company that developed C++ static analysis tools, and this greatly improved my C++ knowledge up to the expert level at that time. C++03 didn't have major changes compared to C++98, and this is why I included it with C++98 for the year 2001. In 2003, things turned out unexpectedly as I moved from full-time development using C++ to full-time memory dump analysis of C++ programs with Mac OS X core dump analysis of user space (BSD) in 2012 and Linux user space core dump analysis in 2015. I continued using C++03 for writing diagnostic tools, though. In 2016, I learned that the language completely changed to C++11/14. I came back to full-time C++ programming in late 2017, where I also started using language features from C++17. In 2020, I moved to functional programming in Scala, which also influenced my C++ coding for new projects. I started using C++20 last year, and this year – C++23. Last year I also switched from Scala to Rust and wrote **Memory Thinking for Rust** book, which was beneficial for me to see certain C and C++ aspects in the new light.

Zinc
https://en.wikipedia.org/wiki/Zinc_Application_Framework

Old CV
https://opentask.com/Vostokov/CV.htm

C and C++ Mastery Process

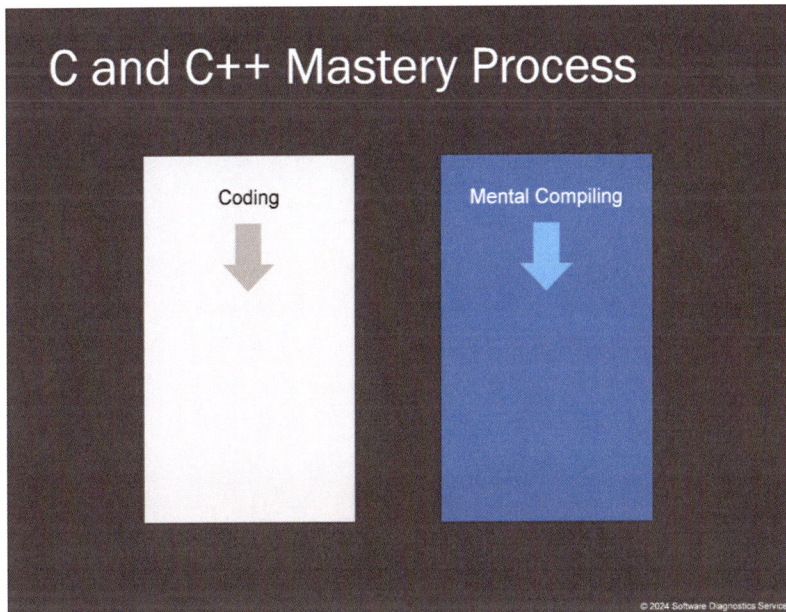

Despite high-level features in C++, there's still much low-level overlap with C, and when I program in C and C++, I mentally compile to memory. This helps when I have a doubt about whether this or that construct is safe. And I also believe that looking at how C and C++ constructs are implemented in memory greatly helps in learning these languages.

Thought Process

This slide about a thought process when using a programming language is perhaps controversial. With C and C++, we think about memory; with Scala/FP, we think about functions; and with Python, we think about data.

Philosophy of Pointers

We start with pointers, the most important concept in C and also in C++. I originally created this approach in 2015 but now extended it for this training. The second edition also adds source code projects in C and several flavors of C++.

Pointer

Conceptually, a pointer is an entity that refers (or points) to some other entity. We say entity, not an object, so as not to confuse it with objects in C++ or objects in object-oriented programming. This can be my finger, for example, pointing to an apple.

Pointer Dereference

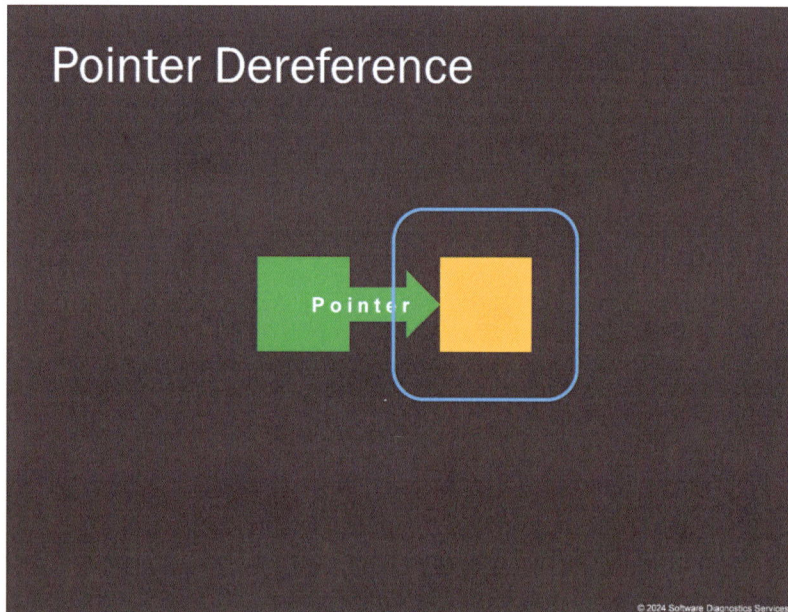

A pointer dereference is an act of getting the entity it references for further inspection or usage. Imagine I point to an apple, and you grab it to eat.

One to Many

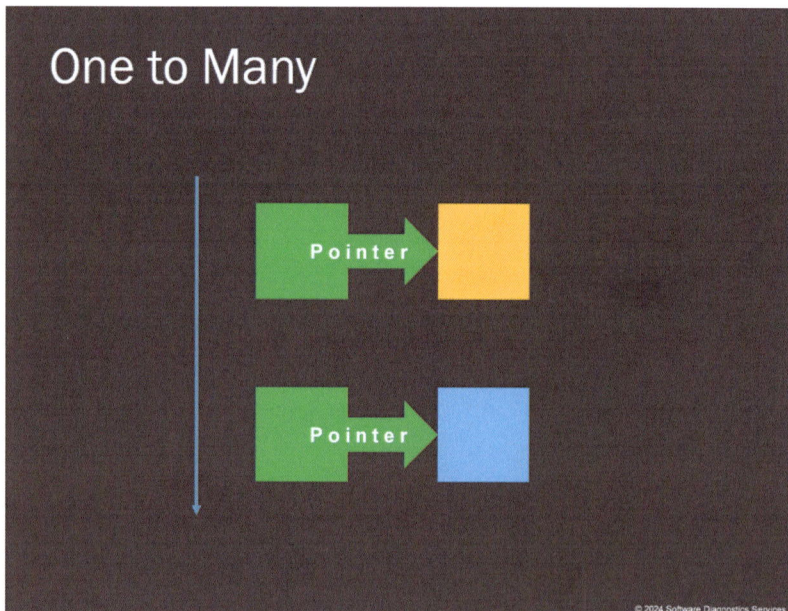

During its lifetime, a pointer may point to different entities. If no pointer points to an entity, it may become lost in certain execution scenarios, the so-called memory leak.

Many to One

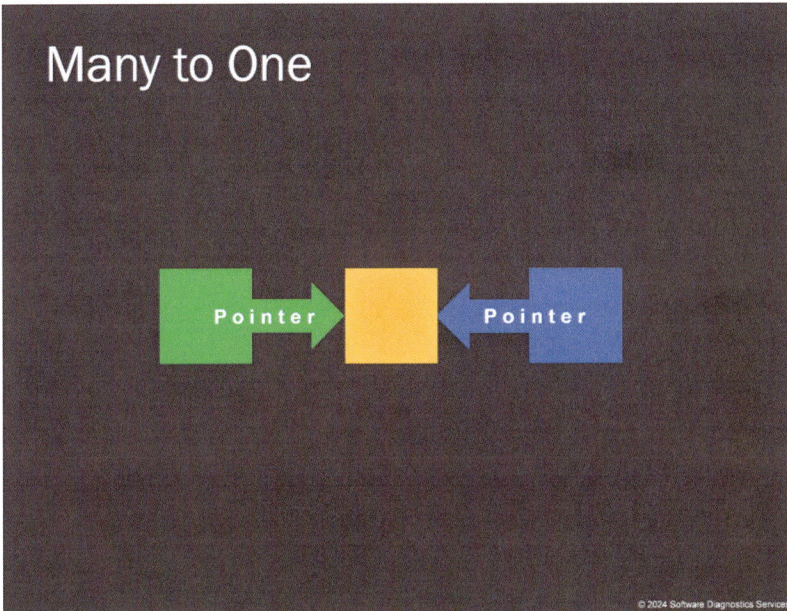

Several pointers can refer (or point) to the same entity. For example, two people are pointing to the same apple. So, conceptually, pointers are distinct from entities they point to. Should we call the latter pointees?

Many to One Dereference

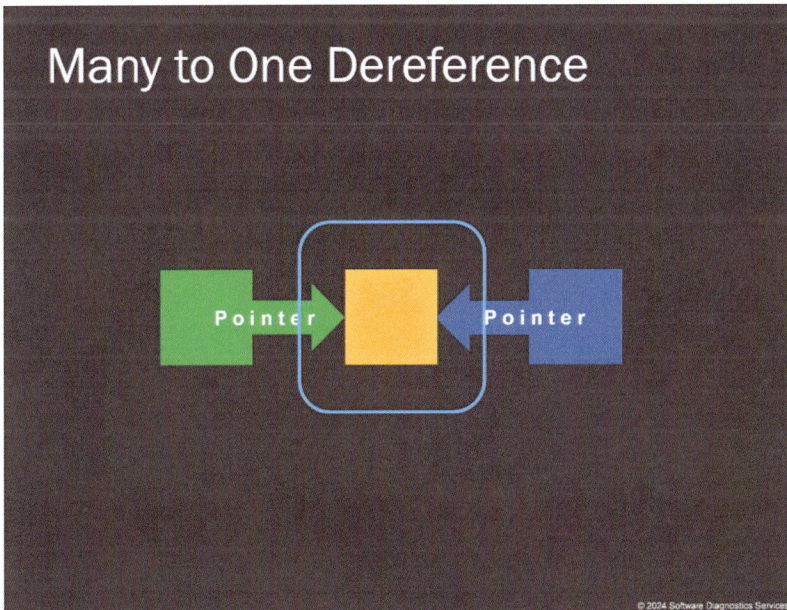

Of course, if you dereference two pointers pointing to the same entity, you get the same entity. If someone else grabs an apple, I point to, at the same time as you do, you both get the same apple.

Invalid Pointer

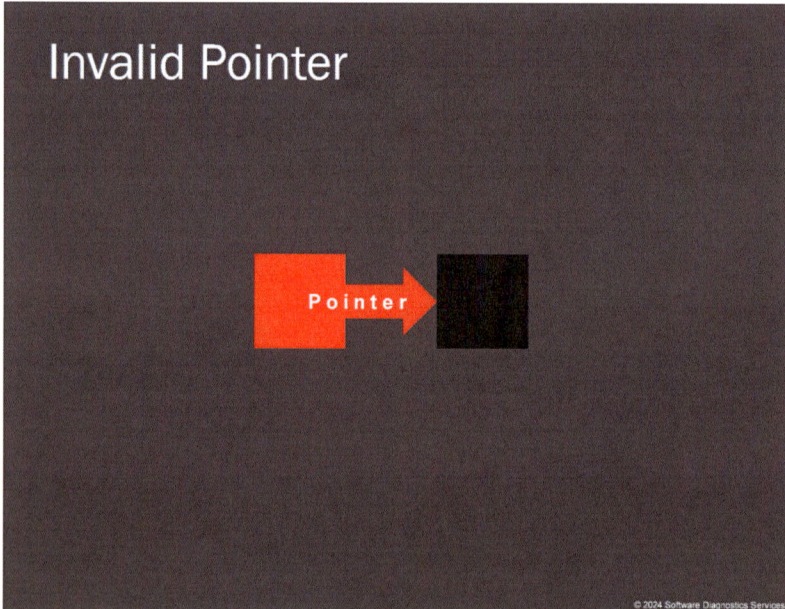

Some pointers may be invalid; for example, I may point to an imaginary apple.

Invalid Pointer Dereference

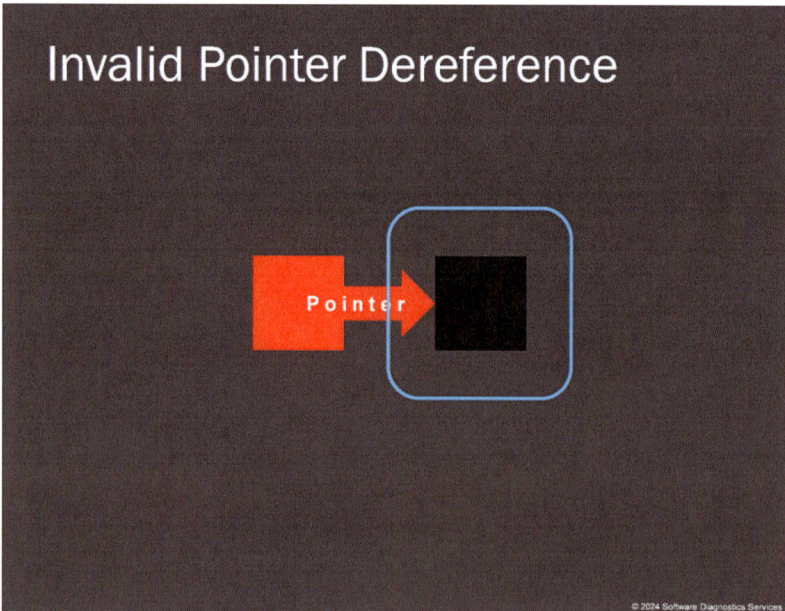

When you dereference an invalid pointer, you get a problem; for example, you fail to get an imaginary apple I point to. Or the apple can be in a cage, inaccessible.

Wild (Dangling) Pointer

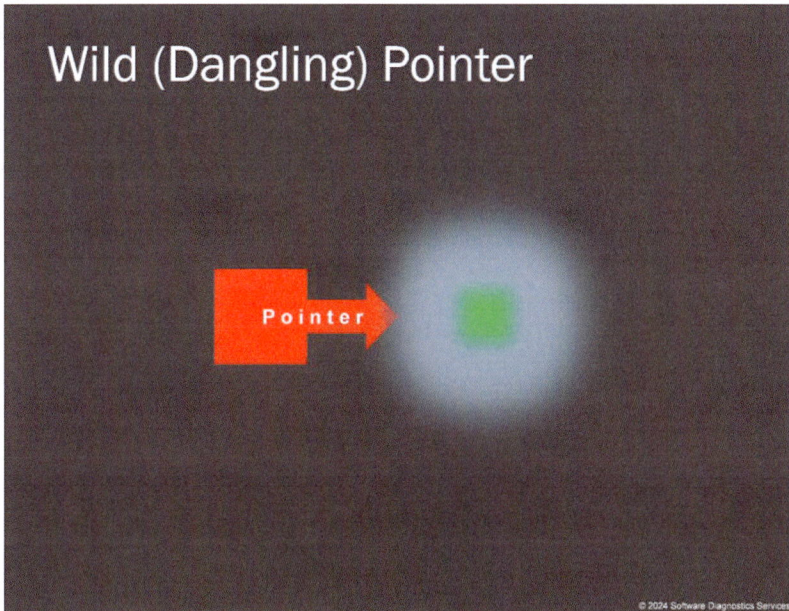

Some pointers are called dangling – they used to point to valid entities some time ago but not anymore, so a dereference fails. You're reaching for an apple that I point to, but someone snatches it a split second ago.

Pointer to Pointer

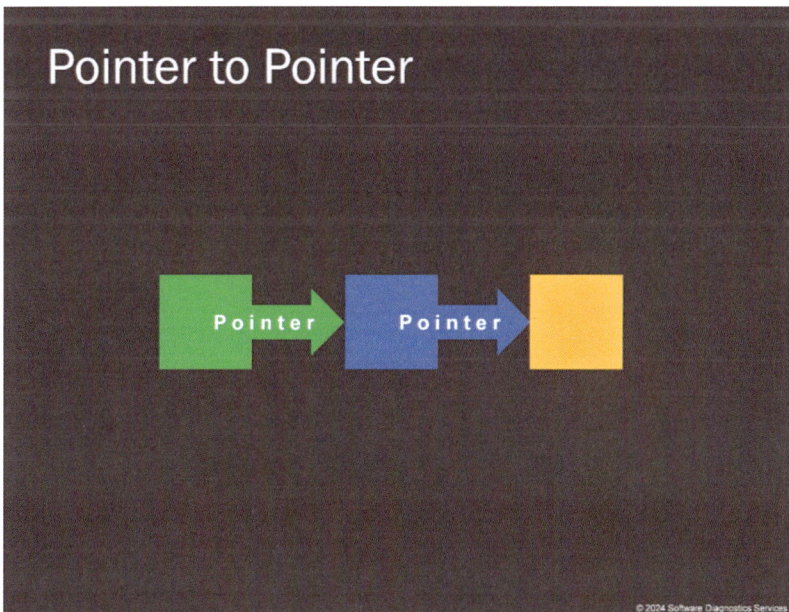

Since a pointer is also an entity that can be pointed to, there can be a chain of pointers. You point to me; I point to an apple.

Pointer to Pointer Dereference

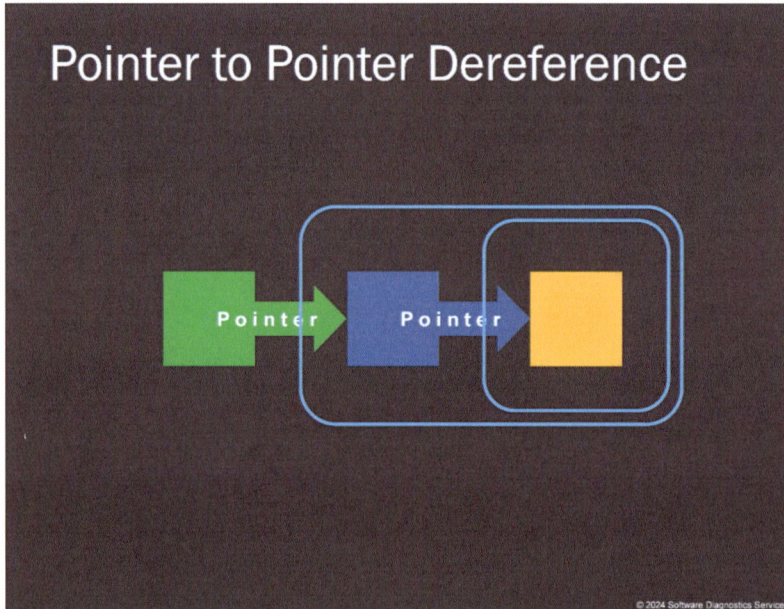

When we dereference the first pointer, we get an entity, another pointer, which we can also dereference to get the underlying entity. You point to me, but an alien snatches me with an apple I point to. Inside a ship, another alien takes an apple for analysis.

Naming Pointers and Entities

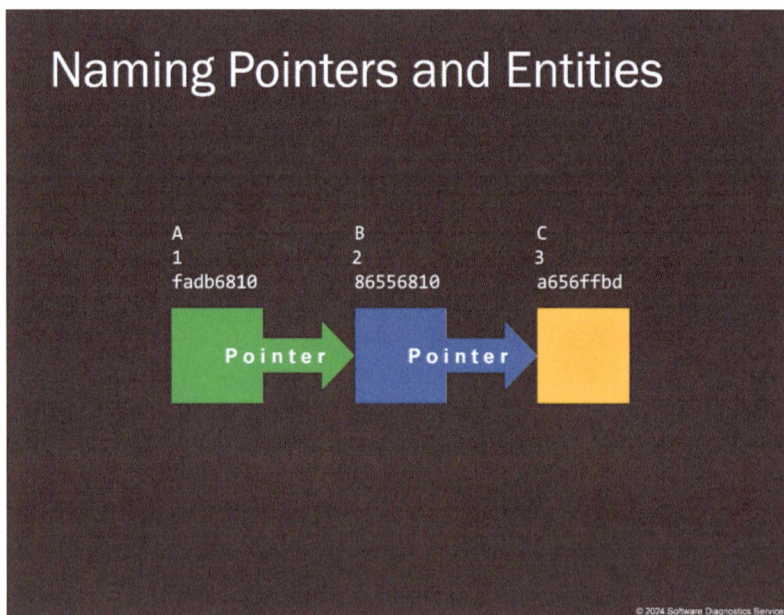

Names are distinct from entities. They can be programming language identifiers or just unique numbers or IDs.

Names as Pointer Content

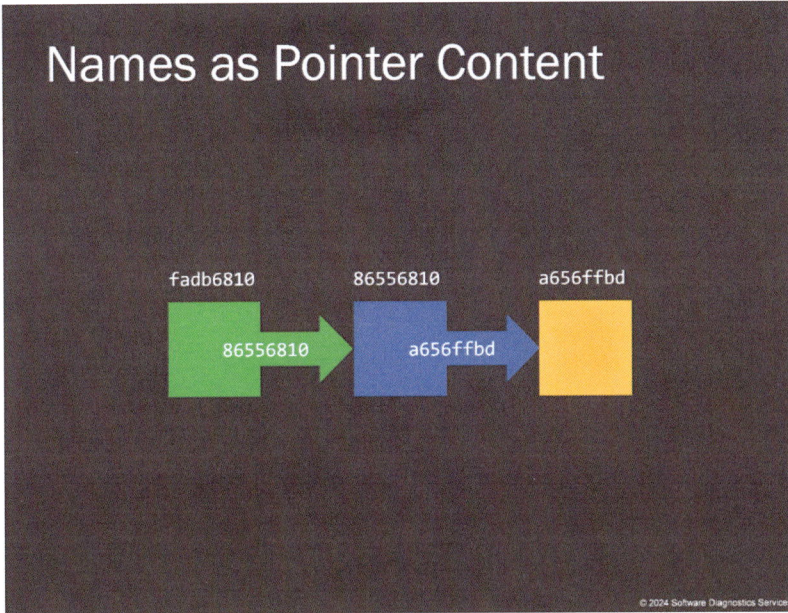

Pointers, as entities, may contain names, and these names may be names of pointers, too. If a pointer contains only a name, we say the pointer value is the name. So, the pointer value can be another pointer name, and the latter pointer value is the name of some other entity.

Pointers as Entities

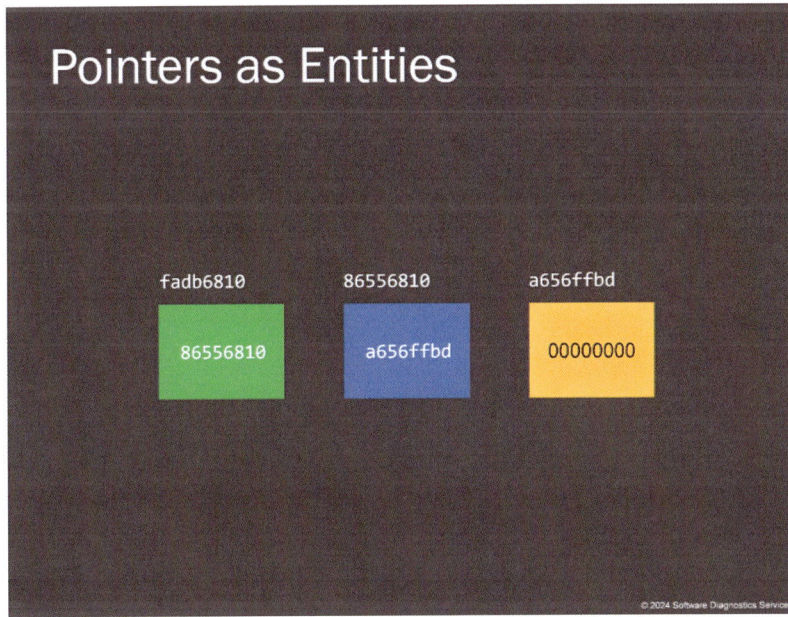

Pointer dereference is an act. If we put acts aside, pointers are just entities with some content that can be interpreted as a name if necessary. All these dereferences happen only at runtime. The pointer content (its value) may be invalid for all time without any problem until we use it.

Pointer Code Examples

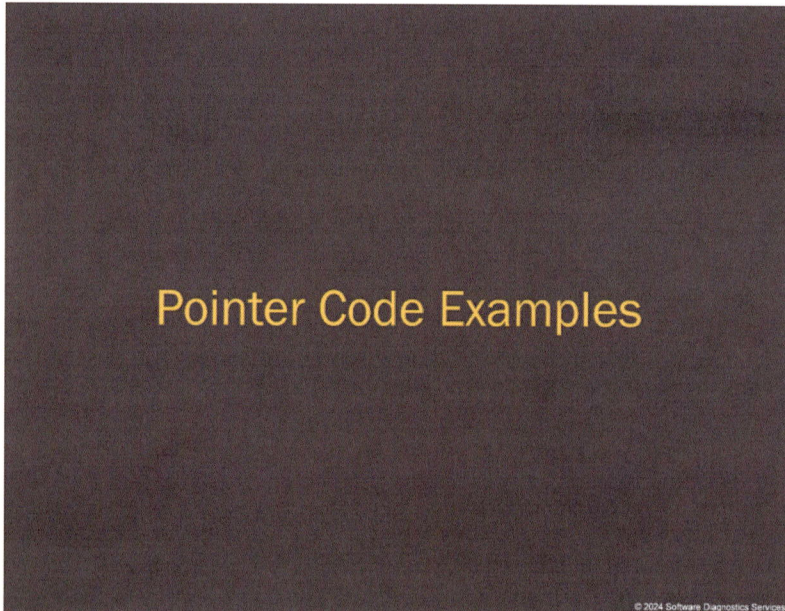

The `pointers` projects:

- `pointers_c`   C
- `pointers_c_cpp`   C++ as a better C
- `pointers_classic_cpp`   Classic C++
- `pointers_modern_cpp`   Modern C++

can be found in the archive[1]. In the following slide descriptions, we only show relevant code snippets and their output.

---

[1] https://www.patterndiagnostics.com/Training/ACPPLD/ACPPLD.tar.gz

Warning

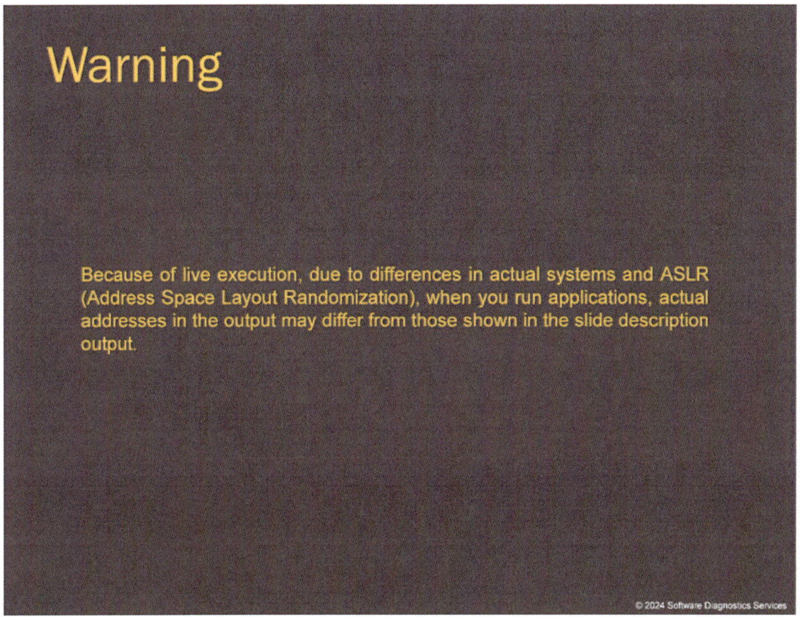

Pointer

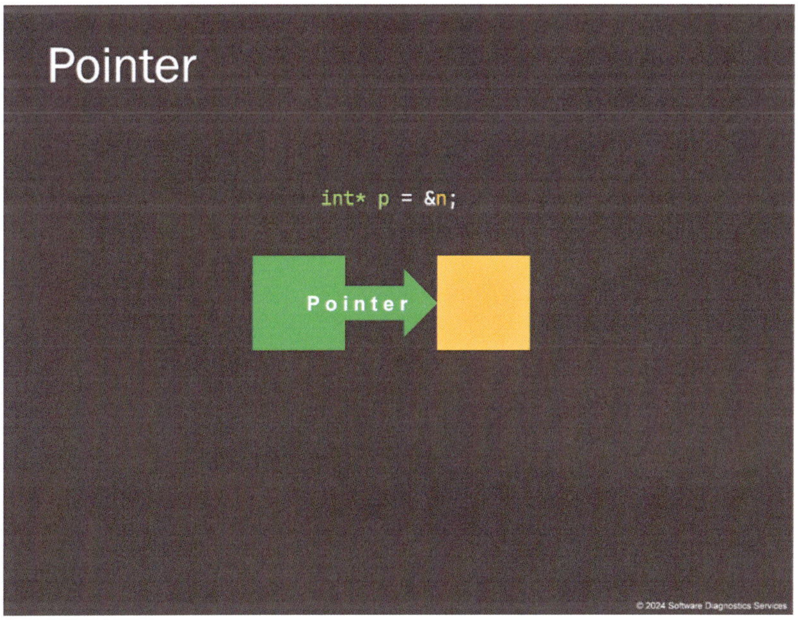

C   C++ as a better C

```
puts("--- Pointer ---");
{
    int n = 0;
    int* p = &n;

    printf("n value: %d address of n: %p \n"
        "p value: %p address of p: %p \n", n, &n, p, &p);
}
```

Classic C++

```
std::cout << "--- Pointer ---" << std::endl;
{
    int n = 0;
    int* p = &n;

    std::cout << "n value: " << n << " address of n: " << &n << std::endl <<
        "p value: " << p << " address of p: " << &p << std::endl;
}
```

Modern C++

```
std::println("--- Pointer ---");
{
    int n{};
    int* p{&n};

    std::println("n value: {:d} address of n: {:016X} \n"
        "p value: {} address of p: {}",
        n, reinterpret_cast<uintptr_t>(&n), p, &p); // why we need custom formatters
}
```

Output (x64)

```
--- Pointer ---
n value: 0 address of n: 0x7fffeaa01d5c
p value: 0x7fffeaa01d5c address of p: 0x7fffeaa01d50
```

* Placement Style

* Placement Style

⊙ int *p; // first edition

⊙ int* p; // second edition

⊙ int * p;

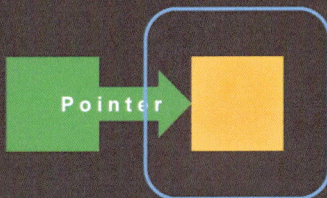

© 2024 Software Diagnostics Services

After writing the book on Rust, I reevaluated how I put types in source code. I used the first variant since I started programming in C almost four decades ago. The * belongs to the type, not the variable. So, in this edition, I switched to the second variant. Also, cppreference.com uses the same variant.

Pointer Dereference

Pointer Dereference

```
assert(*p == n);
```

Pointer

© 2024 Software Diagnostics Services

```c
puts("--- Pointer Dereference ---");
{
    int n = 0;
    int* p = &n;
    assert(*p == n);

    printf("n value: %d address of n: %p \n"
        "p value: %p dereference of p: %d address of p: %p \n",
        n, &n, p, *p, &p);
}
```

Classic C++

```cpp
std::cout << ("--- Pointer Dereference ---") << std::endl;
{
    int n = 0;
    int* p = &n;
    assert(*p == n);

    std::cout << "n value: " << n << " address of n: " << &n << std::endl <<
        "p value: " << p << " dereference of p: " << *p << " address of p: " << &p << std::endl;
}
```

Modern C++

```cpp
std::println("--- Pointer Dereference ---");
{
    int n{};
    int* p{&n};
    assert(*p == n);

    std::println("n value: {:d} address of n: {} \n"
        "p value: {} dereference of p: {:d} address of p: {}",
        n, &n, p, *p, &p);
}
```

Output (x64)

```
--- Pointer Dereference ---
n value: 0 address of n: 0x7fffeaa01d4c
p value: 0x7fffeaa01d4c dereference of p: 0 address of p: 0x7fffeaa01d40
```

One to Many

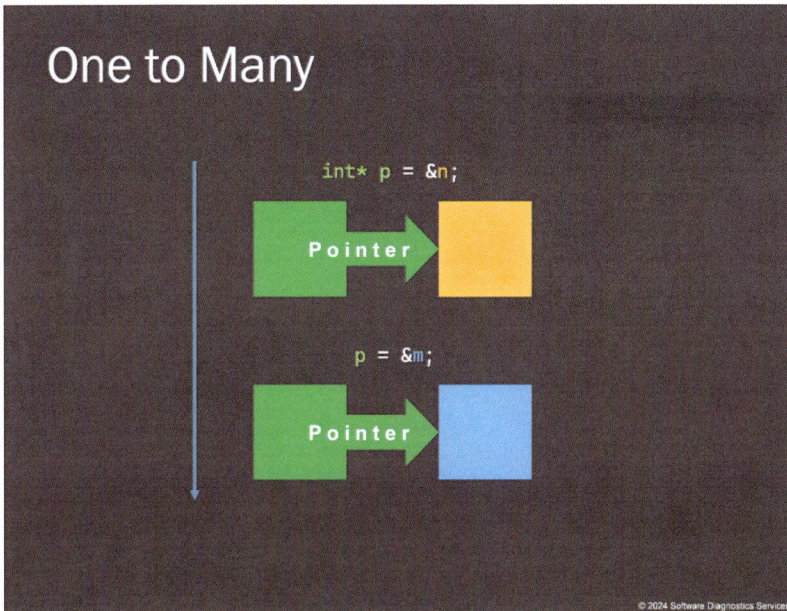

C   C++ as a better C

```c
puts("--- One to Many ---");
{
    int n = 0, m = 0;
    int* p = &n;

    printf("p value: %p dereference of p: %d address of p: %p \n",
        p, *p, &p);

    p = &m; // no leak

    printf("p value: %p dereference of p: %d address of p: %p \n",
        p, *p, &p);
}
```

Classic C++

```cpp
std::cout << ("--- One to Many ---") << std::endl;
{
    int n = 0, m = 0;
    int* p = &n;

    std::cout << "p value: " << p << " dereference of p: " << *p << " address of p: " << &p << std::endl;

    p = &m; // no leak

    std::cout << "p value: " << p << " dereference of p: " << *p << " address of p: " << &p << std::endl;
}
```

```
std::println("--- One to Many ---");
{
    int n{}, m{};
    int* p{&n};

    std::println("p value: {} dereference of p: {:d} address of p: {}",
        p, *p, &p);

    p = &m; // no leak

    std::println("p value: {} dereference of p: {:d} address of p: {}",
        p, *p, &p);
}
```

Output (x64)

```
--- One to Many ---
p value: 0x7fffeaa01d3c dereference of p: 0 address of p: 0x7fffeaa01d30
p value: 0x7fffeaa01d38 dereference of p: 0 address of p: 0x7fffeaa01d30
```

Memory Leak

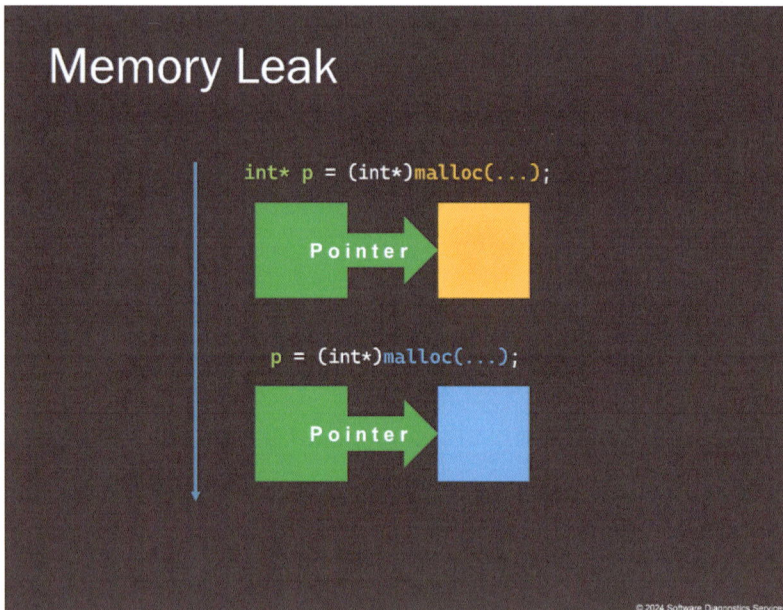

C

```c
puts("--- Memory Leak ---");
{
    int* p = malloc(sizeof(int));
    if (!p) return -1;

    *p = 0;

    printf("p value: %p dereference of p: %d address of p: %p \n",
        p, *p, &p);

    p = malloc(sizeof(int)); // memory leak
    if (!p) return -1;

    *p = 0;

    printf("p value: %p dereference of p: %d address of p: %p \n",
        p, *p, &p);

    free(p);
}
```

C++ as a better C

```cpp
puts("--- Memory Leak ---");
{
    int* p = (int*)malloc(sizeof(int)); // Needs a cast in C++
    if (!p) return -1;

    *p = 0;

    printf("p value: %p dereference of p: %d address of p: %p \n",
        p, *p, &p);

    p = (int*)malloc(sizeof(int)); // memory leak
    if (!p) return -1;

    *p = 0;

    printf("p value: %p dereference of p: %d address of p: %p \n",
        p, *p, &p);

    free(p);

}
```

Classic C++

```cpp
std::cout << ("--- Memory Leak ---") << std::endl;
{
    int* p = new int(0);

    std::cout << "p value: " << p << " dereference of p: " << *p << " address of p: " << &p << std::endl;

    p = new int(0); // memory leak

    std::cout << "p value: " << p << " dereference of p: " << *p << " address of p: " << &p << std::endl;

    delete p;
```

```
}
```

Modern C++

```cpp
std::println("--- Memory Leak ---");
{
    int* p{new int{}};

    std::println("p value: {} dereference of p: {:d} address of p: {}",
        p, *p, &p);

    p = new int{}; // memory leak

    std::println("p value: {} dereference of p: {:d} address of p: {}",
        p, *p, &p);

    delete p;
}
```

Output (x64)

```
--- Memory Leak ---
p value: 0x55dd59c5d6b0 dereference of p: 0 address of p: 0x7fffeaa01d28
p value: 0x55dd59c5d6d0 dereference of p: 0 address of p: 0x7fffeaa01d28
```

Many to One

C C++ as a better C

```c
puts("--- Many to One ---");
{
    int n = 0;
    int* p1 = &n;
    int* p2 = &n;
    assert(p1 == p2);

    printf("n value: %d address of n: %p \n"
        "p1 value: %p address of p1: %p \n"
        "p2 value: %p address of p2: %p \n",
        n, &n, p1, &p1, p2, &p2);
}
```

Classic C++

```cpp
std::cout << ("--- Many to One ---") << std::endl;
{
    int n = 0;
    int* p1 = &n;
    int* p2 = &n;
    assert(p1 == p2);

    std::cout << "n value: " << n << " address of n: " << &n << std::endl <<
        "p1 value: " << p1 << " address of p1: " << &p1 << std::endl <<
        "p2 value: " << p2 << " address of p2: " << &p2 << std::endl;
}
```

Modern C++

```cpp
std::println("--- Many to One ---");
{
    int n{};
    int* p1{&n};
    int* p2{&n};
    assert(p1 == p2);

    std::println("n value: {:d} address of n: {} \n"
        "p1 value: {} address of p1: {} \n"
        "p2 value: {} address of p2: {}",
        n, &n, p1, &p1, p2, &p2);
}
```

Output (x64)

```
--- Many to One ---
n value: 0 address of n: 0x7fffeaa01d24
p1 value: 0x7fffeaa01d24 address of p1: 0x7fffeaa01d18
p2 value: 0x7fffeaa01d24 address of p2: 0x7fffeaa01d10
```

Many to One Dereference

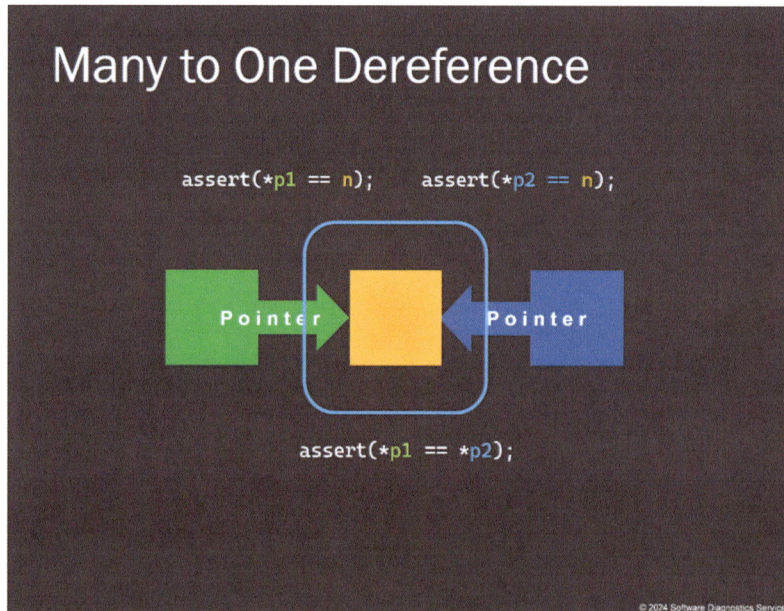

C   C++ as a better C

```
puts("--- Many to One Dereference ---");
{
    int n = 0;
    int* p1 = &n;
    int* p2 = &n;
    assert(*p1 == *p2);

    printf("n value: %d address of n: %p \n"
        "p1 value: %p dereference of p1: %d address of p1: %p \n"
        "p2 value: %p dereference of p2: %d address of p2: %p \n",
        n, &n, p1, *p1, &p1, p2, *p2, &p2);
}
```

Classic C++

```
std::cout << ("--- Many to One Dereference ---") << std::endl;
{
    int n = 0;
    int* p1 = &n;
    int* p2 = &n;
    assert(*p1 == *p2);

    std::cout << "n value: " << n << " address of n: " << &n << std::endl <<
        "p1 value: " << p1 << " dereference of p1: " << *p1 << " address of p1: " << &p1 <<
std::endl <<
        "p2 value: " << p2 << " dereference of p2: " << *p2 << " address of p2: " << &p2 <<
std::endl;
}
```

```cpp
std::println("--- Many to One Dereference ---");
{
    int n{};
    int* p1{&n};
    int* p2{&n};
    assert(*p1 == *p2);

    std::println("n value: {:d} address of n: {} \n"
        "p1 value: {} dereference of p1: {:d} address of p1: {} \n"
        "p2 value: {} dereference of p2: {:d} address of p2: {}",
        n, &n, p1, *p1, &p1, p2, *p2, &p2);
}
```

Output (x64)

```
--- Many to One Dereference ---
n value: 0 address of n: 0x7fffeaa01d0c
p1 value: 0x7fffeaa01d0c dereference of p1: 0 address of p1: 0x7fffeaa01d00
p2 value: 0x7fffeaa01d0c dereference of p2: 0 address of p2: 0x7fffeaa01cf8
```

Invalid Pointer

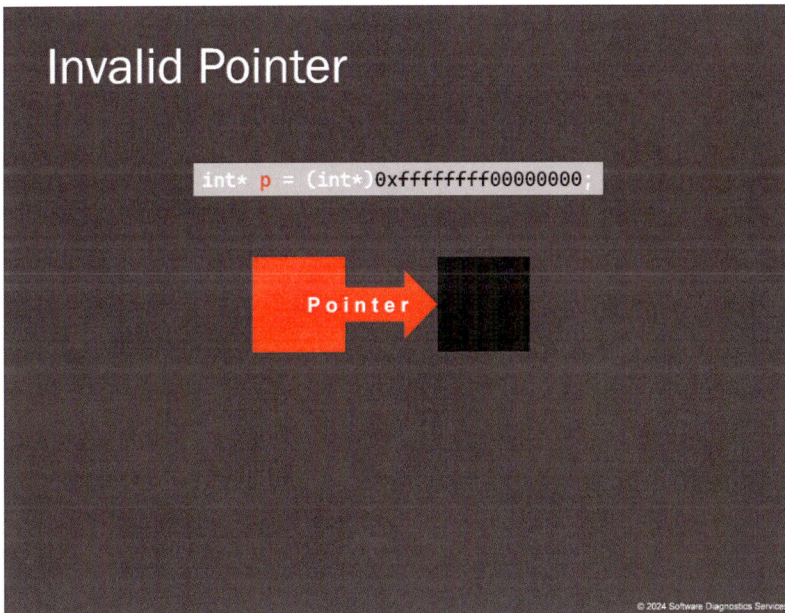

C C++ as a better C

```
puts("--- Invalid Pointer ---");
{
    int* p = (int*)0xffffffff00000000;

    printf("p value: %p address of p: %p \n", p, &p);
}
```

Classic C++

```
std::cout << ("--- Invalid Pointer ---") << std::endl;
{
    int* p = reinterpret_cast<int*>(0xffffffff00000000);

    std::cout << "p value: " << p << " address of p: " << &p << std::endl;
}
```

Modern C++

```
std::println("--- Invalid Pointer ---");
{
    int* p{reinterpret_cast<int*>(0xffffffff00000000)};

    std::println("p value: {} address of p: {}", p, &p);
}
```

Output (x64)

```
--- Invalid Pointer ---
p value: 0xffffffff00000000 address of p: 0x7fffeaa01cf0
```

Invalid Pointer Dereference

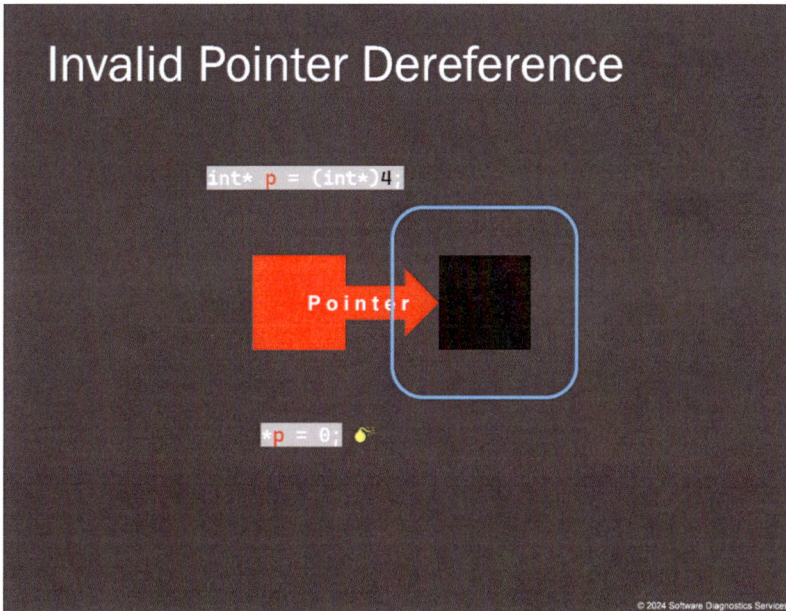

C   C++ as a better C

```
puts("--- Invalid Pointer Dereference ---");
{
    int* p = (int*)4;

    printf("p value: %p address of p: %p \n", p, &p);

    // *p = 0; // crash
}
```

Classic C++

```
std::cout << ("--- Invalid Pointer Dereference ---") << std::endl;
{
    int* p = reinterpret_cast<int*>(4);

    std::cout << "p value: " << p << " address of p: " << &p << std::endl;

    // *p = 0; // crash
}
```

Modern C++

```
std::println("--- Invalid Pointer Dereference ---");
{
    int* p{reinterpret_cast<int*>(4)};

    std::println("p value: {} address of p: {}", p, &p);
```

```
    // *p = 0; // crash
}
```

Output (x64)

```
--- Invalid Pointer Dereference ---
p value: 0x4 address of p: 0x7fffeaa01ce8
```

Wild (Dangling) Pointer

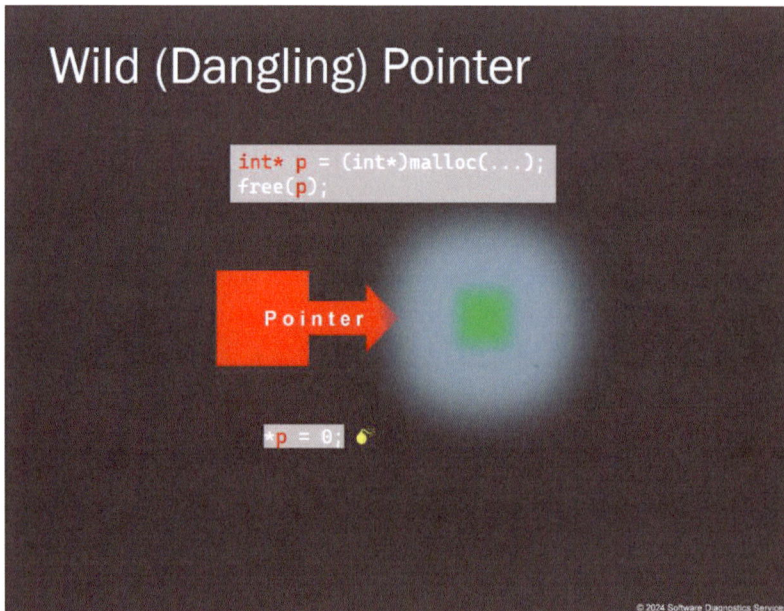

C

```c
puts("--- Wild (Dangling) Pointer ---");
{
    int* p = malloc(sizeof(int));
    if (!p) return -1;

    *p = 0;

    printf("p value: %p dereference of p: %d address of p: %p \n",
        p, *p, &p);

    free(p); // dangling pointer

    printf("p value: %p address of p: %p \n",
        p, &p);

    // printf("p value: %p dereference of p: %d address of p: %p \n",
    //     p, *p, &p);  // may crash
```

```
    // assert(*p == 0); // may crash or fail

    p = NULL; // Not dangling
}
```

 C++ as a better C

```
puts("--- Wild (Dangling) Pointer ---");
{
    int* p = (int*)malloc(sizeof(int)); // needs a cast in C++
    if (!p) return -1;

    *p = 0;

    printf("p value: %p dereference of p: %d address of p: %p \n",
        p, *p, &p);

    free(p); // dangling pointer

    printf("p value: %p address of p: %p \n",
        p, &p);

    // printf("p value: %p dereference of p: %d address of p: %p \n",
    //    p, *p, &p);  // may crash

    // assert(*p == 0); // may crash or fail

    p = NULL; // Not dangling
}
```

<u>Output</u>

```
--- Wild (Dangling) Pointer ---
p value: 0000021602A96FD0 dereference of p: 0 address of p: 000000E5F3CFFB68
p value: 0000021602A96FD0 address of p: 000000E5F3CFFB68
```

Classic C++

```
std::cout << ("--- Wild (Dangling) Pointer ---") << std::endl;
{
    int* p = new int(0);

    std::cout << "p value: " << p << " dereference of p: " << *p << " address of p: " << &p <<
std::endl;

    delete p; // dangling pointer

    std::cout << "p value: " << p << " address of p: " << &p << std::endl;

    // std::cout << "p value: " << p << " dereference of p: " << *p << " address of p: " << &p <<
std::endl; // may crash

    // assert(*p == 0); // may crash or fail

    p = NULL; // Not dangling
}
```

Modern C++

```cpp
std::println("--- Wild (Dangling) Pointer ---");
{
    int* p{new int{}};

    std::println("p value: {} dereference of p: {:d} address of p: {}",
        p, *p, &p);

    delete p; // dangling pointer

    std::println("p value: {} address of p: {}",
        p, &p);

    // std::println("p value: {} dereference of p: {:d} address of p: {}",
    //     p, *p, &p); // may crash

    // assert(*p == 0); // may crash or fail

    p = nullptr; // Not dangling
}
```

<u>Output (x64)</u>

```
--- Wild (Dangling) Pointer ---
p value: 0x55dd59c5d6d0 dereference of p: 0 address of p: 0x7fffeaa01ce0
p value: 0x55dd59c5d6d0 address of p: 0x7fffeaa01ce0
```

Pointer to Pointer

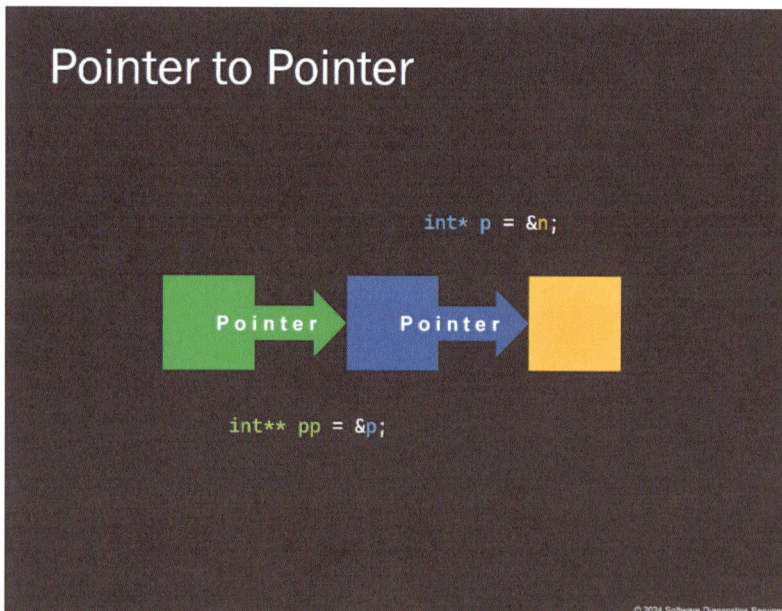

```
puts("--- Pointer to Pointer ---");
{
    int n = 0;
    int* p = &n;
    int** pp = &p;

    printf("n value: %d address of n: %p \n"
        "p value: %p address of p: %p \n"
        "pp value: %p address of pp: %p \n",
        n, &n, p, &p, pp, &pp);
}
```

Classic C++

```
std::cout << ("--- Pointer to Pointer ---") << std::endl;
{
    int n = 0;
    int* p = &n;
    int** pp = &p;

    std::cout << "n value: " << n << " address of n: " << &n << std::endl <<
        "p value: " << p << " address of p: " << &p << std::endl <<
        "pp value: " << pp << " address of pp: " << &pp << std::endl;
}
```

Modern C++

```
std::println("--- Pointer to Pointer ---");
{
    int n{};
    int* p{&n};
    int** pp{&p};

    std::println("n value: {:d} address of n: {} \n"
        "p value: {} address of p: {} \n"
        "pp value: {} address of pp: {}",
        n, &n, p, &p, pp, &pp);
}
```

Output (x64)

```
--- Pointer to Pointer ---
n value: 0 address of n: 0x7fffeaa01cdc
p value: 0x7fffeaa01cdc address of p: 0x7fffeaa01cd0
pp value: 0x7fffeaa01cd0 address of pp: 0x7fffeaa01cc8
```

Pointer to Pointer Dereference

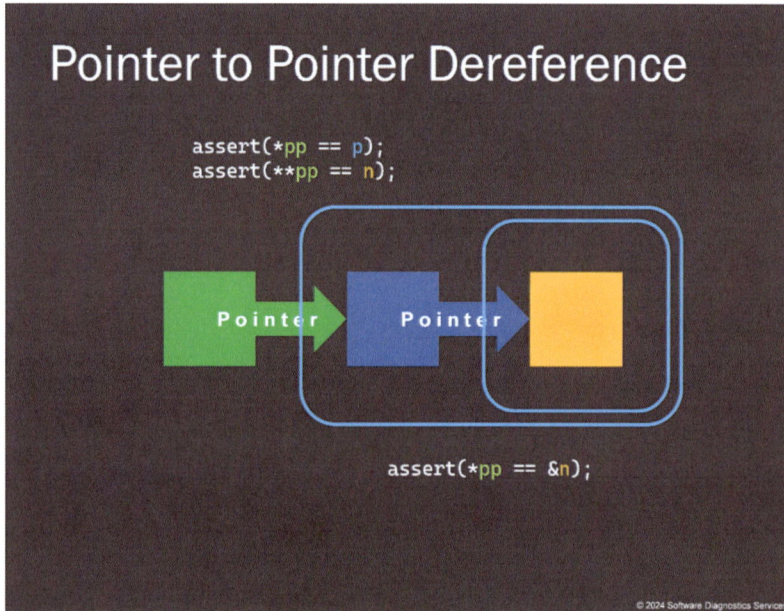

C   C++ as a better C

```
puts("--- Pointer to Pointer Dereference ---");
{
    int n = 0;
    int* p = &n;
    int** pp = &p;
    assert(*pp == p);
    assert(*pp == &n);
    assert(**pp == n);

    printf("n value: %d address of n: %p \n"
        "p value: %p address of p: %p \n"
        "pp value: %p address of pp: %p \n"
        "dereference of pp: %p double dereference of pp: %d \n",
        n, &n, p, &p, pp, &pp, *pp, **pp);
}
```

Classic C++

```
std::cout << ("--- Pointer to Pointer Dereference ---") << std::endl;
{
    int n = 0;
    int* p = &n;
    int** pp = &p;
    assert(*pp == p);
    assert(*pp == &n);
    assert(**pp == n);

    std::cout << "n value: " << n << " address of n: " << &n << std::endl <<
```

```
        "p value: " << p << " address of p: " << &p << std::endl <<
        "pp value: " << pp << " address of pp: " << &pp << std::endl <<
        "dereference of pp: " << *pp << " double dereference of pp: " << **pp << std::endl;
}
```

<mark>Modern C++</mark>

```
std::println("--- Pointer to Pointer Dereference ---");
{
    int n{};
    int* p{&n};
    int** pp{&p};
    assert(*pp == p);
    assert(*pp == &n);
    assert(**pp == n);

    std::println("n value: {:d} address of n: {} \n"
        "p value: {} address of p: {} \n"
        "pp value: {} address of pp: {} \n"
        "dereference of pp: {} double dereference of pp: {:d}",
        n, &n, p, &p, pp, &pp, *pp, **pp);
}
```

Output (x64)

```
--- Pointer to Pointer Dereference ---
n value: 0 address of n: 0x7fffeaa01cc4
p value: 0x7fffeaa01cc4 address of p: 0x7fffeaa01cb8
pp value: 0x7fffeaa01cb8 address of pp: 0x7fffeaa01cb0
dereference of pp: 0x7fffeaa01cc4 double dereference of pp: 0
```

Undefined Behavior

Undefined Behavior

⊚ OK | Corruption | Crash | Spike | Hang | Leak

⊚ Different on different machines

⊚ Different at different times

⊚ Depends on compiler-generated code

⊚ Depends on memory layout

© 2024 Software Diagnostics Services

When looking at `Wild (Dangling) Pointer` code example, you may have noticed a comment that an assertion there may crash or fail. This is an example of the undefined behavior: depending on runtime and memory layout, when we dereference a dangling pointer, its address may be valid or invalid.

Appendix

<u>Output (A64)</u>

```
--- Pointer ---
n value: 0 address of n: 0xffffc16f153c
p value: 0xffffc16f153c address of p: 0xffffc16f1530
--- Pointer Dereference ---
n value: 0 address of n: 0xffffc16f152c
p value: 0xffffc16f152c dereference of p: 0 address of p: 0xffffc16f1520
--- One to Many ---
p value: 0xffffc16f151c dereference of p: 0 address of p: 0xffffc16f1510
p value: 0xffffc16f1518 dereference of p: 0 address of p: 0xffffc16f1510
--- Memory Leak ---
p value: 0x24b006b0 dereference of p: 0 address of p: 0xffffc16f1508
p value: 0x24b006d0 dereference of p: 0 address of p: 0xffffc16f1508
--- Many to One ---
n value: 0 address of n: 0xffffc16f1504
p1 value: 0xffffc16f1504 address of p1: 0xffffc16f14f8
p2 value: 0xffffc16f1504 address of p2: 0xffffc16f14f0
--- Many to One Dereference ---
n value: 0 address of n: 0xffffc16f14ec
p1 value: 0xffffc16f14ec dereference of p1: 0 address of p1: 0xffffc16f14e0
p2 value: 0xffffc16f14ec dereference of p2: 0 address of p2: 0xffffc16f14d8
--- Invalid Pointer ---
p value: 0xffffffff00000000 address of p: 0xffffc16f14d0
--- Invalid Pointer Dereference ---
p value: 0x4 address of p: 0xffffc16f14c8
--- Wild (Dangling) Pointer ---
p value: 0x24b006d0 dereference of p: 0 address of p: 0xffffc16f14c0
p value: 0x24b006d0 address of p: 0xffffc16f14c0
--- Pointer to Pointer ---
n value: 0 address of n: 0xffffc16f14bc
p value: 0xffffc16f14bc address of p: 0xffffc16f14b0
pp value: 0xffffc16f14b0 address of pp: 0xffffc16f14a8
--- Pointer to Pointer Dereference ---
n value: 0 address of n: 0xffffc16f14a4
p value: 0xffffc16f14a4 address of p: 0xffffc16f1498
pp value: 0xffffc16f1498 address of pp: 0xffffc16f1490
dereference of pp: 0xffffc16f14a4 double dereference of pp: 0
```

Memory and Pointers

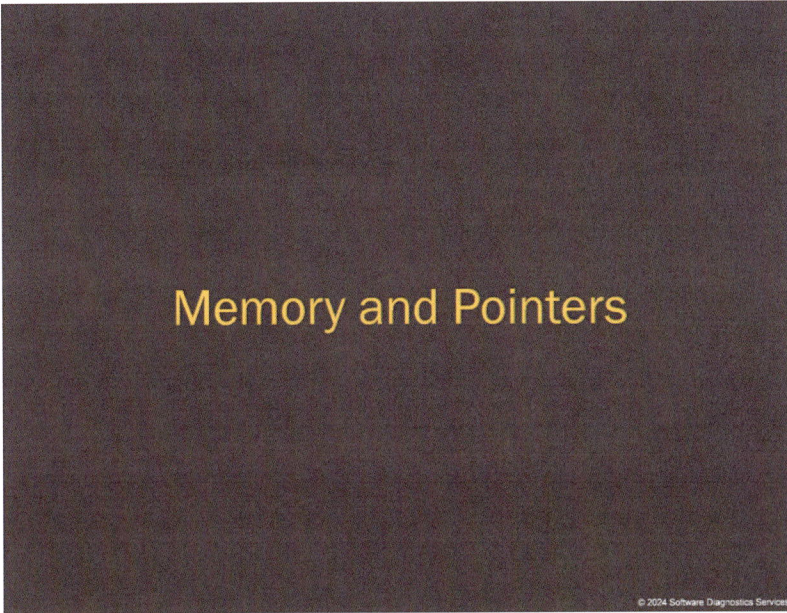

Now, we look at memory representation of pointers and entities they point to.

The `memory_and_pointers` projects:

- `memory_and_pointers_c`   C
- `memory_and_pointers_c_cpp`   C++ as a better C
- `memory_and_pointers_modern_cpp`   Modern C++

can be found in the archive[2]. In the following slide descriptions, we only show relevant code snippets and their output.

---

[2] https://www.patterndiagnostics.com/Training/ACPPLD/ACPPLD.tar.gz

Mental Exercise

Here, in this picture, entities are the so-called memory cells. Memory cells have addresses that start from 0 and are usually incremented by the so-called pointer size, which is 4 on 32-bit systems and 8 on 64-bit systems. Here, for visual clarity, we use memory cells from a 32-bit system.

Debugger Memory Layout

When we use a debugger, it prints memory cell addresses and their contents in a certain layout shown on this slide. Some debugger commands, such as **x** in GDB, use 2-column and some n-column layouts to print memory.

Memory Dereference Layout

For a 2-column format, some debuggers and their commands may interpret the second column as a pointer. In such a case, the third column is a value from a pointer dereference. Also, notice a case when a pointer points to itself. For GDB, it is possible to emulate such behavior using a custom script:

```
define dpp
    set $i = 0
    set $p = $arg0
    while $i < $arg1
        printf "%p: ", $p
        x/gx *(long *)$p
        set $i = $i + 1
        set $p = $p + 8
    end
end
```

Names as Addresses

To repeat, for memory layout, names are interpreted as addresses, and memory cell content (cell value) can also be interpreted as a memory address.

Addresses and Entities

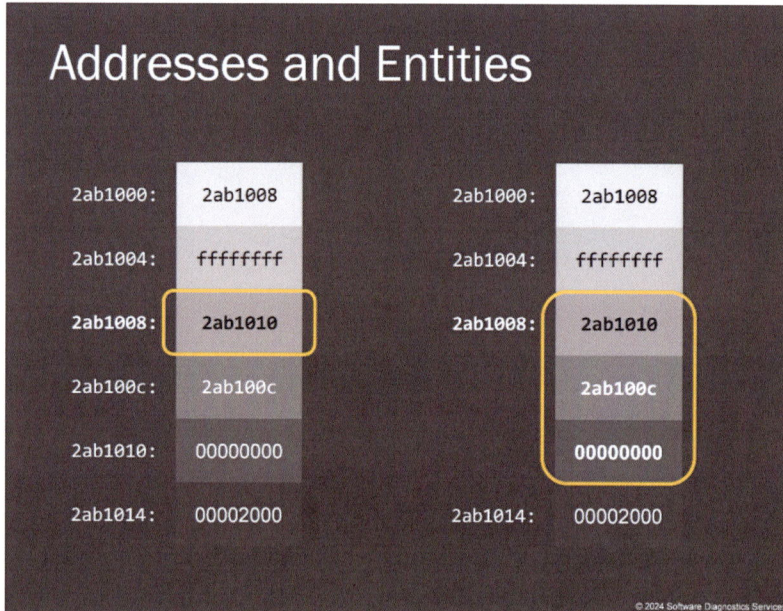

Entities can be either single cells or multicells. Each part of a multicell can be interpreted as a memory address, if necessary, even if it wasn't meant to be a memory address.

Addresses and Structures

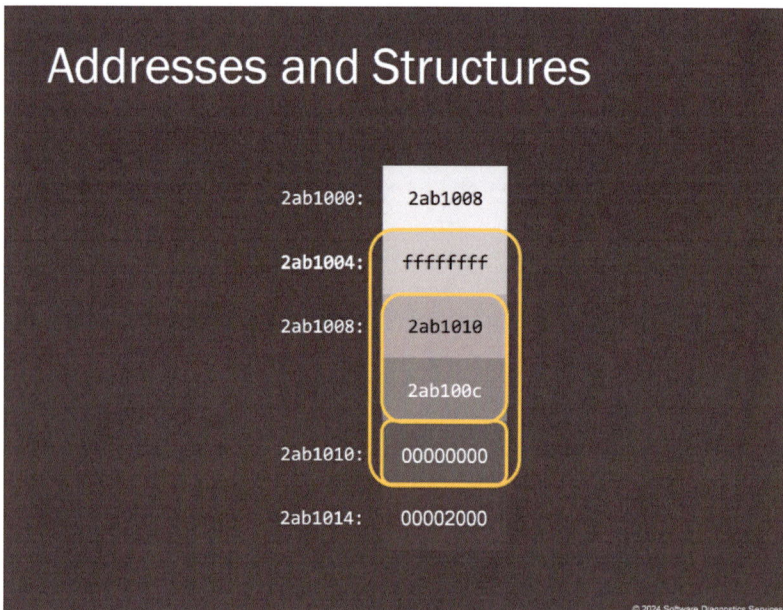

A structure in memory is a sequential collection of memory cells; some may be multicell and themselves substructures. Each part of a structure, its member, or structure field has its own address as well, in addition to the overall address of the structure.

Pointers to Structures

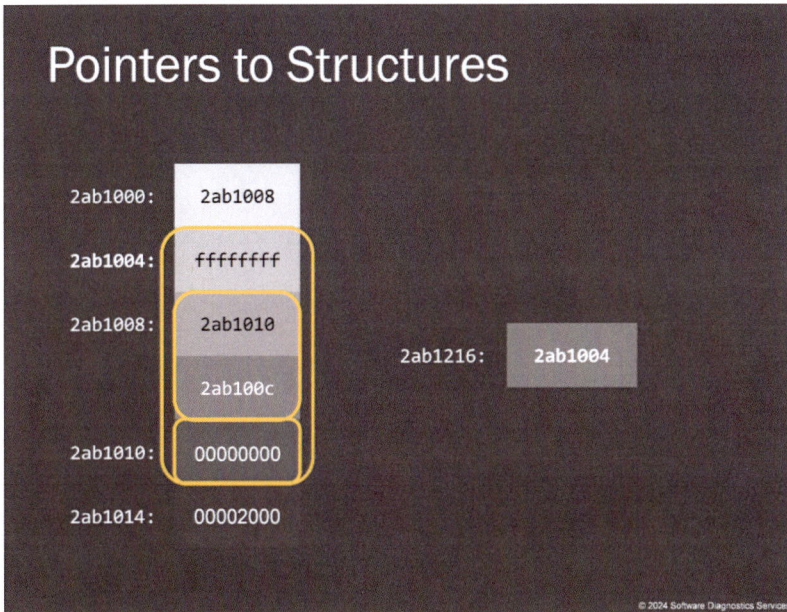

A structure has its address. A pointer to a structure is a memory cell that contains that address. It has its own address. At this point, structures are abstract collections of memory cells. We look at proper C and C++ structures and corresponding source code later.

Arrays

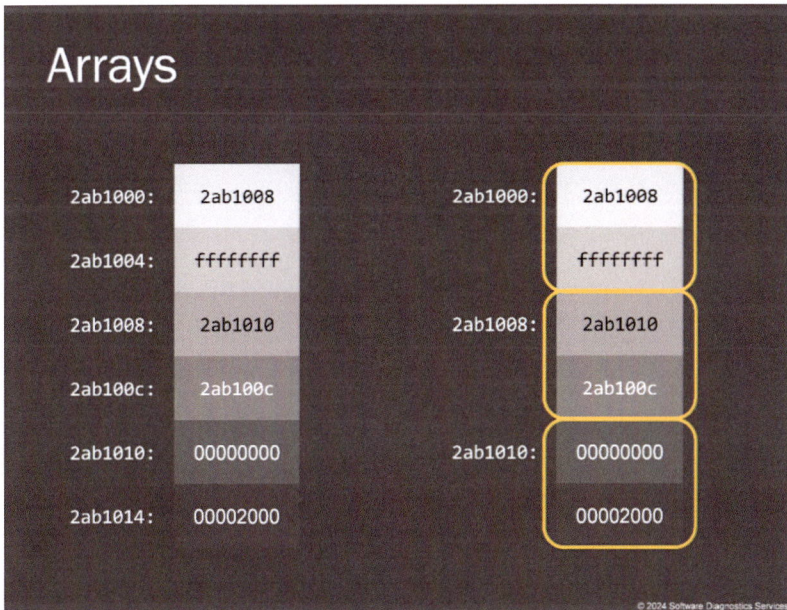

An array is a contiguous sequence of n-cells in memory called array elements. Each array element has its own address. Since the size of each array element is fixed and the same, addressing the random element is fast.

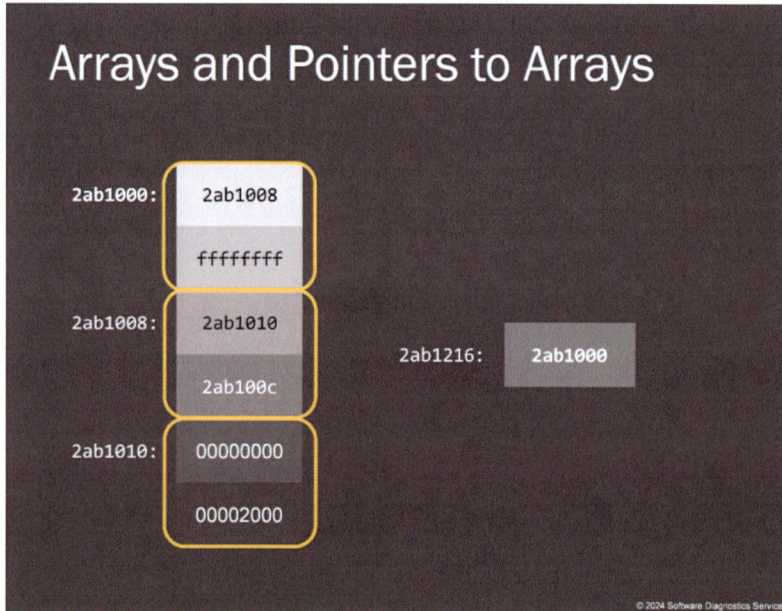

The array address is the address of its first element. But a pointer to an array is a different memory cell that con-tains the array address. This is similar to structures and pointers to struc-tures. An array can be considered as a structure as well.

C   C++ as a better C

```c
puts("--- Arrays and Pointers to Arrays ---");
{
    int arr[10] = { 0, 1, 2, 3, 4, 5, 6, 7, 8, 9 };

    printf("address of arr: %p value of arr: %p address of the first arr element: %p \n",
        &arr, arr, &arr[0]);

    int (*parr)[10] = &arr;

    printf("address of parr: %p value of parr: %p \n",
        &parr, parr);
}
```

Modern C++

```cpp
std::println("--- Arrays and Pointers to Arrays ---");
{
    int arr[10]{ 0, 1, 2, 3, 4, 5, 6, 7, 8, 9 };

    std::println("address of arr: {} value of arr: {} address of the first arr element: {}",
        &arr, arr, &arr[0]);

    int (*parr)[10]{&arr};

    std::println("address of parr: {} value of parr: {}",
        &parr, parr);
}
```

<u>Output (x64)</u>

```
--- Arrays and Pointers to Arrays ---
address of arr: 0x7ffd0f971ef0 value of arr: 0x7ffd0f971ef0 address of the first arr element:
0x7ffd0f971ef0
address of parr: 0x7ffd0f971f28 value of parr: 0x7ffd0f971ef0
```

Strings and Pointers to Strings

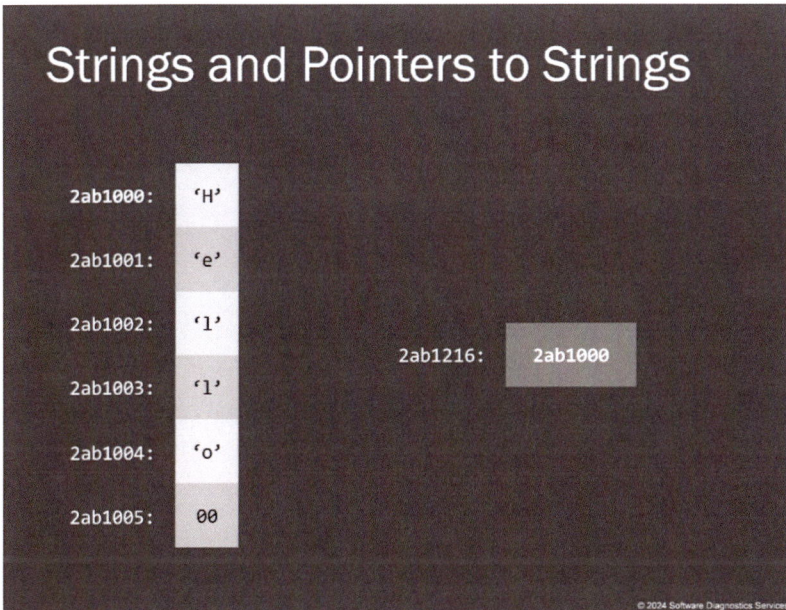

What about strings? An ASCII string is a zero-terminated array of one-byte memory cells. The address of a string is the address of its first byte. Similar to arrays, a pointer to a string is a memory cell that contains the address of the string, the address of its first element – its first character. Please note that **str** is a pointer (it is not an array **str[]**), so its address **&str** is different from the **str** value.

C

```c
puts("--- Strings and Pointers to Strings ---");
{
    char* str = "Hello";

    printf("address of str: %p value of str: %p address of the first str element: %p \n"
        "address of the sixth str element: %p value of the sixth str element: %d \n",
        &str, str, &str[0], &str[5], str[5]);

    char** pstr = &str;

    printf("address of pstr: %p value of pstr: %p \n",
        &pstr, pstr);

    printf("address of the first str element: %p \n"
        "address of the sixth str element: %p value of the sixth str element: %d \n",
        &(*pstr)[0], &(*pstr)[5], (*pstr)[5]);
}
```

C++ as a better C

```cpp
puts("--- Strings and Pointers to Strings ---");
{
    const char* str = "Hello"; // in C++ can't be char*

    printf("address of str: %p value of str: %p address of the first str element: %p \n"
        "address of the sixth str element: %p value of the sixth str element: %d \n",
        &str, str, &str[0], &str[5], str[5]);

    const char** pstr = &str;

    printf("address of pstr: %p value of pstr: %p \n",
        &pstr, pstr);

    printf("address of the first str element: %p \n"
        "address of the sixth str element: %p value of the sixth str element: %d \n",
        &(*pstr)[0], &(*pstr)[5], (*pstr)[5]);
}
```

Modern C++

```cpp
std::println("--- Strings and Pointers to Strings ---");
{
    const char* str{"Hello"}; // str may be interpreted by template code as a value "Hello"

    std::println("address of str: {} value of str: {:016X} address of the first str element:
{:016X} \n"
        "address of the sixth str element: {:016X} value of the sixth str element: {:d}",
        &str, reinterpret_cast<uintptr_t>(str), reinterpret_cast<uintptr_t>(&str[0]),
        reinterpret_cast<uintptr_t>(&str[5]), str[5]);

    const char** pstr{&str};

    std::println("address of pstr: {} value of pstr: {}",
        &pstr, pstr);

    std::println("address of the first str element: {:016X} \n"
        "address of the sixth str element: {:016X} value of the sixth str element: {:d}",
        reinterpret_cast<uintptr_t>(&(*pstr)[0]),
        reinterpret_cast<uintptr_t>(&(*pstr)[5]), (*pstr)[5]);
}
```

Output (x64)

```
--- Strings and Pointers to Strings ---
address of str: 0x7ffd0f971f20 value of str: 0x55c41ce6d0d0 address of the first str element:
0x55c41ce6d0d0
address of the sixth str element: 0x55c41ce6d0d5 value of the sixth str element: 0
address of pstr: 0x7ffd0f971f18 value of pstr: 0x7ffd0f971f20
address of the first str element: 0x55c41ce6d0d0
address of the sixth str element: 0x55c41ce6d0d5 value of the sixth str element: 0
```

Appendix

Output (A64)

```
--- Arrays and Pointers to Arrays ---
address of arr: 0xffffe0f00a60 value of arr: 0xffffe0f00a60 address of the first arr element:
0xffffe0f00a60
address of parr: 0xffffe0f00a98 value of parr: 0xffffe0f00a60
--- Strings and Pointers to Strings ---
address of str: 0xffffe0f00a90 value of str: 0x4008e8 address of the first str element: 0x4008e8
address of the sixth str element: 0x4008ed value of the sixth str element: 0
address of pstr: 0xffffe0f00a88 value of pstr: 0xffffe0f00a90
address of the first str element: 0x4008e8
address of the sixth str element: 0x4008ed value of the sixth str element: 0
```

Basic Types

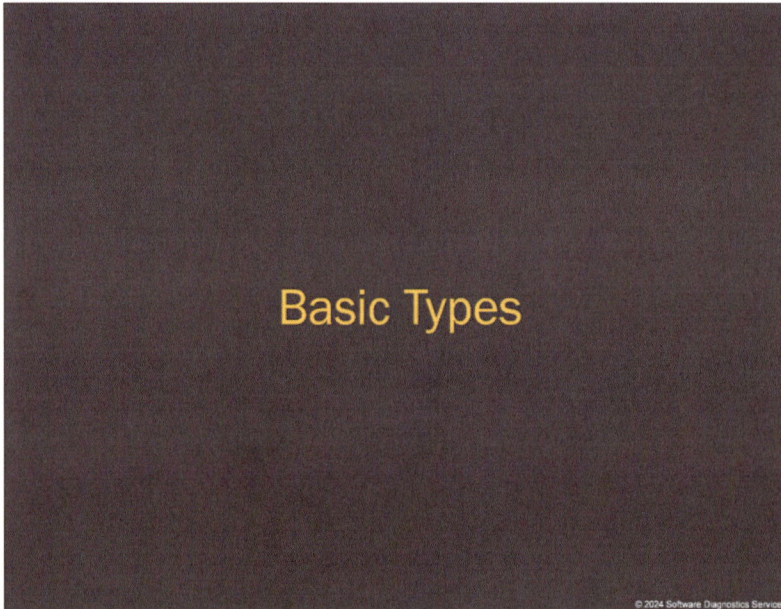

Now, we look at a few fundamental basic types.

The **basic_types** projects:

- `basic_types_c`   C
- `basic_types_c_cpp`   C++ as a better C
- `basic_types_modern_cpp`   Modern C++

can be found in the archive[3]. In the following slide descriptions, we only show relevant code snippets and their output.

---

[3] https://www.patterndiagnostics.com/Training/ACPPLD/ACPPLD.tar.gz

ASCII Characters and Pointers

We have already looked at ASCII zero-terminated strings and pointers conceptually using memory diagrams. Here, we look at some idiomatic C and C++ code.

C   C++ as a better C

```c
puts("--- ASCII Characters and Pointers ---");
{
    char str[] = { 'H', 'e', 'l', 'l', 'o', 0 };

    char* pstr = str;
    printf("value of pstr: %p address of pstr: %p \n", pstr, &pstr);

    char c = *pstr;
    printf("value of c: %c \n", c);

    ++pstr;
    printf("value of pstr: %p \n", pstr);

    c = *pstr;
    printf("value of c: %c \n", c);

    c = *(pstr + 1);
    printf("value of c: %c \n", c);
}
```

Output (x64)

```
--- ASCII Characters and Pointers ---
value of pstr: 0x7fff1d71cf9a address of pstr: 0x7fff1d71cf90
value of c: H
value of pstr: 0x7fff1d71cf9b
value of c: e
value of c: l
```

Bytes and Pointers

Characters are signed with small integer values from -128 to 127. But if we want to work with bytes with unsigned values from 0 to 255, we need to use unsigned characters. Later, we see what other types are available to work with bytes.

C C++ as a better C

```
puts("--- Bytes and Pointers ---");
{
    unsigned char barr[] = { 0x12, 0x34, 0x56, 0x78, 0xab, 0xcd };

    unsigned char* pb = barr;
    printf("value of pb: %p address of pb: %p \n", pb, &pb);

    unsigned char b = *pb;
    printf("value of b: %x \n", b);

    ++pb;
    printf("value of pb: %p \n", pb);

    b = *pb;
    printf("value of b: %x \n", b);

    b = *(pb + 1);
    printf("value of b: %x \n", b);
}
```

Output (x64)

```
--- Bytes and Pointers ---
value of pb: 0x7fff1d71cf8a address of pb: 0x7fff1d71cf80
value of b: 12
value of pb: 0x7fff1d71cf8b
value of b: 34
value of b: 56
```

Wide Characters and Pointers

Wide characters occupy 4 bytes each on x64 and A64 Linux platforms and may be used to represent UNICODE characters.

C   C++ as a better C

```
puts("--- Wide Characters and Pointers ---");
{
    wchar_t wstr[] = { L'H', L'e', L'l', L'l', L'o', 0 };

    wchar_t* pwstr = wstr;
    printf("value of pwstr: %p address of pwstr: %p \n", pwstr, &pwstr);

    wchar_t wc = *pwstr;
    printf("value of wc: %lc \n", wc);

    ++pwstr;
    printf("value of pwstr: %p \n", pwstr);

    wc = *pwstr;
    printf("value of wc: %lc \n", wc);

    wc = *(pwstr + 1);
    printf("value of wc: %lc \n", wc);
}
```

Output (x64)

```
--- Wide Characters and Pointers ---
value of pwstr: 0x7fff1d71cf60 address of pwstr: 0x7fff1d71cf58
value of wc: H
value of pwstr: 0x7fff1d71cf64
value of wc: e
value of wc: l
```

Integers

The next type we look at now is integers, which occupy 4 bytes.

C C++ as a better C

```c
puts("--- Integers ---");
{
    int iarr[] = { 0x2ab1008, -1, 0x2ab1010, 0x2ab100c, 0, 0x2000 };

    int* pi = iarr;
    printf("value of pi: %p address of pi: %p \n", pi, &pi);

    int i = *pi;
    printf("value of i: %x \n", i);

    ++pi;
    printf("value of pi: %p \n", pi);

    i = *pi;
    printf("value of i: %x \n", i);

    i = *(pi + 1);
    printf("value of i: %x \n", i);
}
```

Output (x64)

```
--- Integers ---
value of pi: 0x7fff1d71cf40 address of pi: 0x7fff1d71cf38
value of i: 2ab1008
value of pi: 0x7fff1d71cf44
value of i: ffffffff
value of i: 2ab1010
```

Little-Endian System

When converting between byte sequences and number values, we need to consider the little-endian system where the least significant digits reside at the lowest memory addresses.

C   C++ as a better C

```
puts("--- Little-Endian System ---");
{
    char ba[4] = { 1, 2, 3, 4 };

    int i = *(int*)ba;

    printf("values of ba array: %x, %x, %x, %x value of i: %x \n",
        ba[0], ba[1], ba[2], ba[3], i);
}
```

Output (x64)

```
--- Little-Endian System ---
values of ba array: 1, 2, 3, 4 value of i: 4030201
```

Short Integers

Short integers occupy 2 bytes.

C C++ as a better C

```
puts("--- Short Integers ---");
{
    int iarr[] = { 0x2ab1008, -1, 0x2ab1010, 0x2ab100c, 0, 0x2000 };

    short* ps = (short*)iarr;
    printf("value of ps: %p address of ps: %p \n", ps, &ps);

    short s = *ps;
    printf("value of s: %hx \n", s);

    ++ps;
    printf("value of ps: %p \n", ps);

    s = *ps;
    printf("value of s: %hx \n", s);

    s = *(ps + 1);
    printf("value of s: %hx \n", s);
}
```

Output (x64)

```
--- Short Integers ---
value of ps: 0x7fff1d71cf10 address of ps: 0x7fff1d71cf08
value of s: 1008
value of ps: 0x7fff1d71cf12
value of s: 2ab
value of s: ffff
```

Long and Long Long Integers

If we want 8-byte 64-bit integers, we need to use `long` or `long long` for portability.

C C++ as a better C

```
puts("--- Long and Long Long Integers ---");
{
    int larr[] = { 0x2ab1008, -1, 0x2ab1010, 0x2ab100c, 0, 0x2000 };

    long* pl = (long*)larr;
    printf("value of pl: %p address of pl: %p \n", pl, &pl);

    long l = *pl;
    printf("value of l: %lx \n", l);

    ++pl;
    printf("value of pl: %p \n", pl);

    l = *pl;
    printf("value of l: %lx \n", l);

    l = *(pl + 1);
    printf("value of l: %lx \n", l);
}
```

Output (x64)

```
--- Long and Long Long Integers ---
value of pl: 0x7fff1d71cef0 address of pl: 0x7fff1d71cee8
value of l: ffffffff02ab1008
value of pl: 0x7fff1d71cef8
value of l: 2ab100c02ab1010
value of l: 200000000000
```

Signed and Unsigned Integers

We need to be careful to use unsigned index variables in classic loops. The following code example loops indefi-nitely since the loop variable is always positive:

C | C++ as a better C

```
puts("--- Signed and Unsigned Integers ---");
{
    // for (unsigned i = 0xfff; i >= 0; --i) // hang
    for (signed i = 0xfff; i >= 0; --i)
    {
    }
}
```

Spiking Thread memory analysis pattern

https://www.dumpanalysis.org/blog/index.php/2007/05/11/crash-dump-analysis-patterns-part-14/

Fixed Size Integers

It is also possible to be precise and use portable fixed-size types.

C   C++ as a better C

```
puts("--- Fixed Size Integers ---");
{
    uint8_t b = 0xfe;

    uint32_t dw = 0xfedcba98;

    uint64_t qw = 0x12345678ffffffff;

    uintptr_t p = (uintptr_t)&qw;
}
```

Booleans

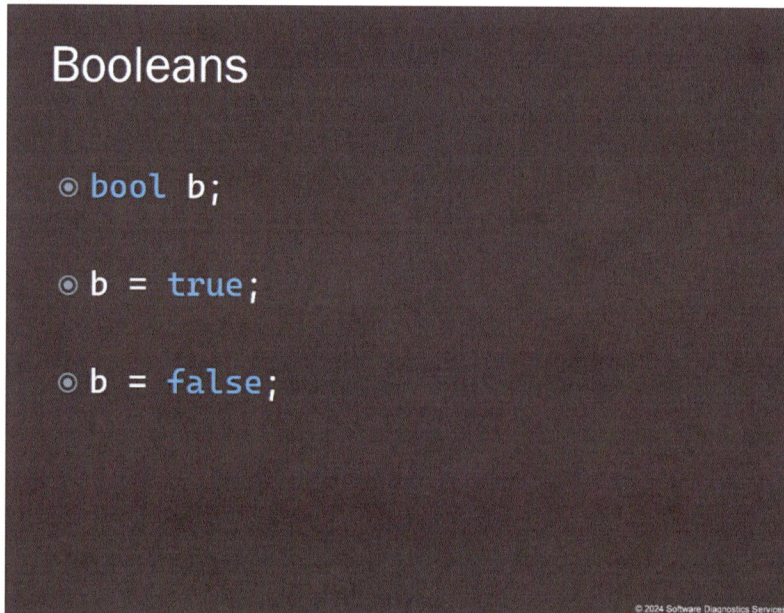

Booleans

⊙ `bool b;`

⊙ `b = true;`

⊙ `b = false;`

© 2024 Software Diagnostics Services

C++ also includes a native type for boolean variables. If you want to use it in pure C, you need to include the *stdbool.h* header.

`C`

```c
puts("--- Booleans ---");
{
    bool b = true; // requires stdbool.h header in C

    b = false;
}
```

C++ as a better C

```cpp
puts("--- Booleans ---");
{
    bool b = true;

    b = false;
}
```

Bytes

The latest C++ standards also include a distinct type for bytes.

Modern C++

```cpp
std::println("--- Bytes ---");
{
    std::byte b{0xab};

    std::println("value of b: {}", b);
}
```

Output (x64)

```
--- Bytes ---
value of b: ab
```

Alignment (C11)

Variables are usually aligned in memory at offsets divisible by their type size value in bytes. In C11, you can get default alignment values using the _Alignof operator and change the default alignment using the _Alignas specifier.

C

```c
puts("--- Alignment (C11) ---");
{
    size_t align = _Alignof(long);

    printf("address of align: %p value of align: %ld \n", &align, align);

    _Alignas(4096) long l = 1;

    printf("address of l: %p \n", &l);
}
```

Output (x64)

```
--- Alignment (C11) ---
address of align: 0x7fff1d71ced8 value of align: 8
address of l: 0x7fff1d71c000
```

Alignment (C++11)

Variables are usually aligned in memory at offsets divisible by their type size value in bytes. In C++11, you can get default alignment values using the `alignof` operator and change the default alignment using the `alignas` specifier.

C++ as a better C

```
puts("--- Alignment (C++11) ---");
{
    size_t align = alignof(long);

    printf("address of align: %p value of align: %ld \n", &align, align);

    alignas(4096) long l = 1;

    printf("address of l: %p \n", &l);
}
```

Output (x64)

```
--- Alignment (C++11) ---
address of align: 0x7ffc93d1eed8 value of align: 8
address of l: 0x7ffc93d1e000
```

Size

The `sizeof` operator can evaluate the size of types, variables, and target result types of expressions (without expression evaluation).

C   C++ as a better C

```c
puts("--- Size ---");
{
    size_t size = sizeof(int);
    printf("value of size: %ld \n", size);

    int i = 0;
    size = sizeof i;
    printf("value of size: %ld \n", size);

    size = sizeof(1 + 1);
    printf("value of size: %ld \n", size);
}
```

Output (x64)

```
--- Size ---
value of size: 4
value of size: 4
value of size: 4
```

LP64

Linux uses the so-called LP64 data model where long integers and pointers are 64-bit.

C   C++ as a better C

```
puts("--- LP64 ---");
{
    printf("size of int: %ld \n"
        "size of int*: %ld \n"
        "size of long: %ld \n"
        "size of long long: %ld \n",
        sizeof(int), sizeof(int*), sizeof(long), sizeof(long long));
}
```

Output (x64)

```
--- LP64 ---
size of int: 4
size of int*: 8
size of long: 8
size of long long: 8
```

Nothing and Anything

- **void foo(void);**

- **void* p;**

© 2024 Software Diagnostics Services

Two distinct types correspond to the concepts of *Nothing* and *Anything* you can find in other programming lan-guages: void and void*. The latter is a pointer to any type.

C   C++ as a better C

```
puts("--- Nothing and Anything ---");
{
    char c;
    char* pc = &c;

    long l;
    long* pl = &l;

    void* p = pc;
    p = pl;
}
```

Automatic Type Inference

C++11 added automatic type specification, so the type is deduced from the initializing expression.

Modern C++

```cpp
auto func(decltype("Hello") cstr) {
    return cstr;
}

std::println("--- Automatic Type Inference ---");
{
    auto a = "Hello";

    std::println("type of a: {}", typeid(a).name());
    std::println("type of func: {}", typeid(func).name());
}
```

Output (x64)

```
$ ./basic_types_modern_cpp
--- Automatic Type Inference ---
type of a: PKc
type of func: FPKcRA6_S_E

$ ./basic_types_modern_cpp | c++filt -t
--- Automatic Type Inference ---
type of signed char: char const*
type of func: char const* (char const (&) [6])
```

Appendix

```
--- ASCII Characters and Pointers ---
value of pstr: 0xffffc7f4e578 address of pstr: 0xffffc7f4e570
value of c: H
value of pstr: 0xffffc7f4e579
value of c: e
value of c: l
--- Bytes and Pointers ---
value of pb: 0xffffc7f4e568 address of pb: 0xffffc7f4e560
value of b: 12
value of pb: 0xffffc7f4e569
value of b: 34
value of b: 56
--- Wide Characters and Pointers ---
value of pwstr: 0xffffc7f4e548 address of pwstr: 0xffffc7f4e540
value of wc: H
value of pwstr: 0xffffc7f4e54c
value of wc: e
value of wc: l
--- Integers ---
value of pi: 0xffffc7f4e528 address of pi: 0xffffc7f4e520
value of i: 2ab1008
value of pi: 0xffffc7f4e52c
value of i: ffffffff
value of i: 2ab1010
--- Little-Endian System ---
values of ba array: 1, 2, 3, 4 value of i: 4030201
--- Short Integers ---
value of ps: 0xffffc7f4e500 address of ps: 0xffffc7f4e4f8
value of s: 1008
value of ps: 0xffffc7f4e502
value of s: 2ab
value of s: ffff
--- Long and Long Long Integers ---
value of pl: 0xffffc7f4e4e0 address of pl: 0xffffc7f4e4d8
value of l: ffffffff02ab1008
value of pl: 0xffffc7f4e4e8
value of l: 2ab100c02ab1010
value of l: 200000000000
--- Signed and Unsigned Integers ---
--- Fixed Size Integers ---
--- Booleans ---
--- Bytes ---
value of bool: ab
--- Alignment (C11) ---
address of align: 0xffffc7f4e4c8 value of align: 8
address of l: 0xffffc7f4e000
--- Alignment (C++11) ---
address of align: 0xffffffaa1e38 value of align: 8
address of l: 0xffffffaa1000
--- Size ---
value of size: 4
value of size: 4
value of size: 4
--- LP64 ---
size of int: 4
size of int*: 8
size of long: 8
size of long long: 8
```

```
--- Nothing and Anything ---
--- Automatic Type Inference ---
type of a: PKc
type of func: FPKcRA6_S_E

$ ./basic_types_modern_cpp | c++filt -t
--- Bytes ---
value of bool: ab
--- Automatic Type Inference ---
type of signed char: char const*
type of func: char const* (char const (&) [6])
```

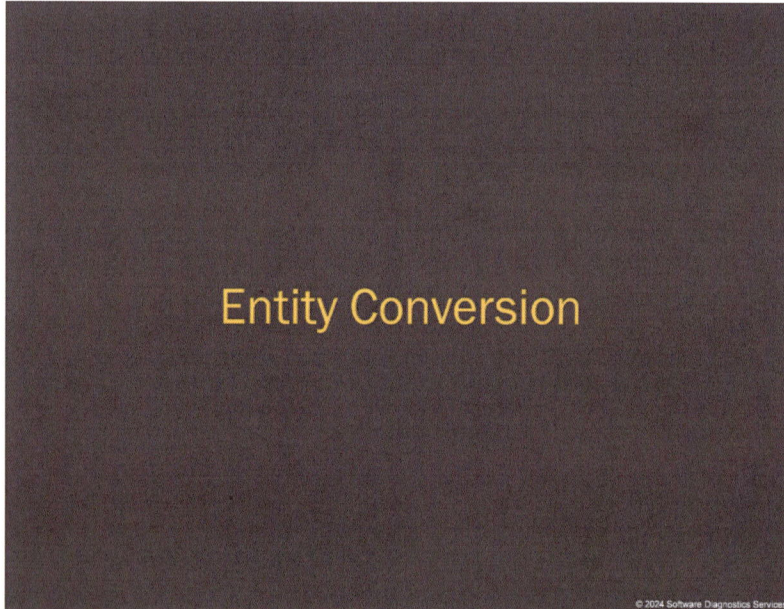

As you anticipate, the same memory cell addresses and their values are the basis of conversion between different entity types. So, let's look at some examples.

The `entity_conversion` projects:

- `entity_conversion_c`   C
- `entity_conversion_c_cpp`   C++ as a better C
- `entity_conversion_classic_cpp` Classic C++

can be found in the archive[4]. In the following slide descriptions, we only show relevant code snippets and their output.

---

[4] https://www.patterndiagnostics.com/Training/ACPPLD/ACPPLD.tar.gz

Pointer Conversion (C-Style)

Pointers can be converted to each other freely because their value is just a memory address. However, when we dereference them, we get the value based on underlying memory contents, which don't change as illustrated here. Please also note that due to the least significant byte endian convention, the integer value we get differs from the memory layout byte order.

C C++ as a better C

```
puts("--- Pointer Conversion (C-Style) ---");
{
    unsigned char barr[] = { 0x12, 0x34, 0x56, 0x78, 0xab, 0xcd };

    unsigned char* pb = barr;
    printf("value of pb: %p address of pb: %p \n", pb, &pb);

    unsigned char b = *pb;
    printf("value of b: %x \n", b);

    int* pi = (int*)pb;

    printf("value of pi: %p address of pi: %p \n", pi, &pi);

    int i = *pi; // Intel LSB endian

    printf("value of i: %x \n", i);
}
```

Output (x64)

```
--- Pointer Conversion (C-Style) ---
value of pb: 0x7ffdb983bb0a address of pb: 0x7ffdb983bb00
value of b: 12
value of pi: 0x7ffdb983bb0a address of pi: 0x7ffdb983baf8
value of i: 78563412
```

Pointer Conversion (C++)

Classic C++

```cpp
std::cout << "--- Pointer Conversion (C++) ---" << std::endl;
{
    unsigned char barr[] = { 0x12, 0x34, 0x56, 0x78, 0xab, 0xcd };

    unsigned char* pb = barr;
    std::cout << "value of pb: " << static_cast<void*>(pb) << // pb is interpreted as a C-string
        " address of pb: " << &pb << std::endl;

    unsigned char b = *pb;
    std::cout << "value of b: " << std::hex << static_cast<int>(b) << std::endl;

    int* pi = reinterpret_cast<int*>(pb);

    std::cout << "value of pi: " << pi << " address of pi: " << &pi << std::endl;

    int i = *pi; // Intel LSB endian

    std::cout << "value of i: " << std::hex << i << std::endl;
}
```

Output (x64)

```
--- Pointer Conversion (C++) ---
value of pb: 0x7fff5fa8778a address of pb: 0x7fff5fa87780
value of b: 12
value of pi: 0x7fff5fa8778a address of pi: 0x7fff5fa87778
value of i: 78563412
```

Numeric Promotion/Conversion

Values from the lesser range of values can be automatically promoted to types with a wider range of values. The opposite automatic conversion may lose some bits of information and should be carefully reviewed.

C   C++ as a better C

```
puts("--- Numeric Promotion/Conversion ---");
{
    char c = 'a';
    int n = c;
    short s = c;

    printf("value of c: %x value of n: %x value of s: %x\n", c, n, s);

    n = 0x1234;
    c = n;

    printf("value of n: %x value of c: %x \n", n, c);
}
```

Classic C++

```
std::cout << "--- Numeric Promotion/Conversion ---" << std::endl;
{
    char c = 'a';
    int n = c;
    short s = c;

    std::cout << "value of c: " << std::hex << static_cast<int>(c) << " value of n: " << n << "
value of s: " << s << std::endl;

    n = 0x1234;
    c = n;
```

```
    std::cout << "value of n: " << n << " value of c: " << static_cast<int>(c) << std::endl;
}
```

Output

```
--- Numeric Promotion/Conversion ---
value of c: 61 value of n: 61 value of s: 61
value of n: 1234 value of c: 34
```

Numeric Conversion

In the absence of automatic conversion for compatible types, we can use C-style casts or explicit, specific C++ casts.

C   C++ as a better C

```
puts("--- Numeric Conversion ---");
{
    for (unsigned i = 0xfff; (int)i >= 0; --i)
    {
    }
}
```

Classic C++

```
std::cout << "--- Numeric Conversion ---" << std::endl;
{
    for (unsigned i = 0xfff; static_cast<int>(i) >= 0; --i)
    {
    }
}
```

Incompatible Types

When types are incompatible, for example, integers and pointers to them, we can use either C-style casts or the specific C++ type reinterpretation cast.

C   C++ as a better C

```
puts("--- Incompatible Type ---");
{
    int* p = (int*)1;
}
```

Classic C++

```
std::cout << "--- Incompatible Type ---" << std::endl;
{
    int* p = reinterpret_cast<int*>(1);
}
```

Forcing

```
Forcing

struct A
{
    unsigned int u1;
    unsigned int u2;
};

struct B
{
    unsigned long ul;
} b;

A a = reinterpret_cast<A>(b);

A a = *(A*)&b;
a = *reinterpret_cast<A*>(&b);
```

© 2024 Software Diagnostics Services

Different structures are even more incompatible with the failing direct C++ reinterpretation cast. However, we can force a reinterpretation of structures by reinterpreting a pointer to a source structure (an address of a source structure) as a pointer to a target structure (an address of a target structure) and then dereferencing it. In such a case, the underlying memory cells are reinterpreted as the target structure field values. You can review the code example after studying the next two sections on structures and memory:

C C++ as a better C

```c
puts("--- Forcing ---");
{
    struct A
    {
        unsigned int u1;
        unsigned int u2;
    };

    struct B
    {
        unsigned long ul;
    } b = {0xFFFFFFFF00000000};

    struct A a = *(struct A*)&b;

    printf("address of a: %p value of a: {%x, %x}: \n", &a, a.u1, a.u2);
    printf("address of b: %p value of b: %lx \n", &b, b.ul); // Intel LSB endian
}
```

Classic C++

```cpp
std::cout << "--- Forcing ---" << std::endl;
{
    struct A
    {
        unsigned int u1;
        unsigned int u2;
    };

    struct B
```

```
{
    unsigned long ul;
} b = { 0xFFFFFFFF00000000 };

struct A a = *reinterpret_cast<A*>(&b);

std::cout << "address of a: " << &a <<
    " value of a: {" << a.u1 << ", " << a.u2 << "}" << std::endl;
std::cout << "address of b: " << &b <<
    " value of b: " << b.ul << std::endl; // Intel LSB endian
}
```

Output (x64)

```
--- Forcing ---
address of a: 0x7ffdb983bae8 value of a: {0, ffffffff}:
address of b: 0x7ffdb983baf0 value of b: ffffffff00000000
```

Uniting

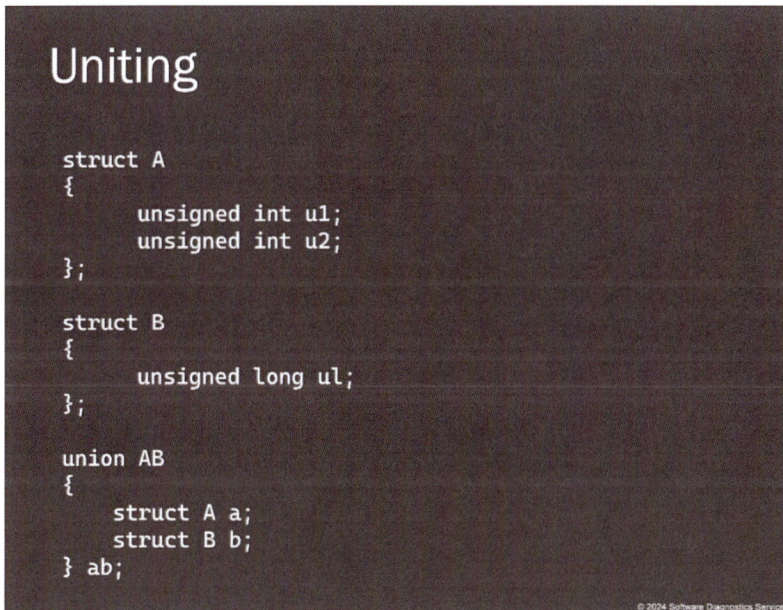

We can superimpose different structures at the same location in memory. In this case, the conversion is automatic when we choose between different discriminating union fields.

```
puts("--- Uniting ---");
{
    struct A
    {
        unsigned int u1;
        unsigned int u2;
    };
```

```
    struct B
    {
        unsigned long ull;
    };

    union AB
    {
        struct A a;
        struct B b;
    } ab = {0};

    ab.b.ul = 0xFFFFFFFF00000000;

    printf("address of ab: %p address of ab.a: %p address of ab.b: %p \n"
        "value of a: {% x, % x} value of b: % llx \n",
        &ab, &ab.a, &ab.b, ab.a.u1, ab.a.u2, ab.b.ul); // Intel LSB endian
}
```

Classic C++

```
std::cout << "--- Uniting ---" << std::endl;
{
    struct A
    {
        unsigned int u1;
        unsigned int u2;
    };

    struct B
    {
        unsigned long ull;
    };

    union AB
    {
        struct A a;
        struct B b;
    } ab = { 0 };

    ab.b.ul = 0xFFFFFFFF00000000;

    std::cout << "address of ab: " << &ab <<
        " address of ab.a: " << &ab.a << " address of ab.b: " << &ab.b <<
        " value of a: {" << ab.a.u1 << ", " << ab.a.u2 << "}" <<
        " value of b: " << ab.b.ul << std::endl; // Intel LSB endian
}
```

Output (x64)

```
--- Uniting ---
address of ab: 0x7ffdb983bae0 address of ab.a: 0x7ffdb983bae0 address of ab.b: 0x7ffdb983bae0
value of a: {0, ffffffff} value of b: ffffffff00000000
```

Appendix

Output (A64)

```
--- Pointer Conversion (C-Style) ---
value of pb: 0xfffff25acec8 address of pb: 0xfffff25acec0
value of b: 12
value of pi: 0xfffff25acec8 address of pi: 0xfffff25aceb8
value of i: 78563412
--- Pointer Conversion (C++) ---
value of pb: 0xfffff5397878 address of pb: 0xfffff5397870
value of b: 12
value of pi: 0xfffff5397878 address of pi: 0xfffff5397868
value of i: 78563412
--- Numeric Promotion/Conversion ---
value of c: 61 value of n: 61 value of s: 61
value of n: 1234 value of c: 34
--- Numeric Conversion ---
--- Incompatible Type ---
--- Forcing ---
address of a: 0xfffff25acea8 value of a: {0, ffffffff}:
address of b: 0xfffff25aceb0 value of b: ffffffff00000000
--- Uniting ---
address of ab: 0xfffff25acea0 address of ab.a: 0xfffff25acea0 address of ab.b: 0xfffff25acea0
value of a: {0, ffffffff} value of b: ffffffff00000000
```

Structures, Classes, and Objects

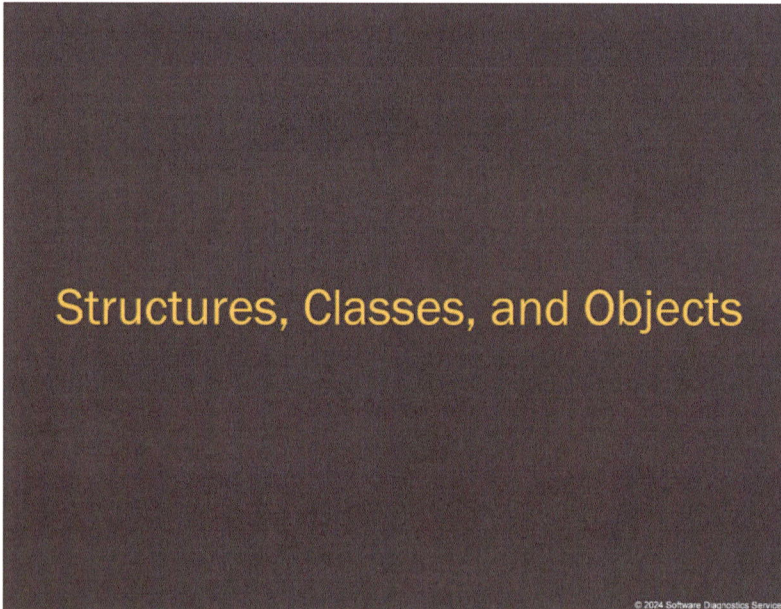

Now, we cover structures, classes, and their objects.

The **structures** projects:

- `structures_c`   C
- `structures_c_cpp`   C++ as a better C
- `structures_classic_cpp` Classic C++

can be found in the archive[5]. In the following slide descriptions, we only show relevant code snippets and their output.

---

[5] https://www.patterndiagnostics.com/Training/ACPPLD/ACPPLD.tar.gz

Structures

We can view structures as collections of fields laid out in memory. Structures may have names or can be anonymous, as on the right.

C

```c
puts("--- Structures ---");
{
    struct MyStruct
    {
        int field;
        // ...
    };

    struct MyStruct myStruct;

    struct MyStruct* pMyStruct;

    struct
    {
        int field;
        // ...
    } myOtherStruct;

    struct
    {
        int field;
        // ...
    }* pMyOtherStruct;
}
```

C++ as a better C

```cpp
puts("--- Structures ---");
{
    struct MyStruct
    {
        int field;
        // ...
    };

    MyStruct myStruct; // in C++ struct keyword can be omitted

    MyStruct* pMyStruct;

    struct
    {
        int field;
        // ...
    } myOtherStruct;

    struct
    {
        int field;
        // ...
    }* pMyOtherStruct;
}
```

Access Level

Fields with the private access specifier cannot be referenced from the outside.

Classic C++

```cpp
std::cout << "--- Access Level ---" << std::endl;
{
    struct MyStruct
    {
        // public:
        int field1;
    private:
        int field2;
    } myStruct;

    myStruct.field1 = 1;
    // myStruct.field2 = 2; // error
}
```

Reading/Writing Private Fields

Reading/Writing Private Fields

```cpp
struct MyStruct
{
// public:
    int field1;
private:
    int field2;
} myStruct;



*((int*)&myStruct+1);

*(reinterpret_cast<int*>(&myStruct)+1);
```

© 2024 Software Diagnostics Services

Nevertheless, we can access private fields' memory locations through casting and pointer arithmetic. Such manupulations depend on field alignment.

Classic C++

```cpp
std::cout << "--- Reading/Writing Private Fields ---" << std::endl;
{
    struct MyStruct
    {
        // public:
        int field1;
    private:
        int field2;
```

```
    } myStruct;

    std::cout << "value of field1: " << *reinterpret_cast<int*>(&myStruct) <<
        " value of field2: " << *(reinterpret_cast<int*>(&myStruct)+1) << std::endl;

    myStruct.field1 = 1;
    *(reinterpret_cast<int*>(&myStruct)+1) = 2;

    std::cout << "value of field1: " << *reinterpret_cast<int*>(&myStruct) <<
        " value of field2: " << *(reinterpret_cast<int*>(&myStruct)+1) << std::endl;
}
```

Output (x64)

```
--- Reading/Writing Private Fields ---
value of field1: 1 value of field2: 0
value of field1: 1 value of field2: 2
```

Classes and Objects

Classes have the same structure.

Classic C++

```
std::cout << "--- Classes and Objects ---" << std::endl;
{
    class MyClass {
        int field;
    };

    MyClass myStruct; // class keyword can be omitted
```

```
MyClass* pMyStruct;

class {
    int field;
} myOtherClass;

class
{
    int field;
}* pMyOtherClass;
}
```

Structures and Classes

Both structures and classes are completely the same in C++ and can be used interchangeably. This is why you can always see struct in good modern C++ books. The only difference (if we ignore inheritance for now) is the field access, which is public by default in structures and private in classes.

Classic C++

```
std::cout << "--- Structures and Classes ---" << std::endl;
{
    struct tagStruct
    {
    // public:
        int field;
    };

    class tagClass
    {
    public: // (private:)
        int field;
    };
}
```

Pointer to Structure

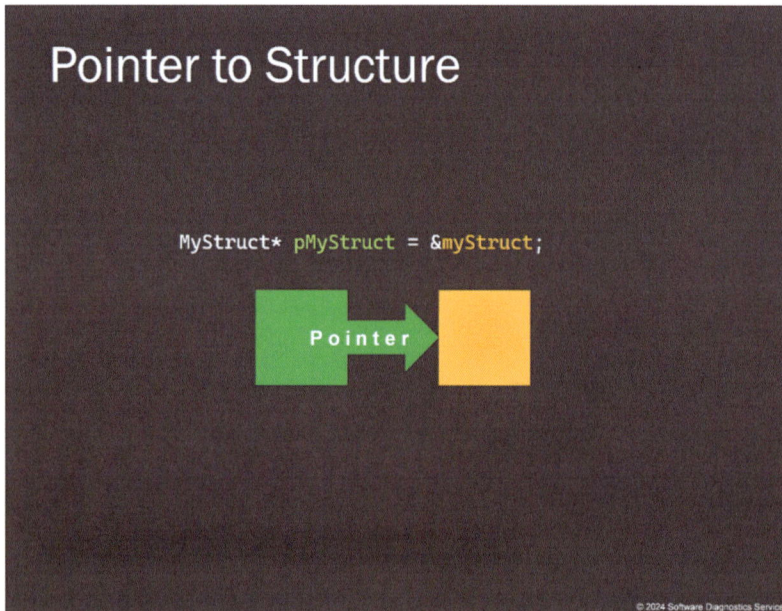

Here, we go again through our conceptual philosophy of pointers pictures and annotate them with C and C++ code.

C

```c
puts("--- Pointer to Structure ---");
{
    struct MyStruct
    {
        int field;
        // ...
    } myStruct;

    struct MyStruct* pMyStruct = &myStruct;

    printf("address of myStruct: %p address of pMyStruct: %p value of pMyStruct: %p \n",
        &myStruct, &pMyStruct, pMyStruct);
}
```

C++ as a better C

```cpp
puts("--- Pointer to Structure ---");
{
    struct MyStruct
    {
        int field;
        // ...
    } myStruct;

    MyStruct* pMyStruct = &myStruct;

    printf("address of myStruct: %p address of pMyStruct: %p value of pMyStruct: %p \n",
        &myStruct, &pMyStruct, pMyStruct);
}
```

<u>Output (x64)</u>

```
--- Pointer to Structure ---
address of myStruct: 0x7ffdf3736714 address of pMyStruct: 0x7ffdf3736708 value of pMyStruct:
0x7ffdf3736714
```

Pointer to Structure Dereference

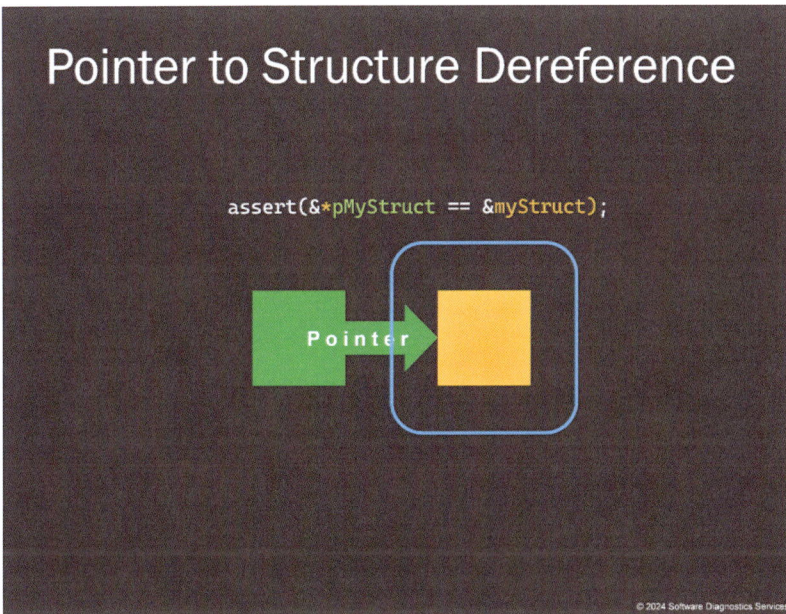

Here, we dereference a pointer to some structure. We get the structure value.

C

```
puts("--- Pointer to Structure Dereference ---");
{
    struct MyStruct
    {
        int field;
        // ...
    } myStruct;

    struct MyStruct* pMyStruct = &myStruct;

    printf("address of myStruct: %p address of pMyStruct: %p value of pMyStruct: %p \n",
        &myStruct, &pMyStruct, pMyStruct);

    assert(&*pMyStruct == &myStruct);

    printf("address of pMyStruct dereference: %p address of myStruct: %p \n",
        &*pMyStruct, &myStruct);
}
```

C++ as a better C

```
puts("--- Pointer to Structure Dereference ---");
{
    struct MyStruct
    {
        int field;
        // ...
    } myStruct;

    MyStruct* pMyStruct = &myStruct;

    printf("address of myStruct: %p address of pMyStruct: %p value of pMyStruct: %p \n",
        &myStruct, &pMyStruct, pMyStruct);

    assert(&*pMyStruct == &myStruct);

    printf("address of pMyStruct dereference: %p address of myStruct: %p \n",
        &*pMyStruct, &myStruct);
}
```

Output (x64)

```
--- Pointer to Structure Dereference ---
address of myStruct: 0x7ffdf3736704 address of pMyStruct: 0x7ffdf37366f8 value of pMyStruct:
0x7ffdf3736704
address of pMyStruct dereference: 0x7ffdf3736704 address of myStruct: 0x7ffdf3736704
```

One to Many

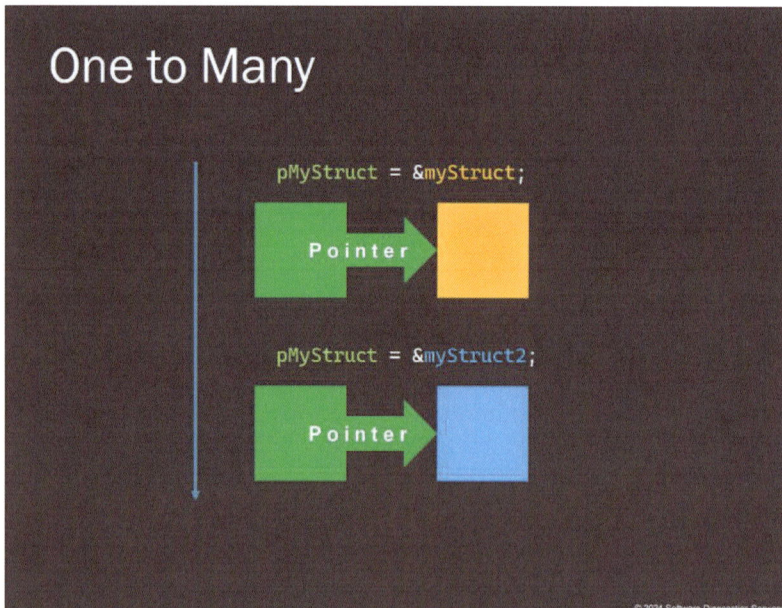

A pointer may contain memory addresses of different structure objects during its lifetime. If such objects are dynamically allocated (not in static or stack memory) then we may have a possibility of a memory leak.

`C`

```
puts("--- One to Many ---");
{
    struct MyStruct
    {
        int field;
        // ...
    } myStruct, myStruct2;

    struct MyStruct* pMyStruct = &myStruct;

    printf("address of myStruct: %p address of pMyStruct: %p value of pMyStruct: %p \n",
        &myStruct, &pMyStruct, pMyStruct);

    pMyStruct = &myStruct2; // no leak

    printf("address of myStruct2: %p address of pMyStruct: %p value of pMyStruct: %p \n",
        &myStruct2, &pMyStruct, pMyStruct);
}
```

C++ as a better C

```
puts("--- One to Many ---");
{
    struct MyStruct
    {
        int field;
        // ...
    } myStruct, myStruct2;

    MyStruct* pMyStruct = &myStruct;

    printf("address of myStruct: %p address of pMyStruct: %p value of pMyStruct: %p \n",
        &myStruct, &pMyStruct, pMyStruct);

    pMyStruct = &myStruct2; // no leak

    printf("address of myStruct2: %p address of pMyStruct: %p value of pMyStruct: %p \n",
        &myStruct2, &pMyStruct, pMyStruct);
}
```

Output (x64)

```
--- One to Many ---
address of myStruct: 0x7ffdf37366f4 address of pMyStruct: 0x7ffdf37366e8 value of pMyStruct:
0x7ffdf37366f4
address of myStruct2: 0x7ffdf37366f0 address of pMyStruct: 0x7ffdf37366e8 value of pMyStruct:
0x7ffdf37366f0
```

Memory Leak

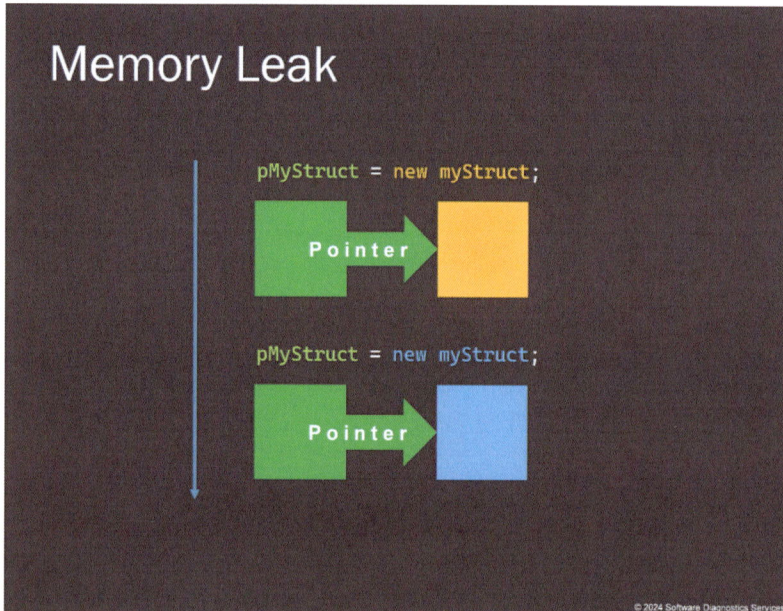

C

```c
puts("--- Memory Leak ---");
{
    struct MyStruct
    {
        int field;
        // ...
    };

    struct MyStruct* pMyStruct = malloc(sizeof(struct MyStruct));

    printf("address of pMyStruct: %p value of pMyStruct: %p \n", &pMyStruct, pMyStruct);

    // free(pMyStruct);

    pMyStruct = malloc(sizeof(struct MyStruct)); // leak

    printf("address of pMyStruct: %p value of pMyStruct: %p \n", &pMyStruct, pMyStruct);

    free(pMyStruct);
}
```

C++ as a better C

```c
puts("--- Memory Leak ---");
{
    struct MyStruct
    {
        int field;
        // ...
    };

    MyStruct* pMyStruct = (MyStruct*)malloc(sizeof(MyStruct)); // needs casting in C++

    printf("address of pMyStruct: %p value of pMyStruct: %p \n", &pMyStruct, pMyStruct);

    // free(pMyStruct);

    pMyStruct = (MyStruct*)malloc(sizeof(MyStruct)); // leak

    printf("address of pMyStruct: %p value of pMyStruct: %p \n", &pMyStruct, pMyStruct);

    free(pMyStruct);
}
```

Classic C++

```cpp
std::cout << "--- Memory Leak ---" << std::endl;
{
    struct MyStruct
    {
        int field;
        // ...
    };

    MyStruct* pMyStruct = new MyStruct;

    std::cout << "address of pMyStruct: " << &pMyStruct <<
        " value of pMyStruct: " << pMyStruct << std::endl;

    // delete pMyStruct;

    pMyStruct = new MyStruct; // leak

    std::cout << "address of pMyStruct: " << &pMyStruct <<
        " value of pMyStruct: " << pMyStruct << std::endl;

    delete pMyStruct;
}
```

Output (x64)

```
--- Memory Leak ---
address of pMyStruct: 0x7ffdf37366e0 value of pMyStruct: 0xc54cb0
address of pMyStruct: 0x7ffdf37366e0 value of pMyStruct: 0xc54cd0
```

Many Pointers to One Structure

Here, we assign the value of one pointer to another, and both now point to the same structure.

C

```c
puts("--- Many Pointers to One Structure ---");
{
    struct MyStruct
    {
        int field;
        // ...
    } myStruct;

    struct MyStruct* pMyStruct = &myStruct;

    printf("address of myStruct: %p address of pMyStruct: %p value of pMyStruct: %p \n",
        &myStruct, &pMyStruct, pMyStruct);

    struct MyStruct* pMyStruct2 = &myStruct;

    printf("address of myStruct: %p address of pMyStruct2: %p value of pMyStruct2: %p \n",
        &myStruct, &pMyStruct2, pMyStruct2);
}
```

C++ as a better C

```cpp
puts("--- Many Pointers to One Structure ---");
{
    struct MyStruct
    {
        int field;
        // ...
    } myStruct;

    MyStruct* pMyStruct = &myStruct;
```

```
printf("address of myStruct: %p address of pMyStruct: %p value of pMyStruct: %p \n",
    &myStruct, &pMyStruct, pMyStruct);

MyStruct* pMyStruct2 = &myStruct;

printf("address of myStruct: %p address of pMyStruct2: %p value of pMyStruct2: %p \n",
    &myStruct, &pMyStruct2, pMyStruct2);
}
```

Output (x64)

```
--- Many Pointers to One Structure ---
address of myStruct: 0x7ffdf37366dc address of pMyStruct: 0x7ffdf37366d0 value of pMyStruct:
0x7ffdf37366dc
address of myStruct: 0x7ffdf37366dc address of pMyStruct2: 0x7ffdf37366c8 value of pMyStruct2:
0x7ffdf37366dc
```

Many to One Dereference

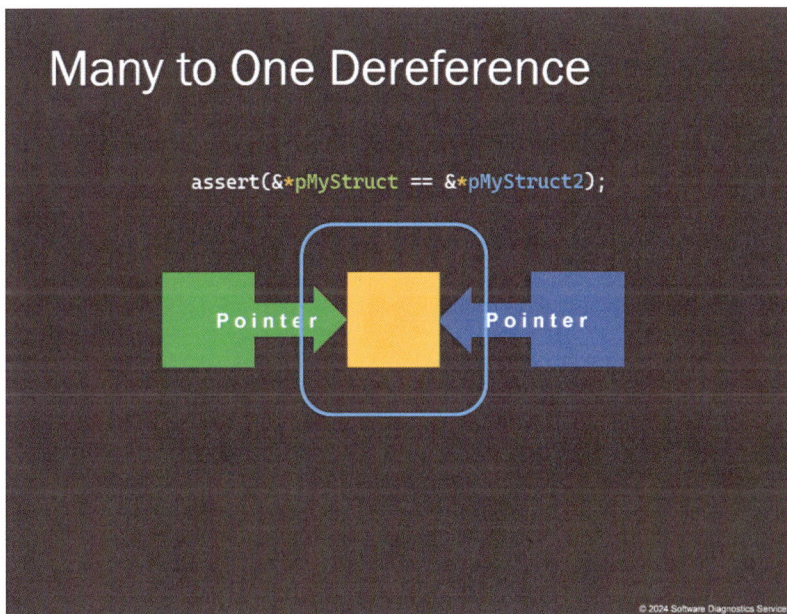

If we dereference both, we get the same value with the same address.

C

```
puts("--- Many to One Dereference ---");
{
    struct MyStruct
    {
        int field;
        // ...
    } myStruct;

    struct MyStruct* pMyStruct = &myStruct;
```

```cpp
    struct MyStruct* pMyStruct2 = &myStruct;

    assert(&*pMyStruct == &*pMyStruct2);

    printf("address of myStruct: %p address of pMyStruct: %p value of pMyStruct: %p \n",
        &myStruct, &pMyStruct, pMyStruct);
    printf("address of myStruct: %p address of pMyStruct2: %p value of pMyStruct2: %p \n",
        &myStruct, &pMyStruct2, pMyStruct2);
    printf("address of pMyStruct dereference: %p address of pMyStruct2 dereference: %p \n",
        &*pMyStruct, &*pMyStruct2);
}
```

C++ as a better C

```cpp
puts("--- Many to One Dereference ---");
{
    struct MyStruct
    {
        int field;
        // ...
    } myStruct;

    MyStruct* pMyStruct = &myStruct;
    MyStruct* pMyStruct2 = &myStruct;

    assert(&*pMyStruct == &*pMyStruct2);

    printf("address of myStruct: %p address of pMyStruct: %p value of pMyStruct: %p \n",
        &myStruct, &pMyStruct, pMyStruct);
    printf("address of myStruct: %p address of pMyStruct2: %p value of pMyStruct2: %p \n",
        &myStruct, &pMyStruct2, pMyStruct2);
    printf("address of pMyStruct dereference: %p address of pMyStruct2 dereference: %p \n",
        &*pMyStruct, &*pMyStruct2);
}
```

<u>Output (x64)</u>

```
--- Many to One Dereference ---
address of myStruct: 0x7ffdf37366c4 address of pMyStruct: 0x7ffdf37366b8 value of pMyStruct:
0x7ffdf37366c4
address of myStruct: 0x7ffdf37366c4 address of pMyStruct2: 0x7ffdf37366b0 value of pMyStruct2:
0x7ffdf37366c4
address of pMyStruct dereference: 0x7ffdf37366c4 address of pMyStruct2 dereference: 0x7ffdf37366c4
```

Invalid Pointer to Structure

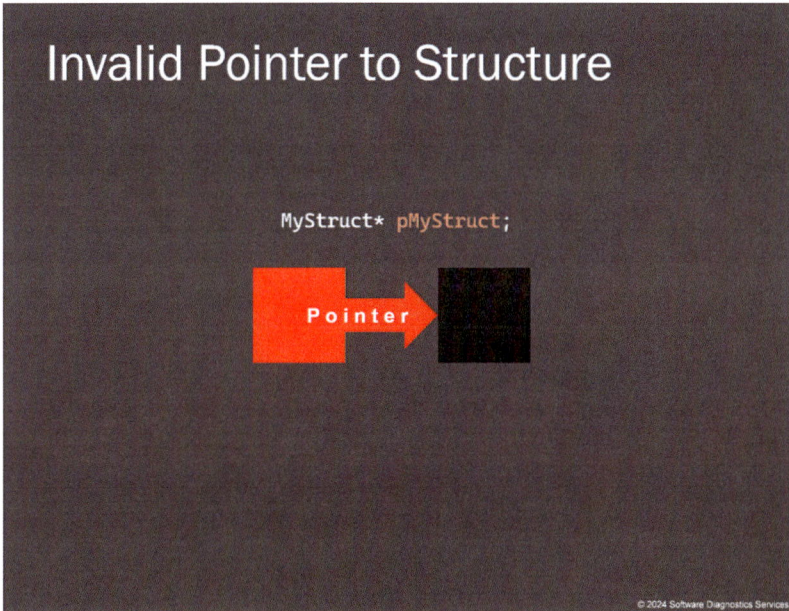

Here, we depict an uninitialized pointer that, depending on the memory storage type, can be a NULL pointer or some random value.

C

```c
puts("--- Invalid Pointer to Structure ---");
{
    struct MyStruct
    {
        int field;
        // ...
    } myStruct;

    struct MyStruct* pMyStruct = (struct MyStruct*)0xffffffff00000000;

    printf("address of pMyStruct: %p value of pMyStruct: %p \n", &pMyStruct, pMyStruct);

    struct MyStruct* pUninitialized;

    printf("address of pUninitialized: %p value of pUninitialized: %p \n", &pUninitialized,
pUninitialized);
}
```

C++ as a better C

```c
puts("--- Invalid Pointer to Structure ---");
{
    struct MyStruct
    {
        int field;
        // ...
    } myStruct;

    MyStruct* pMyStruct = (MyStruct*)0xffffffff00000000;

    printf("address of pMyStruct: %p value of pMyStruct: %p \n", &pMyStruct, pMyStruct);

    MyStruct* pUninitialized;

    printf("address of pUninitialized: %p value of pUninitialized: %p \n", &pUninitialized,
pUninitialized);
}
```

Output (x64)

```
--- Invalid Pointer to Structure ---
address of pMyStruct: 0x7ffdf37366a0 value of pMyStruct: 0xffffffff00000000
address of pUninitialized: 0x7ffdf3736698 value of pUninitialized: 0
```

Classic C++

```cpp
puts("--- Invalid Pointer to Structure ---");
{
    struct MyStruct
    {
        int field;
        // ...
    } myStruct;

    MyStruct* pMyStruct = reinterpret_cast<MyStruct*>(0xffffffff00000000);

    std::cout << "address of pMyStruct: " << &pMyStruct <<
        " value of pMyStruct: " << pMyStruct << std::endl;

    MyStruct* pUninitialized;

    std::cout << "address of pUninitialized: " << &pUninitialized << " value of pUninitialized: "
<< pUninitialized << std::endl;
}
```

Output (x64)

```
--- Invalid Pointer to Structure ---
address of pMyStruct: 0x7ffe5de4dc30 value of pMyStruct: 0xffffffff00000000
address of pUninitialized: 0x7ffe5de4dc28 value of pUninitialized: 0x12000
```

Invalid Pointer Dereference

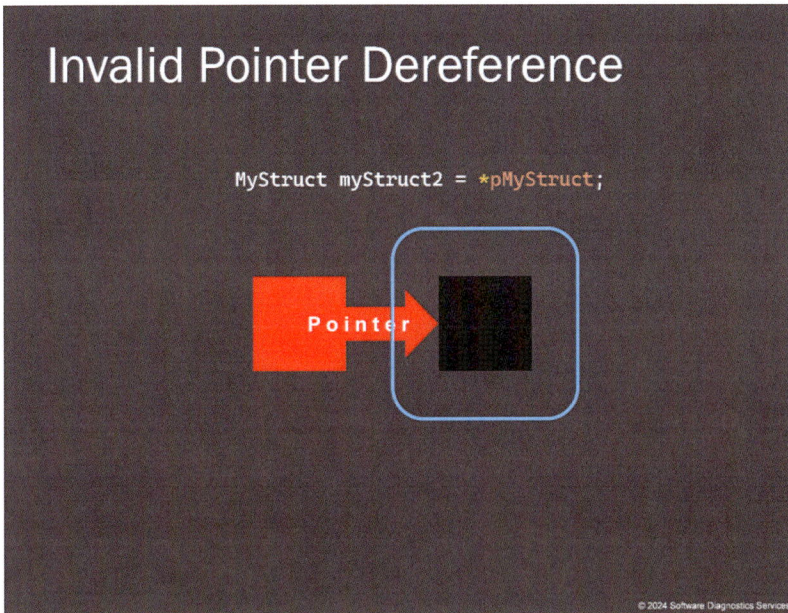

Dereferencing an uninitialized pointer can have undefined behavior, most likely an access violation leading to a crash.

C

```
puts("--- Invalid Pointer Dereference ---");
{
    struct MyStruct
    {
        int field;
        // ...
    } myStruct;

    struct MyStruct* pMyStruct = (struct MyStruct*)4;

    printf("address of pMyStruct: %p value of pMyStruct: %p \n", &pMyStruct, pMyStruct);

    // struct MyStruct myStruct2 = *pMyStruct; // crash
}
```

C++ as a better C

```
puts("--- Invalid Pointer Dereference ---");
{
    struct MyStruct
    {
        int field;
        // ...
    } myStruct;

    MyStruct* pMyStruct = (MyStruct*)4;

    printf("address of pMyStruct: %p value of pMyStruct: %p \n", &pMyStruct, pMyStruct);

    // MyStruct myStruct2 = *pMyStruct; // crash
}
```

Classic C++

```cpp
puts("--- Invalid Pointer Dereference ---");
{
    struct MyStruct
    {
        int field;
        // ...
    } myStruct;

    MyStruct* pMyStruct = reinterpret_cast<MyStruct*>(4);

    std::cout << "address of pMyStruct: " << &pMyStruct <<
        " value of pMyStruct: " << pMyStruct << std::endl;

    // MyStruct myStruct2 = *pMyStruct; // crash
}
```

Output (x64)

```
--- Invalid Pointer Dereference ---
address of pMyStruct: 0x7ffdf3736688 value of pMyStruct: 0x4
```

Wild (Dangling) Pointer

Memory for a structure can be dynamically allocated and then deallocated, but if a pointer is not reset to some value easy to check, such as 0, then we have a dangling pointer with its dereferencing resulting in undefined behavior that could lead to further corruption.

C

```c
puts("--- Wild (Dangling) Pointer ---");
{
    struct MyStruct
    {
        int field;
        // ...
    };

    struct MyStruct* pMyStruct = malloc(sizeof(struct MyStruct));
    if (pMyStruct == NULL) return -1;

    *(int*)pMyStruct = 0x12345678;

    printf("address of pMyStruct: %p value of pMyStruct: %p dereference of pMyStruct: %x \n",
        &pMyStruct, pMyStruct, *(int*)pMyStruct);

    free(pMyStruct); // dangling pointer

    printf("address of pMyStruct: %p value of pMyStruct: %p \n",
        &pMyStruct, pMyStruct);

    // printf("dereference of pMyStruct: %x \n", *(int*)pMyStruct); // may crash

    // assert(*(int*)pMyStruct == 0x12345678); // may fail or crash

    pMyStruct = NULL; // Not dangling
}
```

C++ as a better C

```c
puts("--- Wild (Dangling) Pointer ---");
{
    struct MyStruct
    {
        int field;
        // ...
    };

    MyStruct* pMyStruct = (MyStruct*)malloc(sizeof(MyStruct));
    if (pMyStruct == NULL) return -1;

    *(int*)pMyStruct = 0x12345678;

    printf("address of pMyStruct: %p value of pMyStruct: %p dereference of pMyStruct: %x \n",
        &pMyStruct, pMyStruct, *(int*)pMyStruct);

    free(pMyStruct); // dangling pointer

    printf("address of pMyStruct: %p value of pMyStruct: %p \n",
        &pMyStruct, pMyStruct);

    // printf("dereference of pMyStruct: %x \n", *(int*)pMyStruct); // may crash

    // assert(*(int*)pMyStruct == 0x12345678); // may fail or crash

    pMyStruct = NULL; // Not dangling
}
```

Output (x64)

```
--- Wild (Dangling) Pointer ---
address of pMyStruct: 0x7ffdf3736680 value of pMyStruct: 0xc54cd0 dereference of pMyStruct: 12345678
address of pMyStruct: 0x7ffdf3736680 value of pMyStruct: 0xc54cd0
```

Classic C++

```cpp
puts("--- Wild (Dangling) Pointer ---");
{
    struct MyStruct
    {
        int field;
        // ...
    };

    MyStruct* pMyStruct = new MyStruct;

    *reinterpret_cast<int*>(pMyStruct) = 0x12345678;

    std::cout << "address of pMyStruct: " << &pMyStruct << " value of pMyStruct: " <<
        pMyStruct << " dereference of pMyStruct: " << *reinterpret_cast<int*>(pMyStruct) <<
std::endl;

    delete pMyStruct; // dangling pointer

    std::cout << "address of pMyStruct: " << &pMyStruct <<
        " value of pMyStruct: " << pMyStruct << std::endl;

    // std::cout << " dereference of pMyStruct: "
    //     << *reinterpret_cast<int*>(pMyStruct) << std::endl; // may crash

    // assert(*reinterpret_cast<int*>(pMyStruct) == 0x12345678); // may fail or crash

    pMyStruct = NULL; // Not dangling
    // pMyStruct = nullptr;  // C++11
}
```

Output (x64)

```
--- Wild (Dangling) Pointer ---
address of pMyStruct: 0x7ffe5de4dc10 value of pMyStruct: 0x1808d20 dereference of pMyStruct: 12345678
address of pMyStruct: 0x7ffe5de4dc10 value of pMyStruct: 0x1808d20
```

Pointer to Pointer to Structure

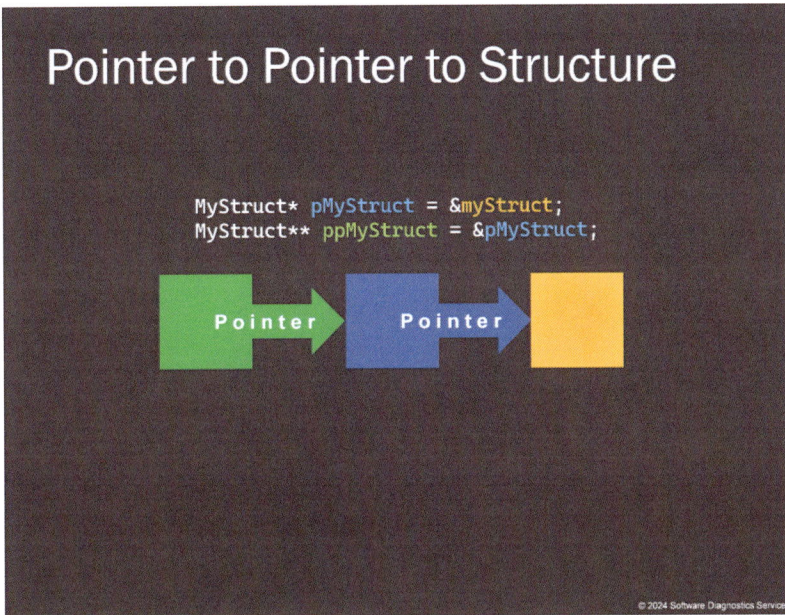

We can also have pointers to pointers to structures and so on, with double and more dereferences needed to get the value. We'll see why we need double-pointers later when we discuss passing parameters to functions.

C

```c
puts("--- Pointer to Pointer to Structure ---");
{
    struct MyStruct
    {
        int field;
        // ...
    } myStruct;

    struct MyStruct* pMyStruct = &myStruct;

    printf("address of myStruct: %p address of pMyStruct: %p value of pMyStruct: %p \n",
        &myStruct, &pMyStruct, pMyStruct);

    struct MyStruct** ppMyStruct = &pMyStruct;

    printf("address of ppMyStruct: %p value of ppMyStruct: %p \n",
        &ppMyStruct, ppMyStruct);
}
```

C++ as a better C

```cpp
puts("--- Pointer to Pointer to Structure ---");
{
    struct MyStruct
    {
        int field;
        // ...
    } myStruct;

    MyStruct* pMyStruct = &myStruct;
```

```c
    printf("address of myStruct: %p address of pMyStruct: %p value of pMyStruct: %p \n",
        &myStruct, &pMyStruct, pMyStruct);

    MyStruct** ppMyStruct = &pMyStruct;

    printf("address of ppMyStruct: %p value of ppMyStruct: %p \n",
        &ppMyStruct, ppMyStruct);
}
```

Output (x64)

```
--- Pointer to Pointer to Structure ---
address of myStruct: 0x7ffdf373667c address of pMyStruct: 0x7ffdf3736670 value of pMyStruct:
0x7ffdf373667c
address of ppMyStruct: 0x7ffdf3736668 value of ppMyStruct: 0x7ffdf3736670
```

Pointer to Pointer Dereference

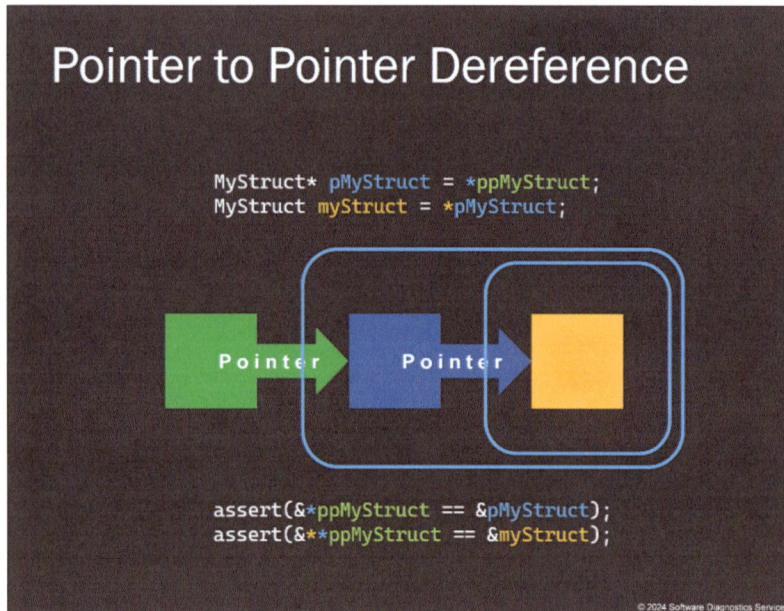

Here, we have double dereference illustrated. Please notice an example of Hungarian notation.

C

```c
puts("--- Pointer to Pointer to Dereference ---");
{
    struct MyStruct
    {
        int field;
        // ...
    } myStruct;

    struct MyStruct* pMyStruct = &myStruct;
```

```c
    printf("address of myStruct: %p address of pMyStruct: %p value of pMyStruct: %p \n",
        &myStruct, &pMyStruct, pMyStruct);

    struct MyStruct** ppMyStruct = &pMyStruct;

    printf("address of ppMyStruct: %p value of ppMyStruct: %p value of ppMyStruct dereference: %p \n",
        &ppMyStruct, ppMyStruct, *ppMyStruct);

    assert(&*ppMyStruct == &pMyStruct);

    printf("address of ppMyStruct dereference: %p address of pMyStruct: %p \n",
        &*ppMyStruct, &pMyStruct);

    assert(&**ppMyStruct == &myStruct);

    printf("address of ppMyStruct double dereference: %p address of myStruct: %p \n",
        &**ppMyStruct, &myStruct);
}
```

C++ as a better C

```cpp
puts("--- Pointer to Pointer to Dereference ---");
{
    struct MyStruct
    {
        int field;
        // ...
    } myStruct;

    MyStruct* pMyStruct = &myStruct;

    printf("address of myStruct: %p address of pMyStruct: %p value of pMyStruct: %p \n",
        &myStruct, &pMyStruct, pMyStruct);

    MyStruct** ppMyStruct = &pMyStruct;

    printf("address of ppMyStruct: %p value of ppMyStruct: %p value of ppMyStruct dereference: %p \n",
        &ppMyStruct, ppMyStruct, *ppMyStruct);

    assert(&*ppMyStruct == &pMyStruct);

    printf("address of ppMyStruct dereference: %p address of pMyStruct: %p \n",
        &*ppMyStruct, &pMyStruct);

    assert(&**ppMyStruct == &myStruct);

    printf("address of ppMyStruct double dereference: %p address of myStruct: %p \n",
        &**ppMyStruct, &myStruct);
}
```

Output (x64)

```
--- Pointer to Pointer Dereference ---
address of myStruct: 0x7ffdf3736664 address of pMyStruct: 0x7ffdf3736658 value of pMyStruct:
0x7ffdf3736664
address of ppMyStruct: 0x7ffdf3736650 value of ppMyStruct: 0x7ffdf3736658 value of ppMyStruct dereference:
0x7ffdf3736664
address of ppMyStruct dereference: 0x7ffdf3736658 address of pMyStruct: 0x7ffdf3736658
address of ppMyStruct double dereference: 0x7ffdf3736664 address of myStruct: 0x7ffdf3736664
```

Appendix

Output (A64, structures_c)

```
--- Structures ---
--- Pointer to Structure ---
address of myStruct: 0xffffeba50598 address of pMyStruct: 0xffffeba50590 value of pMyStruct:
0xffffeba50598
--- Pointer to Structure Dereference ---
address of myStruct: 0xffffeba50588 address of pMyStruct: 0xffffeba50580 value of pMyStruct:
0xffffeba50588
address of pMyStruct dereference: 0xffffeba50588 address of myStruct: 0xffffeba50588
--- One to Many ---
address of myStruct: 0xffffeba50578 address of pMyStruct: 0xffffeba50568 value of pMyStruct:
0xffffeba50578
address of myStruct2: 0xffffeba50570 address of pMyStruct: 0xffffeba50568 value of pMyStruct:
0xffffeba50570
--- Memory Leak ---
address of pMyStruct: 0xffffeba50560 value of pMyStruct: 0x17773b50
address of pMyStruct: 0xffffeba50560 value of pMyStruct: 0x17773b70
--- Many Pointers to One Structure ---
address of myStruct: 0xffffeba50558 address of pMyStruct: 0xffffeba50550 value of pMyStruct:
0xffffeba50558
address of myStruct: 0xffffeba50558 address of pMyStruct2: 0xffffeba50548 value of pMyStruct2:
0xffffeba50558
--- Many to One Dereference ---
address of myStruct: 0xffffeba50540 address of pMyStruct: 0xffffeba50538 value of pMyStruct:
0xffffeba50540
address of myStruct: 0xffffeba50540 address of pMyStruct2: 0xffffeba50530 value of pMyStruct2:
0xffffeba50540
address of pMyStruct dereference: 0xffffeba50540 address of pMyStruct2 dereference: 0xffffeba50540
--- Invalid Pointer to Structure ---
address of pMyStruct: 0xffffeba50520 value of pMyStruct: 0xffffffff00000000
address of pUninitialized: 0xffffeba50518 value of pUninitialized: 100
--- Invalid Pointer Dereference ---
address of pMyStruct: 0xffffeba50508 value of pMyStruct: 0x4
--- Wild (Dangling) Pointer ---
address of pMyStruct: 0xffffeba50500 value of pMyStruct: 0x17773b70 dereference of pMyStruct: 12345678
address of pMyStruct: 0xffffeba50500 value of pMyStruct: 0x17773b70
--- Pointer to Pointer to Structure ---
address of myStruct: 0xffffeba504f8 address of pMyStruct: 0xffffeba504f0 value of pMyStruct:
0xffffeba504f8
address of ppMyStruct: 0xffffeba504e8 value of ppMyStruct: 0xffffeba504f0
--- Pointer to Pointer Dereference ---
address of myStruct: 0xffffeba504e0 address of pMyStruct: 0xffffeba504d8 value of pMyStruct:
0xffffeba504e0
address of ppMyStruct: 0xffffeba504d0 value of ppMyStruct: 0xffffeba504d8 value of ppMyStruct dereference:
0xffffeba504e0
address of ppMyStruct dereference: 0xffffeba504d8 address of pMyStruct: 0xffffeba504d8
address of ppMyStruct double dereference: 0xffffeba504e0 address of myStruct: 0xffffeba504e0
```

Output (A64, structures_classic_cpp)

```
--- Access Level ---
--- Reading/Writing Private Fields ---
value of field1: 1 value of field2: 0
value of field1: 1 value of field2: 2
--- Classes and Objects ---
--- Structures and Classes ---
--- Memory Leak ---
address of pMyStruct: 0xffffe341a428 value of pMyStruct: 0x4cd5bc0
```

```
address of pMyStruct: 0xffffe341a428 value of pMyStruct: 0x4cd5be0
--- Invalid Pointer to Structure ---
address of pMyStruct: 0xffffe341a418 value of pMyStruct: 0xffffffff00000000
address of pUninitialized: 0xffffe341a410 value of pUninitialized: 0xb
--- Invalid Pointer Dereference ---
address of pMyStruct: 0xffffe341a400 value of pMyStruct: 0x4
--- Wild (Dangling) Pointer ---
address of pMyStruct: 0xffffe341a3f8 value of pMyStruct: 0x4cd5be0 dereference of pMyStruct: 12345678
address of pMyStruct: 0xffffe341a3f8 value of pMyStruct: 0x4cd5be0
```

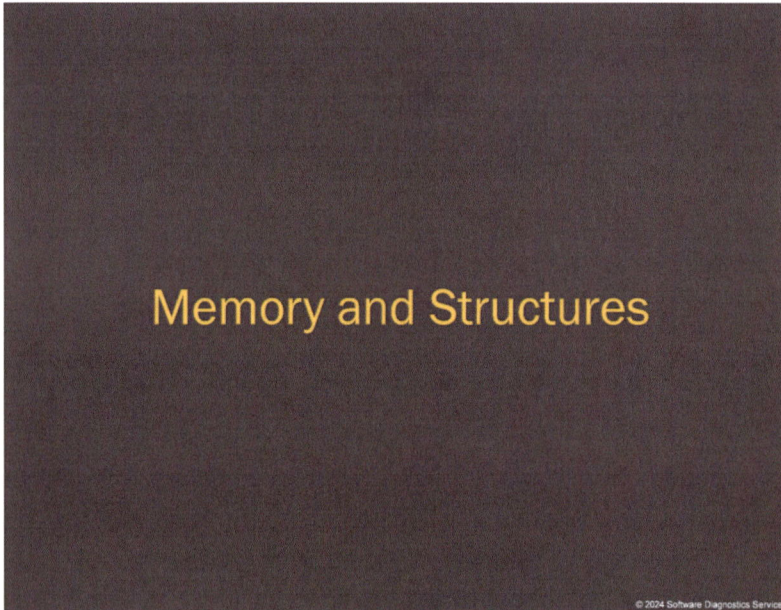

Now, we look at the memory representation of structures.

The `memory_and_structures` projects:

- `memory_and_structures_c`   C

- `memory_and_structures_c_cpp`   C++ as a better C

- `memory_and_structures_classic_cpp` Classic C++

can be found in the archive[6]. In the following slide descriptions, we only show relevant code snippets and their
output.

---

[6] https://www.patterndiagnostics.com/Training/ACPPLD/ACPPLD.tar.gz

Addresses and Structures

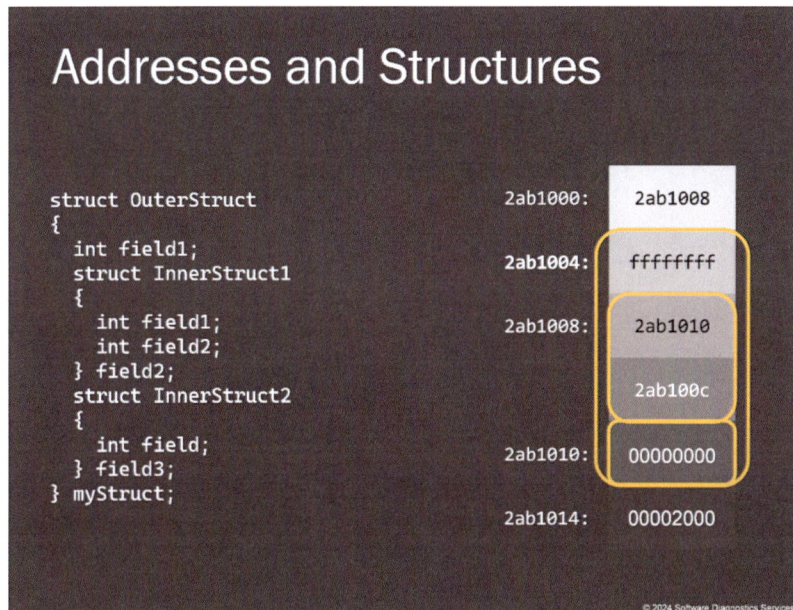

A structure in memory is a sequential collection of memory cells; some may be multicell and themselves substructures. Each part of a structure, its member, or structure field has its own address as well, in addition to the overall address of the structure.

C   C++ as a better C

```
puts("--- Addresses and Structures ---");
{
    struct OuterStruct
    {
        int field1;
        struct InnerStruct1
        {
            int field1;
            int field2;
        } field2;
        struct InnerStruct2
        {
            int field;
        } field3;
    } myStruct;

    printf("address of myStruct: %p address of field2: %p address of field3: %p \n",
        &myStruct, &myStruct.field2, &myStruct.field3);
}
```

Output (x64)

```
--- Addresses and Structures ---
address of myStruct: 0x7ffc217864d0 address of field2: 0x7ffc217864d4 address of field3: 0x7ffc217864dc
```

Structure Field Access

This example shows field addresses and access when we have a structure value.

C

```
puts("--- Structure Field Access  ---");
{
    struct OuterStruct
    {
        int field1;
        struct InnerStruct1
        {
            int field1;
            int field2;
        } field2;
        struct InnerStruct2
        {
            int field;
        } field3;
    } myStruct = { 0xffffffff, { 0x2ab1010, 0x2ab100c }, { 0 } };

    printf("&myStruct: %p \n"
        "&myStruct.field1: %p \n"
        "myStruct.field1: %x \n"
        "&myStruct.field2: %p \n"
        "&myStruct.field2.field1: %p \n"
        "myStruct.field2.field1: %x \n"
        "&myStruct.field2.field2: %p \n"
        "myStruct.field2.field2: %x \n"
        "&myStruct.field3: %p \n"
        "&myStruct.field3.field: %p \n"
        "myStruct.field3.field: %x \n",
        &myStruct,
        &myStruct.field1,
        myStruct.field1,
```

```
            &myStruct.field2,
            &myStruct.field2.field1,
            myStruct.field2.field1,
            &myStruct.field2.field2,
            myStruct.field2.field2,
            &myStruct.field3,
            &myStruct.field3.field,
            myStruct.field3.field);
}
```

C++ as a better C

```
puts("--- Structure Field Access  ---");
{
    struct OuterStruct
    {
        int field1;
        struct InnerStruct1
        {
            int field1;
            int field2;
        } field2;
        struct InnerStruct2
        {
            int field;
        } field3;
    } myStruct = { -1, { 0x2ab1010, 0x2ab100c }, { 0 } }; // warning about unsigned int -> int
conversion in C++

    printf("&myStruct: %p \n"
        "&myStruct.field1: %p \n"
        "myStruct.field1: %x \n"
        "&myStruct.field2: %p \n"
        "&myStruct.field2.field1: %p \n"
        "myStruct.field2.field1: %x \n"
        "&myStruct.field2.field2: %p \n"
        "myStruct.field2.field2: %x \n"
        "&myStruct.field3: %p \n"
        "&myStruct.field3.field: %p \n"
        "myStruct.field3.field: %x \n",
        &myStruct,
        &myStruct.field1,
        myStruct.field1,
        &myStruct.field2,
        &myStruct.field2.field1,
        myStruct.field2.field1,
        &myStruct.field2.field2,
        myStruct.field2.field2,
        &myStruct.field3,
        &myStruct.field3.field,
        myStruct.field3.field);
}
```

Output (x64)

```
--- Structure Field Access  ---
&myStruct: 0x7ffc217864c0
&myStruct.field1: 0x7ffc217864c0
myStruct.field1: ffffffff
&myStruct.field2: 0x7ffc217864c4
&myStruct.field2.field1: 0x7ffc217864c4
myStruct.field2.field1: 2ab1010
&myStruct.field2.field2: 0x7ffc217864c8
```

```
myStruct.field2.field2: 2ab100c
&myStruct.field3: 0x7ffc217864cc
&myStruct.field3.field: 0x7ffc217864cc
myStruct.field3.field: 0
```

Pointers to Structures

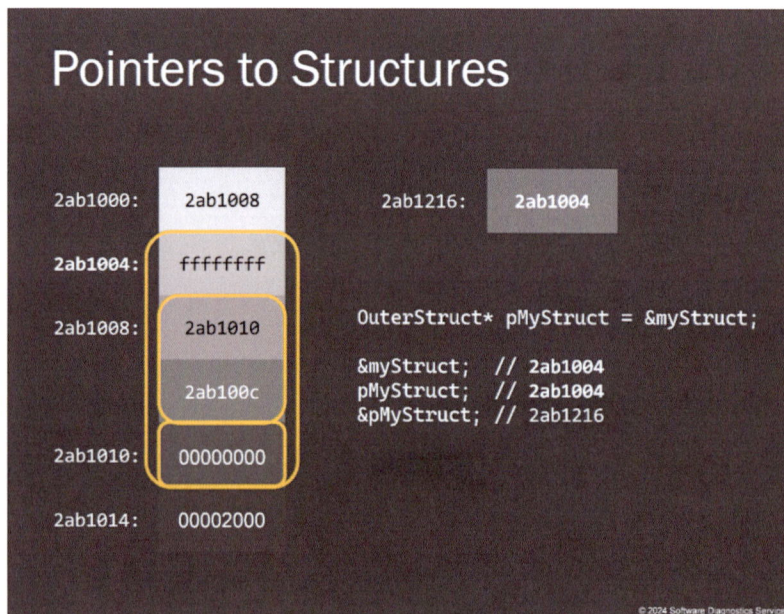

A structure has its address. A pointer to a structure is a memory cell that contains that address. It has its own address.

C

```c
puts("--- Pointers to Structures ---");
{
    struct OuterStruct
    {
        int field1;
        struct InnerStruct1
        {
            int field1;
            int field2;
        } field2;
        struct InnerStruct2
        {
            int field;
        } field3;
    } myStruct;

    struct OuterStruct* pMyStruct = &myStruct;

    printf("address of myStruct: %p address of pMyStruct: %p value of pMyStruct: %p \n",
        &myStruct, &pMyStruct, pMyStruct);
}
```

C++ as a better C

```cpp
puts("--- Pointers to Structures ---");
{
    struct OuterStruct
    {
        int field1;
        struct InnerStruct1
        {
            int field1;
            int field2;
        } field2;
        struct InnerStruct2
        {
            int field;
        } field3;
    } myStruct;

    OuterStruct* pMyStruct = &myStruct; // struct keyword can be omitted in C++

    printf("address of myStruct: %p address of pMyStruct: %p value of pMyStruct: %p \n",
        &myStruct, &pMyStruct, pMyStruct);
}
```

Output (x64)

```
--- Pointers to Structures ---
address of myStruct: 0x7ffc217864b0 address of pMyStruct: 0x7ffc217864a8 value of pMyStruct:
0x7ffc217864b0
```

Pointers to Structure Fields

This example shows field addresses and access when we have a pointer to a structure value.

C

```c
puts("--- Pointers to Structure Fields ---");
{
    struct OuterStruct
    {
        int field1;
        struct InnerStruct1
        {
            int field1;
            int field2;
        } field2;
        struct InnerStruct2
        {
            int field;
        } field3;
    } myStruct = { 0xffffffff, { 0x2ab1010, 0x2ab100c }, { 0 } };

    struct OuterStruct* pMyStruct = &myStruct;

    printf("pMyStruct: %p \n"
        "&pMyStruct->field1: %p \n"
        "pMyStruct->field1: %x \n"
        "&pMyStruct->field2: %p \n"
        "&pMyStruct->field2.field1: %p \n"
        "pMyStruct->field2.field1: %x \n"
        "&pMyStruct->field2.field2: %p \n"
        "pMyStruct->field2.field2: %x \n"
        "&pMyStruct->field3: %p \n"
        "&pMyStruct->field3.field: %p \n"
        "pMyStruct->field3.field: %x \n",
        pMyStruct,
        &pMyStruct->field1,
        pMyStruct->field1,
        &pMyStruct->field2,
        &pMyStruct->field2.field1,
        pMyStruct->field2.field1,
        &pMyStruct->field2.field2,
        pMyStruct->field2.field2,
        &pMyStruct->field3,
        &pMyStruct->field3.field,
        pMyStruct->field3.field);
}
```

C++ as a better C

```cpp
puts("--- Pointers to Structure Fields ---");
{
    struct OuterStruct
    {
        int field1;
        struct InnerStruct1
        {
            int field1;
            int field2;
        } field2;
        struct InnerStruct2
        {
            int field;
        } field3;
    } myStruct = { -1, { 0x2ab1010, 0x2ab100c }, { 0 } };

    OuterStruct* pMyStruct = &myStruct;
```

```
    printf("pMyStruct: %p \n"
        "&pMyStruct->field1: %p \n"
        "pMyStruct->field1: %x \n"
        "&pMyStruct->field2: %p \n"
        "&pMyStruct->field2.field1: %p \n"
        "pMyStruct->field2.field1: %x \n"
        "&pMyStruct->field2.field2: %p \n"
        "pMyStruct->field2.field2: %x \n"
        "&pMyStruct->field3: %p \n"
        "&pMyStruct->field3.field: %p \n"
        "pMyStruct->field3.field: %x \n",
        pMyStruct,
        &pMyStruct->field1,
        pMyStruct->field1,
        &pMyStruct->field2,
        &pMyStruct->field2.field1,
        pMyStruct->field2.field1,
        &pMyStruct->field2.field2,
        pMyStruct->field2.field2,
        &pMyStruct->field3,
        &pMyStruct->field3.field,
        pMyStruct->field3.field);
}
```

Output (x64)

```
--- Pointers to Structure Fields ---
pMyStruct: 0x7ffc21786490
&pMyStruct->field1: 0x7ffc21786490
pMyStruct->field1: ffffffff
&pMyStruct->field2: 0x7ffc21786494
&pMyStruct->field2.field1: 0x7ffc21786494
pMyStruct->field2.field1: 2ab1010
&pMyStruct->field2.field2: 0x7ffc21786498
pMyStruct->field2.field2: 2ab100c
&pMyStruct->field3: 0x7ffc2178649c
&pMyStruct->field3.field: 0x7ffc2178649c
pMyStruct->field3.field: 0
```

Structure Inheritance

Structures can inherit fields from other structures. In the case of the same field names, the derived structure hides the base structure fields, but they can be accessed by explicit base structure name qualification.

Classic C++

```cpp
std::cout << "--- Structure Inheritance ---" << std::endl;
{
    struct Base
    {
        int field;
    };

    struct Derived : Base
    {
        int field;
        int field2;
    } myDerived = { -1, 0x2ab1010, 0x2ab100c };

    std::cout << std::hex << "address of myDerived: " << &myDerived << std::endl <<
        "address of myDerived.field: " << &myDerived.field <<
        " value of myDerived.field: " << myDerived.field << std::endl <<
        "address of myDerived.Base::field: " << &myDerived.Base::field <<
        " value of myDerived.Base::field: " << myDerived.Base::field << std::endl;

    Base* pMyBase = &myDerived;

    std::cout << std::hex << "address of myDerived: " << &myDerived <<
        " address of pMyBase: " << &pMyBase << " value of pMyBase: " << pMyBase << std::endl <<
        "address of pMyBase->field: " << &pMyBase->field <<
        " value of pMyBase->field: " << pMyBase->field << std::endl;
}
```

<u>Output (x64)</u>

```
--- Structure Inheritance ---
address of myDerived: 0x7ffd23efcd04
address of myDerived.field: 0x7ffd23efcd08 value of myDerived.field: 2ab1010
address of myDerived.Base::field: 0x7ffd23efcd04 value of myDerived.Base::field: ffffffff
address of myDerived: 0x7ffd23efcd04 address of pMyBase: 0x7ffd23efccf8 value of pMyBase: 0x7ffd23efcd04
address of pMyBase->field: 0x7ffd23efcd04 value of pMyBase->field: ffffffff
```

Structure Slicing

It is possible to copy a derived structure to a base structure variable, but in this case, the former contents are sliced since the base structure occupies less memory. The other way around, from the base structure to the derived, is forbidden by default because the compiler doesn't know how to fill the new derived-only fields. However, this can be forced with a static cast where the derived fields may be either default initialized with zeroes or filled with the existing adja-cent memory content, which can be completely random. The same down-cast can be done between pointers, but when we try to dereference a tar-get pointer to the derived structure later, we may get random data.

Classic C++

```cpp
std::cout << "--- Structure Slicing ---" << std::endl;
{
    struct Base
    {
        int field;
    };

    struct Derived : Base
    {
        int field2;
    } myDerived = { 0, 1 };

    Base myBase = myDerived;
    // myDerived = myBase; // error

    std::cout << "address of myDerived: " << &myDerived <<
```

```cpp
        " value of myDerived: { " << myDerived.field << ", " << myDerived.field2 << " }" <<
std::endl <<
        "address of myBase: " << &myBase << " value of myBase: " << myBase.field << std::endl;

    Base myBase2 = { 0 };
    Derived myDerived2 = static_cast<Derived>(myBase2);

    std::cout << "address of myBase2: " << &myBase2 << " value of myBase2: " << myBase2.field <<
std::endl <<
        "address of myDerived2: " << &myDerived2 <<
        " value of myDerived2: { " << myDerived2.field << ", " << myDerived2.field2 << " }" <<
std::endl;

    Base* pMyBase = &myDerived;
    // Derived* pMyDerived = pMyBase; // error

    Derived* pMyDerived = static_cast<Derived*>(pMyBase);

    std::cout << "address of pMyBase: " << &pMyBase << " value of pMyBase: " << pMyBase <<
std::endl <<
        "address of pMyDerived: " << &pMyDerived << " value of pMyDerived: " << pMyDerived <<
std::endl <<
        " value of pMyDerived dereference: { " << (*pMyDerived).field << ", " <<
(*pMyDerived).field2 << " }" << std::endl;

    Base myBase3 = { 0 };
    Derived* pMyDerived3 = static_cast<Derived*>(&myBase3);

    std::cout << "address of myBase3: " << &myBase3 << " value of myBase3: " << myBase3.field <<
std::endl <<
        "address of pMyDerived3: " << &pMyDerived3 << " value of pMyDerived3: " << pMyDerived3 <<
std::endl <<
        " value of pMyDerived3 dereference: { " << (*pMyDerived3).field << ", " <<
(*pMyDerived3).field2 << " }" << std::endl;
}
```

Output (x64)

```
--- Structure Slicing ---
address of myDerived: 0x7ffd23efccf0 value of myDerived: { 0, 1 }
address of myBase: 0x7ffd23efccec value of myBase: 0
address of myBase2: 0x7ffd23efcce8 value of myBase2: 0
address of myDerived2: 0x7ffd23efcce0 value of myDerived2: { 0, 0 }
address of pMyBase: 0x7ffd23efccd8 value of pMyBase: 0x7ffd23efccf0
address of pMyDerived: 0x7ffd23efccd0 value of pMyDerived: 0x7ffd23efccf0
 value of pMyDerived dereference: { 0, 1 }
address of myBase3: 0x7ffd23efcccc value of myBase3: 0
address of pMyDerived3: 0x7ffd23efccc0 value of pMyDerived3: 0x7ffd23efcccc
 value of pMyDerived3 dereference: { 0, 23efccf0 }
```

Inheritance Access Level

It is possible to inherit privately. In such a case, the base structure fields are inaccessible from the outside, even with the explicit qualification.

Classic C++

```cpp
std::cout << "--- Inheritance Access Level ---" << std::endl;
{
    struct Base {
        int field;
    };

    struct Derived : private Base
    {
        int field;
        int field2;
    } myDerived;

    myDerived.field;
    // myDerived.Base::field; // error

    // Base* pMyBase = &myDerived; // error
    // pMyBase->field;
}
```

Structures and Classes II

Again, structures and classes are almost equivalent except for the default inheritance access (and field access), which is, by default, public for structures and private for classes. Public access needs to be specified explicitly for classes. We do not discuss protected access in this training, which is not really relevant for memory thinking when we look at built code.

`Classic C++`

```cpp
std::cout << "--- Structures and Classes II ---" << std::endl;
{
    class Base
    {
    public:
        int field;
    };

    class Derived : public Base // (private by default)
    {
        // ...
    };
}
```

Reading/Writing Private Base

Nevertheless, we can access private base memory locations through casting.

```cpp
std::cout << "--- Reading/Writing Private Base ---" << std::endl;
{
    struct Base
    {
        int field;
    };

    struct Derived : private Base
    {
        int field;
        int field2;
    } myDerived;

    std::cout << "value of Base.field: " << (reinterpret_cast<Base*>(&myDerived))->field <<
std::endl;

    (reinterpret_cast<Base*>(&myDerived))->field = 2;

    std::cout << "value of Base.field: " << (reinterpret_cast<Base*>(&myDerived))->field <<
std::endl;
}
```

Output (x64)

```
--- Reading/Writing Private Base ---
value of Base.field: 90
value of Base.field: 2
```

Internal Structure Alignment

Fields may be aligned according to their default type alignment, which may introduce gaps, increasing the overall structure size.

Classic C++

```cpp
std::cout << "--- Internal Structure Alignment ---" << std::endl;
{
    struct Struct
    {
        bool field1;
        short field2;
        long field8;
    } myStruct;

    #pragma pack(1)
    alignas(8) struct StructPacked
    {
        bool field1;
        short field2;
        long field8;
    } myStructPacked;

    std::cout << "address of myStruct: " << &myStruct <<
        " size of myStruct: " << std::dec << sizeof(myStruct) << std::endl <<
        "address of myStruct.field2: " << &myStruct.field2 <<
        " address of myStruct.field8: " << &myStruct.field8 << std::endl <<
        "address of myStructPacked: " << &myStructPacked <<
        " size of myStructPacked: " << std::dec << sizeof(myStructPacked) << std::endl <<
        "address of myStructPacked.field2: " << &myStructPacked.field2 <<
        " address of myStructPacked.field8: " << &myStructPacked.field8 << std::endl;
}
```

Output (x64)

```
--- Internal Structure Alignment ---
address of myStruct: 0x7ffd23efcc90 size of myStruct: 16
address of myStruct.field2: 0x7ffd23efcc92 address of myStruct.field8: 0x7ffd23efcc98
address of myStructPacked: 0x7ffd23efcc80 size of myStructPacked: 11
address of myStructPacked.field2: 0x7ffd23efcc81 address of myStructPacked.field8: 0x7ffd23efcc83
```

Static Structure Fields

Static structure field values are shared between the different objects of the same structure type. They occupy uniquely separate memory cells from the objects' memory.

Classic C++

```cpp
struct MyStructS
{
    int field;
    static unsigned sharedField;
};

unsigned MyStructS::sharedField = 123;

// ...

std::cout << "--- Static Structure Fields ---" << std::endl;
{
    MyStructS myStruct1, myStruct2;

    myStruct1.field = 0;
    myStruct1.sharedField = 0x123;
    myStruct2.field = 1;

    std::cout << "address of myStruct1: " << &myStruct1 <<
        " address of myStruct2: " << &myStruct2 << std::endl <<
```

```
           "address of myStruct1.sharedField: " << &myStruct1.sharedField <<
           " value of myStruct1.sharedField: " << myStruct1.sharedField << std::endl <<
           "address of myStruct2.sharedField: " << &myStruct2.sharedField <<
           " value of myStruct2.sharedField: " << myStruct2.sharedField << std::endl;
}
```

Output (x64)

```
--- Static Structure Fields ---
address of myStruct1: 0x7ffd23efcc7c address of myStruct2: 0x7ffd23efcc78
address of myStruct1.sharedField: 0x5d6130 value of myStruct1.sharedField: 291
address of myStruct2.sharedField: 0x5d6130 value of myStruct2.sharedField: 291
```

Appendix

Output (A64, memory_and_structures_c)

```
--- Addresses and Structures ---
address of myStruct: 0xffffd363f2d8 address of field2: 0xffffd363f2dc address of field3: 0xffffd363f2e4
--- Structure Field Access  ---
&myStruct: 0xffffd363f2c8
&myStruct.field1: 0xffffd363f2c8
myStruct.field1: ffffffff
&myStruct.field2: 0xffffd363f2cc
&myStruct.field2.field1: 0xffffd363f2cc
myStruct.field2.field1: 2ab1010
&myStruct.field2.field2: 0xffffd363f2d0
myStruct.field2.field2: 2ab100c
&myStruct.field3: 0xffffd363f2d4
&myStruct.field3.field: 0xffffd363f2d4
myStruct.field3.field: 0
--- Pointers to Structures ---
address of myStruct: 0xffffd363f2b8 address of pMyStruct: 0xffffd363f2b0 value of pMyStruct:
0xffffd363f2b8
--- Pointers to Structure Fields ---
pMyStruct: 0xffffd363f2a0
&pMyStruct->field1: 0xffffd363f2a0
pMyStruct->field1: ffffffff
&pMyStruct->field2: 0xffffd363f2a4
&pMyStruct->field2.field1: 0xffffd363f2a4
pMyStruct->field2.field1: 2ab1010
&pMyStruct->field2.field2: 0xffffd363f2a8
pMyStruct->field2.field2: 2ab100c
&pMyStruct->field3: 0xffffd363f2ac
&pMyStruct->field3.field: 0xffffd363f2ac
pMyStruct->field3.field: 0
--- Internal Structure Alignment ---
address of myStruct: 0xffffd363f290 size of myStruct: 16
address of myStruct.field2: 0xffffd363f292 address of myStruct.field8: 0xffffd363f298
address of myStructPacked: 0xffffd363f280 size of myStructPacked: 11
address of myStructPacked.field2: 0xffffd363f281 address of myStructPacked.field8: 0xffffd363f283
```

<u>Output (A64, memory_and_structures_classic_cpp)</u>

```
--- Structure Inheritance ---
address of myDerived: 0xffffc08a9270
address of myDerived.field: 0xffffc08a9274 value of myDerived.field: 2ab1010
address of myDerived.Base::field: 0xffffc08a9270 value of myDerived.Base::field: ffffffff
address of myDerived: 0xffffc08a9270 address of pMyBase: 0xffffc08a9268 value of pMyBase: 0xffffc08a9270
address of pMyBase->field: 0xffffc08a9270 value of pMyBase->field: ffffffff
--- Structure Slicing ---
address of myDerived: 0xffffc08a9260 value of myDerived: { 0, 1 }
address of myBase: 0xffffc08a9258 value of myBase: 0
address of myBase2: 0xffffc08a9250 value of myBase2: 0
address of myDerived2: 0xffffc08a9248 value of myDerived2: { 0, 0 }
address of pMyBase: 0xffffc08a9240 value of pMyBase: 0xffffc08a9260
address of pMyDerived: 0xffffc08a9238 value of pMyDerived: 0xffffc08a9260
 value of pMyDerived derefernce: { 0, 1 }
address of myBase3: 0xffffc08a9230 value of myBase3: 0
address of pMyDerived3: 0xffffc08a9228 value of pMyDerived3: 0xffffc08a9230
 value of pMyDerived3 derefernce: { 0, 0 }
--- Inheritance Access Level ---
--- Structures and Classes II ---
--- Reading/Writing Private Base ---
value of Base.field: 5841e8
value of Base.field: 2
--- Internal Structure Alignment ---
address of myStruct: 0xffffc08a91f8 size of myStruct: 16
address of myStruct.field2: 0xffffc08a91fa address of myStruct.field8: 0xffffc08a9200
address of myStructPacked: 0xffffc08a91e8 size of myStructPacked: 11
address of myStructPacked.field2: 0xffffc08a91e9 address of myStructPacked.field8: 0xffffc08a91eb
--- Static Structure Fields ---
address of myStruct1: 0xffffc08a91e0 address of myStruct2: 0xffffc08a91d8
address of myStruct1.sharedField: 0x58f048 value of myStruct1.sharedField: 291
address of myStruct2.sharedField: 0x58f048 value of myStruct2.sharedField: 291
```

Uniform Initialization

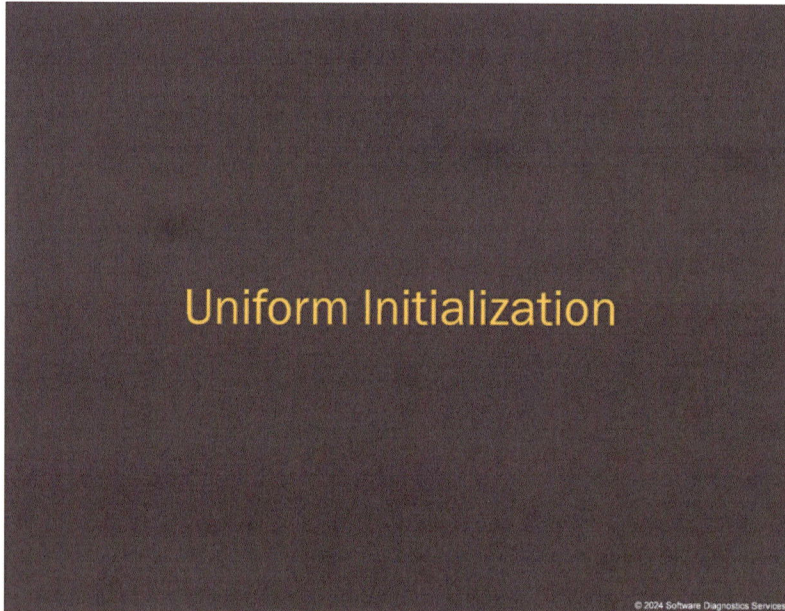

Throughout C++ history, there were several ways to initialize variables. Finally, there is some uniform way to do it consistently.

The `uniform_initialization` project:

- `uniform_initialization_modern_cpp`   Modern C++

can be found in the archive[7]. In the following slide descriptions, we only show relevant code snippets and their output.

---

[7] https://www.patterndiagnostics.com/Training/ACPPLD/ACPPLD.tar.gz

Old Initialization Ways

When we omit an initialization value, a variable is considered uninitialized if its memory belongs to certain memory classes, such as stack. For static memory, it may be default-initialized with zero memory values.

Modern C++

```cpp
std::println("--- Old Initialization Ways ---");
{
    struct OuterStruct
    {
        int field1;
        struct InnerStruct1
        {
            int field1;
            int field2;
        } field2;
        struct InnerStruct2
        {
            int field;
        } field3;
    };

    OuterStruct* pMyStruct1; // uninitialized
    OuterStruct* pMyStruct2 = NULL;
    OuterStruct* pMyStruct3(NULL);
    OuterStruct* pMyStruct4 = nullptr;
}
```

New Way {}

When we use the new way of initialization in modern C++, we can use empty {} to signal default initialization even for stack memory.

Modern C++

```cpp
std::println("--- New Way {{}} ---"); // prints --- New Way {} ---
{
    struct OuterStruct
    {
        int field1;
        struct InnerStruct1
        {
            int field1;
            int field2;
        } field2;
        struct InnerStruct2
        {
            int field;
        } field3;
    } myStruct;

    OuterStruct* pMyStruct1{};
    OuterStruct* pMyStruct2{NULL};
    OuterStruct* pMyStruct3{nullptr};
    OuterStruct* pMyStruct4{&myStruct};
}
```

Uniform Structure Initialization

It is possible to uniformly initialize the structure outside or provide default field initializers in the structure definition.

Modern C++

```cpp
std::println("--- Uniform Structure Initialization ---");
{
    struct OuterStructA
    {
        int field1;
        struct InnerStruct1
        {
            int field1;
            int field2;
        } field2;
        struct InnerStruct2
        {
            int field;
        } field3;
    } myStructA{ 1, {2, 3}, {4} };

    std::println("value of myStructA: {{ {}, {{{}, {}}}, {{{}}} }}",
        myStructA.field1, myStructA.field2.field1, myStructA.field2.field2,
myStructA.field3.field);

    struct OuterStructB
    {
        int field1{1};
        struct InnerStruct1
        {
            int field1{2};
            int field2{3};
        } field2;
        struct InnerStruct2
        {
```

```
            int field{4};
        } field3;
    } myStructB;

    std::println("value of myStructB: {{ {}, {{{}, {}}}, {{{}}} }}",
        myStructB.field1, myStructB.field2.field1, myStructB.field2.field2,
myStructB.field3.field);

    OuterStructB myStructC;

    std::println("value of myStructC: {{ {}, {{{}, {}}}, {{{}}} }}",
        myStructC.field1, myStructC.field2.field1, myStructC.field2.field2,
myStructC.field3.field);
}
```

Output

```
--- Uniform Structure Initialization ---
value of myStructA: { 1, {2, 3}, {4} }
value of myStructB: { 1, {2, 3}, {4} }
value of myStructC: { 1, {2, 3}, {4} }
```

Static Field Initialization

The latest C++ standards allow static field initialization inside the structure definition instead of the classic C++ ways of outside initialization (shown in comments).

Modern C++

```cpp
struct MyStructS
{
    int field;
    inline static unsigned sharedField{123};
};

// ...

std::println("--- Static Field Initialization ---");
{
    MyStructS myStruct1, myStruct2;

    myStruct1.field = 0;
    assert(myStruct1.sharedField == 123);
    myStruct2.field = 1;

    std::println("value of myStruct1: {{ {}, {} }} value of myStruct2: {{ {}, {} }}",
        myStruct1.field, myStruct1.sharedField, myStruct2.field, myStruct2.sharedField);
}
```

Output

```
--- Static Field Initialization ---
value of myStruct1: { 0, 123 } value of myStruct2: { 1, 123 }
```

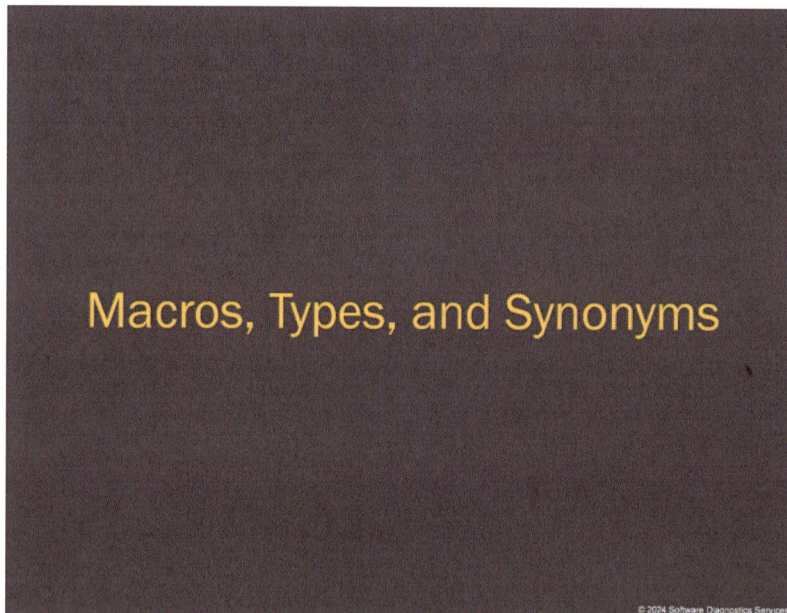

Type names may be long or inconvenient. There are some ways to construct easier type names.

The `macros_types_synonyms` projects:

- `macros_types_synonyms_c`   C
- `macros_types_synonyms_c_cpp`   C++ as a better C
- `macros_types_synonyms_modern_cpp`   Modern C++

can be found in the archive[8]. In the following slide descriptions, we only show relevant code snippets and their output.

---

[8] https://www.patterndiagnostics.com/Training/ACPPLD/ACPPLD.tar.gz

Macros

C

```c
puts("--- Macros ---");
{
#define TRUE 1
#define byte_t unsigned char
#define p_byte_t unsigned char*

    struct MyStruct { byte_t _dummy; } myStruct = {TRUE};

#define p_MyStruct_t struct MyStruct*

    p_MyStruct_t pMyStruct = NULL;
}
```

C++ as a better C

```c
puts("--- Macros ---");
{
#define TRUE 1
#define byte_t unsigned char
#define p_byte_t unsigned char*

    struct MyStruct {} myStruct; // In C++ structs can be without members

    printf("size of myStruct: %ld \n", sizeof(myStruct));

#define p_MyStruct_t struct MyStruct*

    p_MyStruct_t pMyStruct = NULL;
}
```

Output

```
--- Macros ---
size of myStruct: 1
```

Old Way

C

```
puts("--- Old Way ---");
{
#undef byte_t
#undef p_byte_t
#undef p_MyStruct_t

    typedef unsigned char byte_t;
    typedef unsigned char* p_byte_t;
    typedef unsigned char byte_t, * p_byte_t;
    typedef struct { byte_t _dummy; } MyStruct, * p_MyStruct_t;

    MyStruct myStruct = {TRUE};
    p_MyStruct_t pMyStruct = &myStruct;
}
```

C++ as a better C

```
puts("--- Old Way ---");
{
#undef byte_t
#undef p_byte_t
#undef p_MyStruct_t

    typedef unsigned char byte_t;
    typedef unsigned char* p_byte_t;
    typedef unsigned char byte_t, * p_byte_t;
    typedef struct {} MyStruct, * p_MyStruct_t;

    MyStruct myStruct;
    p_MyStruct_t pMyStruct = &myStruct;
}
```

New Way

New Way

⊙ using byte_t = unsigned char;

⊙ using p_byte_t = unsigned char*;

⊙ using MyStruct = struct {};

© 2024 Software Diagnostics Services

Modern C++

```
std::println("--- New Way ---");
{
    using byte_t = unsigned char;
    using p_byte_t = unsigned char*;
    using MyStruct = struct { byte_t field; };

    MyStruct myStruct{1};
}
```

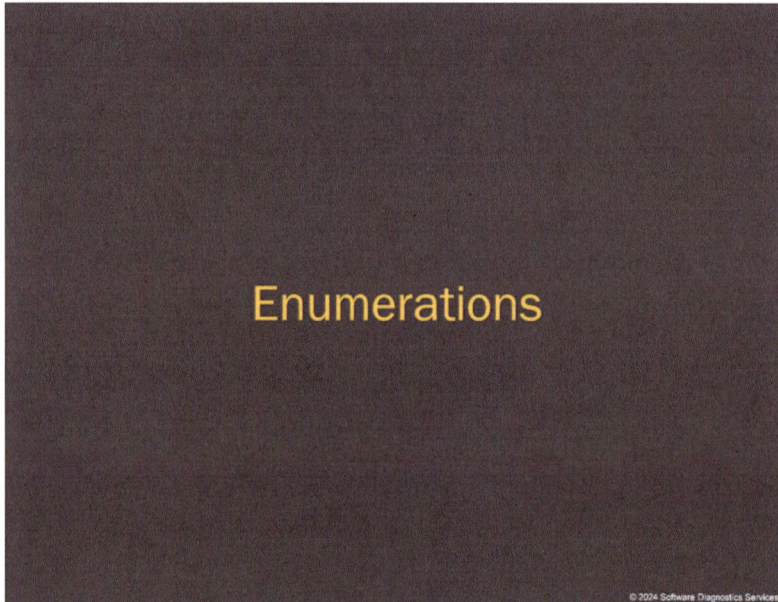

The **enumerations** projects:

- `enumerations_c`   C
- `enumerations_c_cpp`   C++ as a better C
- `enumerations_modern_cpp`   Modern C++

can be found in the archive[9]. In the following slide descriptions, we only show relevant code snippets and their output.

---

[9] https://www.patterndiagnostics.com/Training/ACPPLD/ACPPLD.tar.gz

Old Way

When using the old C-style enums, you cannot reuse the same enum value names for other enums, for example, when extending them. Also, all such enums have the same type.

`C`

```
puts("--- Old Way ---");
{
    enum MEMORY_DUMP_TYPE { PROCESS = 1, KERNEL, COMPLETE = 10 };

    enum MEMORY_DUMP_TYPE dumpType = KERNEL;

    printf("address of dumpType: %p size of dumpType: %lx value of dumpType: %x \n",
        &dumpType, sizeof(dumpType), dumpType);

    assert(sizeof(enum MEMORY_DUMP_TYPE) == 4);

    int d = dumpType;

    dumpType = 3;

    printf("value of dumpType: %x \n", dumpType);

    // enum MEMORY_DUMP_TYPE_EX { PROCESS, KERNEL, COMPLETE, ACTIVE }; // error
}
```

C++ as a better C

```
puts("--- Old Way ---");
{
    enum MEMORY_DUMP_TYPE { PROCESS = 1, KERNEL, COMPLETE = 10 };

    MEMORY_DUMP_TYPE dumpType = KERNEL; // enum can omitted in C++

    printf("address of dumpType: %p size of dumpType: %lx value of dumpType: %x \n",
        &dumpType, sizeof(dumpType), dumpType);
```

```
    assert(sizeof(MEMORY_DUMP_TYPE) == 4);

    int d = dumpType;

    dumpType = (MEMORY_DUMP_TYPE)3; // requires a cast

    printf("value of dumpType: %x \n", dumpType);

    // enum MEMORY_DUMP_TYPE_EX { PROCESS = 1, KERNEL, COMPLETE = 10, ACTIVE }; // error
}
```

<u>Output (x64)</u>

```
--- Old Way ---
address of dumpType: 0x7ffefc7f6a58 size of dumpType: 4 value of dumpType: 2
value of dumpType: 3
```

New Way

The modern C++ way allows reusing enum value names since the type of each enum is distinct; we have to qualify the value names.

Modern C++

```
std::println("--- New Way ---");
{
    enum class MEMORY_DUMP_TYPE
    {
        PROCESS = 1, KERNEL, COMPLETE = 10
    };

    MEMORY_DUMP_TYPE dumpType = MEMORY_DUMP_TYPE::KERNEL;

    std::println("address of dumpType: {} size of dumpType: {} value of dumpType: {}",
```

```cpp
        reinterpret_cast<uintptr_t>(&dumpType), sizeof(dumpType), static_cast<int>(dumpType));

    assert(sizeof(MEMORY_DUMP_TYPE) == 4);

    int d = static_cast<int>(dumpType);

    dumpType = static_cast<MEMORY_DUMP_TYPE>(3);

    std::println("value of dumpType: {}", static_cast<int>(dumpType));

    enum class MEMORY_DUMP_TYPE_EX {
        PROCESS = MEMORY_DUMP_TYPE::PROCESS,
        KERNEL = MEMORY_DUMP_TYPE::KERNEL, COMPLETE = MEMORY_DUMP_TYPE::COMPLETE,
        ACTIVE
    };
}
```

Output (x64)

```
--- Old Way ---
address of dumpType: 0x7ffefc7f6a58 size of dumpType: 4 value of dumpType: 2
value of dumpType: 3
```

Appendix

Output (A64, enumerations_c)

```
--- Old Way ---
address of dumpType: 0xffffe31b5548 size of dumpType: 4 value of dumpType: 2
value of dumpType: 3
```

Output (A64, enumerations_modern_cpp)

```
--- New Way ---
address of dumpType: 0000FFFFCAF7E57C size of dumpType: 4 value of dumpType: 2
value of dumpType: 3
```

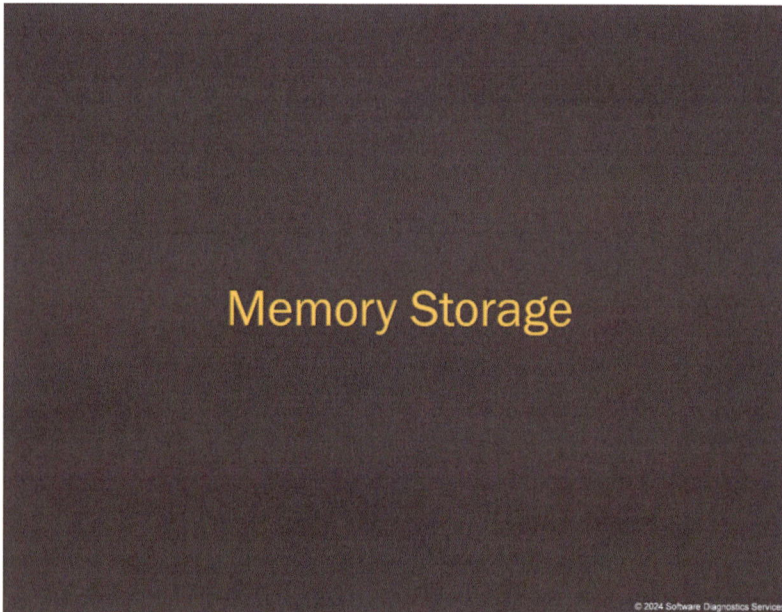

What memory storage is used to store values ultimately influences program behavior and possible defects.

The `memory_storage` projects:

- `memory_storage_c`   C
- `memory_storage_c_cpp`   C++ as a better C
- `memory_storage_classic_cpp`   Classic C++

can be found in the archive[10]. In the following slide descriptions, we only show relevant code snippets and their output.

---

[10] https://www.patterndiagnostics.com/Training/ACPPLD/ACPPLD.tar.gz

Overview

Here, we show the list of different storage types and talk about them in detail later. We cover the polymorphic allocators in the next edition.

Memory Regions

All computer memory is physical memory. However, unless you write specific hardware-related kernel-mode drivers or modules, you don't really work with physical memory in your applications and services. You work with the so-called virtual memory, an abstraction that allows you to think that your process works with linearly ordered computer memory cells, each with its own memory address. Processes allocate memory in pages of virtual memory. But they can dedicate some of the virtual memory regions for specialized purposes. The **SSH** abbreviation is a good mnemonic for static, stack, and heap types of memory regions. We now look at these three region types separately.

Dynamic Virtual Memory

Dynamic Virtual Memory

◉ OS managed

◉ Base for static, stack, and heap

◉ `mmap`

© 2024 Software Diagnostics Services

Virtual memory is dynamic – we have terabytes of virtual memory for an x64 process. But it is not really a memory you can write or read to. It needs to be committed – physical memory pages associated with virtual memory regions. All these committed virtual memory regions are used as underlying memory pages for static data, stack, and heap regions. Even large heap blocks are allocated using this mechanism. You can use Linux API to allocate large chunks of virtual memo-ry for your own usage.

Static Memory

Static Memory

◉ Per process

◉ Program data

◉ Can be read-only

◉ Shared between all threads

◉ "Always there"

◉ Persists across function calls

© 2024 Software Diagnostics Services

Static memory is per process and usually contains program data, such as string literals. It can be read-only memory pages. Static memory is shared between all process threads, so caution is needed for multithreaded access. It is "always there", having a static lifetime, so any pointers or references to it are valid for the duration of the process.

Stack Memory

Stack memory regions are separate for each process thread and provide some degree of isolation. The purpose of stack memory is to have some space for function frame data such as parameters and local values. Such frames are temporary: once a function returns to its caller frame, frame memory can be reused by subsequent function calls, so we should treat memory values before and after each call as undefined, containing garbage. However, for the duration of a function call, frame memory values can point to (contain addresses of) static, stack, and heap memory.

Thread Stack Frames

When a function is called, a stack frame is allocated in the thread stack memory region to hold local variables' values.

Local Variable Value Lifecycle

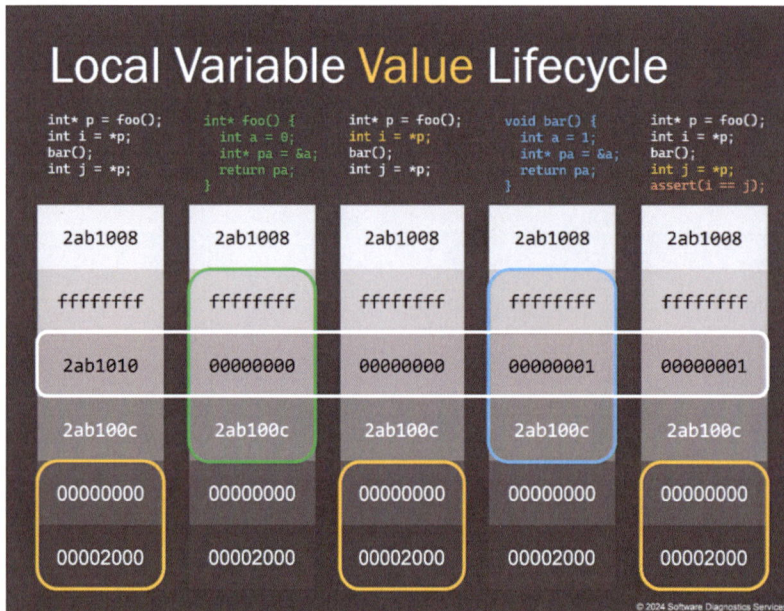

Since the stack frame memory values can be overwritten after the return from the function by subsequent function calls, local variable values have definite values only during the function call where they were initialized.

The code examples correspond to the memory diagrams.

Before calling the **foo** function, the memory values below the current stack frame are undefined:

```
int* p = foo();
int i = *p;
bar();
int j = *p;
```

When we enter the **foo** function, the corresponding stack frame is created. The function code also initializes the local variable a with 0 value. The function also returns the stack address of that local variable:

```
int* foo()
{
    int a = 0;
    int* pa = &a;
    return pa;
}
```

In the caller, we save that value at that address in the i variable. Then we call the **bar** function:

```
int* p = foo();
int i = *p;
bar();
int j = *p;
```

When we enter the **bar** function, the corresponding stack frame is created. The function code also initializes the local variable a with 1. Coincidentally, the variable a occupies the same stack memory location as the local variable a in the previous **foo** function call:

```
void bar()
{
    int a = 1;
    int* pa = &a;
    return pa;
}
```

Upon the return from the **bar** function, we dereference the same p address but get a different value:

```
int* p = foo();
int i = *p;
bar();
int j = *p;
assert(i == j);
```

C   C++ as a better C

```
int* foo(void)
{
    int a = 0;
    int* pa = &a;
    return pa;
}

int* bar(void)
{
    int a = 1;
    int* pa = &a;
    return pa;
}

// ...

puts("--- Local Variable Value Lifecycle ---");
{
    int* p = foo();
    int i = *p;
    bar();
    int j = *p;

    printf("value of i: %d value of j: %d \n", i, j);

    // assert(i == j); // fails
}
```

Output (x64)

```
--- Local Variable Value Lifecycle ---
value of i: 0 value of j: 1
```

Scope

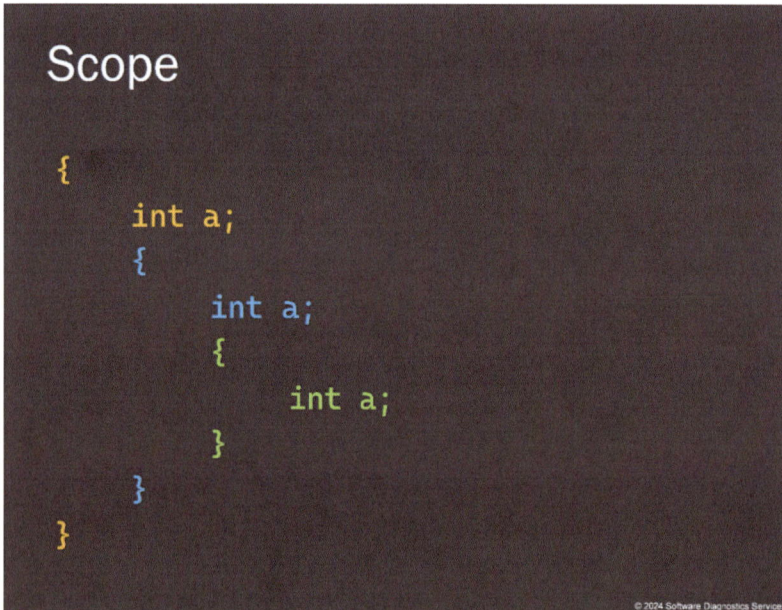

Scopes of variables can be nested with variable names in the nested scope, hiding variables with the same name in the enclosing scope.

C   C++ as a better C

```c
puts("--- Scope ---");
{
    int a = 0;
    int b = 0xb;
    {
        int a = 1;
        {
            int a = 2;
            printf("value of a: %d value of b: %x \n", a, b);
        }
        printf("value of a: %d value of b: %x \n", a, b);
    }
    printf("value of a: %d value of b: %x \n", a, b);
}
```

Output (x64)

```
--- Scope ---
value of a: 2 value of b: b
value of a: 1 value of b: b
value of a: 0 value of b: b
```

Stack Allocation Pitfalls

Please don't forget that stack frame memory for all function local variables is allocated at the entrance of the function, but individual variables may be initialized at a later time.

The code example corresponding to the memory diagram:

```
foo(1);
```

When we enter the **foo** function, the allocated stack frame includes the local variable c, which is initially uninitialized:

```
void foo(int i) {
...
}
```

If the value of the **i** function parameter is positive, the initialization of the local variable c is skipped, and the assertion is failed.

`C`

```c
puts("--- Stack Allocation Pitfalls ---");
{
    int a = 0;

    {
        int b = 0;
    }

    if (/*some condition*/ 1)
        goto end;

    int c = 0x78563412;

end:;

    printf("value of c: %x \n", c);
    // assert(c == 0x78563412); // fail
}
```

Output (x64)

```
--- Stack Allocation Pitfalls ---
value of c: 0
```

```
puts("--- Stack Allocation Pitfalls ---");
{
    int a = 0;

    {
        int b = 0;
    }

    if (/*some condition*/ 1)
        goto end; // requires /Zc:gotoScope-

        // int c = 0x78563412;
        // fails with the error with the note: crosses initialization of 'int c'

end:;

    // printf("value of c: %x \n", c);
    // assert(c == 0x78563412); // fail
}
```

Explicit Local Allocation

It is possible to explicitly allocate memory on the thread stack, for example, for some variable-length array storage. However, be aware of the possible stack overflow.

```
puts("--- Explicit Local Allocation ---");
{
    int i;

    void* pBlock = alloca(0x200);

    int j;

    printf("address of i: %p address of j: %p address of pBlock: %p value of pBlock: %p \n",
        &i, &j, &pBlock, pBlock);

    int k;

    printf("address of i: %p address of j: %p address of k: %p \n"
        "address of pBlock: %p value of pBlock: %p \n",
        &i, &j, &k, &pBlock, pBlock);
}
```

Output (x64)

```
--- Explicit Local Allocation ---
address of i: 0x7ffd1e686a70 address of j: 0x7ffd1e686a64 address of pBlock: 0x7ffd1e686a68 value of
pBlock: 0x7ffd1e686850
address of i: 0x7ffd1e686a70 address of j: 0x7ffd1e686a64 address of k: 0x7ffd1e686a60
address of pBlock: 0x7ffd1e686a68 value of pBlock: 0x7ffd1e686850
```

Heap Memory

Like static memory, heap memory is also accessible to and shared between all process threads. It is also dynamic, with the total amount of allocated memory changing over time. After heap-allocated memory is freed or released, its contents become undefined due to subsequent allocations or heap compactification. Values allocated from the heap may contain pointers to static and other heap memory. Generally, if heap memory contains pointers to stack memory, it may be a red flag since stack memory is defined only for the duration of the function call unless heap memory is also released before the return of the function call.

Dynamic Allocation (C-style)

Dynamic Allocation (C-style)

- Persistent across function calls

- (m|c|re)alloc

- free

- Can be replaced

© 2024 Software Diagnostics Services

There are some advantages to a dynamic memory allocation compared to a local stack allocation. The allocated memory and its values persist across function calls. Since allocations are implemented by library calls, they can be replaced with other libraries and custom code that provides debugging capabilities for tracking memory allocations and deallocations, as well as other checks.

Dynamic Allocation (C++)

Dynamic Allocation (C++)

- Persistent across function calls

- Global operators

- Structure-specific operators

- Can be replaced

© 2024 Software Diagnostics Services

C++ has its own implementation of dynamic memory that is often internally implemented by underlying C-style calls and Linux API. However, these high-level allocation facilities are more flexible and customizable to the needs of structure designers. It provides replaceable operators for global allocations for chunks of memory and structure-specific allocations.

Memory Expressions

Memory Expressions

- Use memory operators

- new

- delete / delete[]

- new throws std::bad_alloc exception (do not check for nullptr) unless told not to via std::nothrow value

© 2024 Software Diagnostics Services

Memory allocation expressions are used for allocating memory for values, structures, and their arrays. Internally, they may use memory operators. The same advice for non-array/array deallocation and checking return addresses is applicable here.

Memory Operators

Memory Operators

- operator new / operator delete

- operator new[] / operator delete[]

- operator new throws std::bad_alloc exception (do not check for nullptr) unless told not to via std::nothrow value

© 2024 Software Diagnostics Services

When freeing globally allocated memory, always pay attention to whether it was allocated in the array form to avoid memory leaks, crashes, and other undefined behavior. Also, never check the allocated memory address for nullptr as done in the C-style allocations: C++ allocation operators throw an exception in-stead.

Classic C++

```cpp
// allocate from the stack instead of heap

void* operator new(std::size_t size)
{
    std::cout << "operator new(std::size_t size) called" << std::endl;

    void* p = alloca(size);
    if (p) return p;

    throw std::bad_alloc{};
}

void* operator new(std::size_t size, const std::nothrow_t&) noexcept
{
    std::cout << "operator new(std::size_t size, const std::nothrow_t&) called" << std::endl;

    return alloca(size);
}

void* operator new[](std::size_t size)
{
    std::cout << "operator new[](std::size_t size) called" << std::endl;

    void* p = alloca(size);
    if (p) return p;

    throw std::bad_alloc{};
}

void* operator new[](std::size_t size, const std::nothrow_t&) noexcept
{
    std::cout << "operator new[](std::size_t size, const std::nothrow_t&) called" << std::endl;

    return alloca(size);
}

void operator delete(void* p) noexcept
{
    std::cout << "operator delete(void* p) called" << std::endl;
}

void operator delete(void* p, std::size_t size) noexcept
{
    std::cout << "operator delete(void* p, std::size_t size) called" << std::endl;
}

void operator delete[](void* p) noexcept
{
    std::cout << "operator delete[](void* p) called" << std::endl;
}

void operator delete[](void* p, std::size_t size) noexcept
{
    std::cout << "operator delete[](void* p, std::size_t size) called" << std::endl;
}

// ...
```

```cpp
std::cout << "--- Memory Expressions ---" << std::endl;
{
    int* pi = new int;
    int* iarr = new int[10];

    std::cout << "address of pi: " << &pi << " value of pi: " << pi << std::endl;
    std::cout << "address of iarr: " << &iarr << " value of iarr: " << iarr << std::endl;

    delete[] iarr;
    delete pi;

    pi = new(std::nothrow) int;
    iarr = new(std::nothrow) int[10];

    std::cout << "address of pi: " << &pi << " value of pi: " << pi << std::endl;
    std::cout << "address of iarr: " << &iarr << " value of iarr: " << iarr << std::endl;

    delete[] iarr;
    delete pi;
}

std::cout << "--- Memory Operators ---" << std::endl;
{
    // see above
}
```

Output (x64)

```
--- Memory Expressions ---
operator new(std::size_t size) called
operator new[](std::size_t size) called
address of pi: 0x7ffe878f0128 value of pi: 0x7ffe878f00c0
address of iarr: 0x7ffe878f0120 value of iarr: 0x7ffe878f00a0
operator delete[](void* p) called
operator delete(void* p) called
operator new(std::size_t size, const std::nothrow_t&) called
operator new[](std::size_t size, const std::nothrow_t&) called
address of pi: 0x7ffe878f0128 value of pi: 0x7ffe878f00e0
address of iarr: 0x7ffe878f0120 value of iarr: 0x7ffe878f00c0
operator delete[](void* p) called
operator delete(void* p) called
```

Local Pointers (Manual)

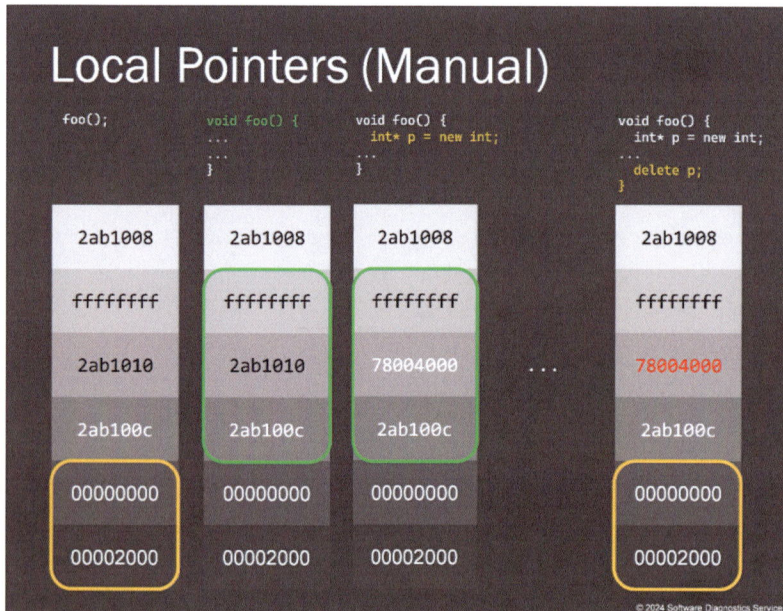

When allocating memory dynamically and assigning the memory address to a local variable, we must not forget to free/delete memory before returning from the function to avoid a memory leak.

The code example corresponds to the memory diagram.

```
foo();
```

When we enter the **foo** function, the allocated stack frame includes the local variables:

```
void foo()
{
...
...
}
```

The local variable p contains the address of the allocated memory for an integer value:

```
void foo()
{
  int* p = new int;
...
}
```

However, before exiting the function, we must free the memory; otherwise, there is a memory leak. Please note that neither delete nor **free** change the value of the variable p. It becomes a dangling pointer but it is ok because it goes out of scope here and is not reused for dereferencing unless saved somewhere else.

```
void foo()
{
  int* p = new int;
...
  delete p;
}
```

In-place Allocation

If we want to reuse existing memory buffers, we can use placement new.

Classic C++

```cpp
std::cout << "--- In-place Allocation ---" << std::endl;
{
    char buf[sizeof(int)];
    int* pi = new(buf) int;
    *pi = 1;

    std::cout << "address of buf: " << &buf << " value of pi: " << pi << std::endl;

    char* pbuf = new char[sizeof(int)];
    pi = new(pbuf) int;
    *pi = 2;

    std::cout << "value of pbuf: " << static_cast<void*>(pbuf) << " value of pi: " << pi <<
std::endl;

    delete[] pbuf;
}
```

Output (x64)

```
--- In-place Allocation ---
address of buf: 0x7ffe878f011c value of pi: 0x7ffe878f011c
operator new[](std::size_t size) called
value of pbuf: 0x7ffe878f00c0 value of pi: 0x7ffe878f00c0
operator delete[](void* p) called
```

Useful GDB Commands

Useful GDB Commands

- break main

- run

- info proc mappings

- disassemble main

- info types / locals / ptype / vtbl

- x/a \<address>

- x/s \<address>

- thread apply \<thread> \<command>

Appendix

Output (A64, memory_storage_c)

```
--- Local Variable Value Lifecycle ---
value of i: 0 value of j: 1
--- Scope ---
value of a: 2 value of b: b
value of a: 1 value of b: b
value of a: 0 value of b: b
--- Stack Allocation Pitfalls ---
value of c: 0
--- Explicit Local Allocation ---
address of i: 0xffffc9c57df0 address of j: 0xffffc9c57de4 address of pBlock: 0xffffc9c57de8 value of
pBlock: 0xffffc9c57bd0
address of i: 0xffffc9c57df0 address of j: 0xffffc9c57de4 address of k: 0xffffc9c57de0
address of pBlock: 0xffffc9c57de8 value of pBlock: 0xffffc9c57bd0
```

Output (A64, memory_storage_classic_cpp)

```
--- Memory Expressions ---
operator new(std::size_t size) called
operator new[](std::size_t size) called
address of pi: 0x7fffd5695838 value of pi: 0x7fffd56957d0
address of iarr: 0x7fffd5695830 value of iarr: 0x7fffd56957b0
operator delete[](void* p) called
operator delete(void* p) called
operator new(std::size_t size, const std::nothrow_t&) called
operator new[](std::size_t size, const std::nothrow_t&) called
address of pi: 0x7fffd5695838 value of pi: 0x7fffd56957f0
address of iarr: 0x7fffd5695830 value of iarr: 0x7fffd56957d0
operator delete[](void* p) called
operator delete(void* p) called
--- Memory Operators ---
--- In-place Allocation ---
address of buf: 0x7fffd569582c value of pi: 0x7fffd569582c
operator new[](std::size_t size) called
value of pbuf: 0x7fffd56957d0 value of pi: 0x7fffd56957d0
operator delete[](void* p) called
```

Source Code Organisation

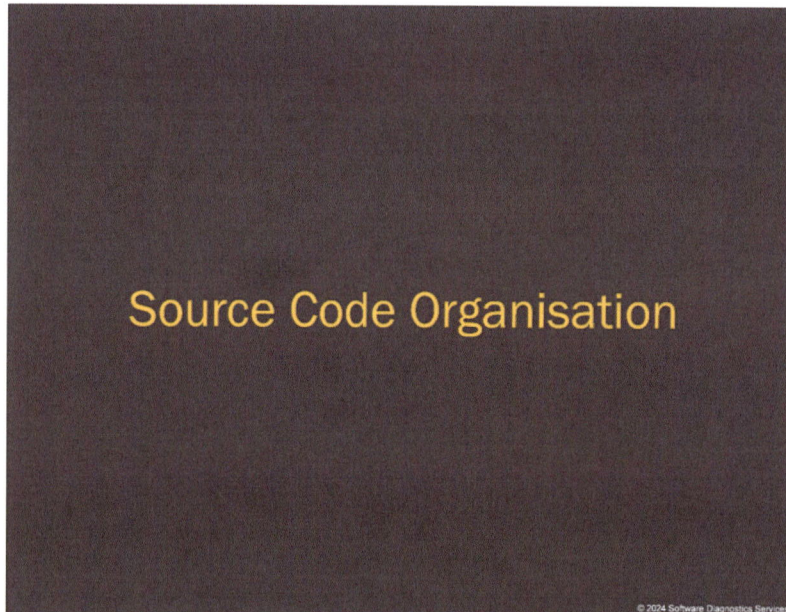

We now discuss C and C++ source code organization.

The **source_code_organization** project:

- **source_code_organization_classic_cpp**   Classic C++

can be found in the archive[11]. In the following slide descriptions, we only show relevant code snippets and their output.

---

[11] https://www.patterndiagnostics.com/Training/ACPPLD/ACPPLD.tar.gz

Logical Layer (Translation Units)

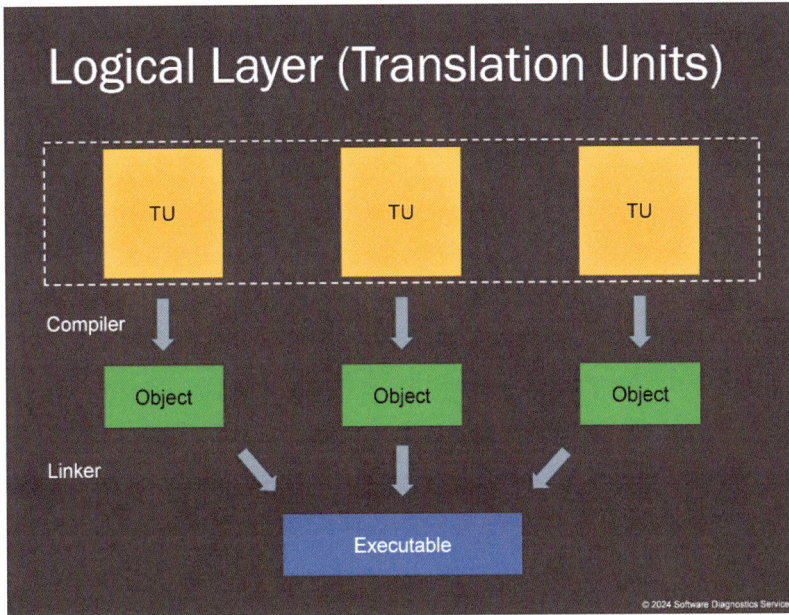

From a compiler perspective, it works with a translation unit as a whole and converts the source code of a translation unit to an object file. Several object files are combined by a linker into an executable file.

Physical Layer (Source Files)

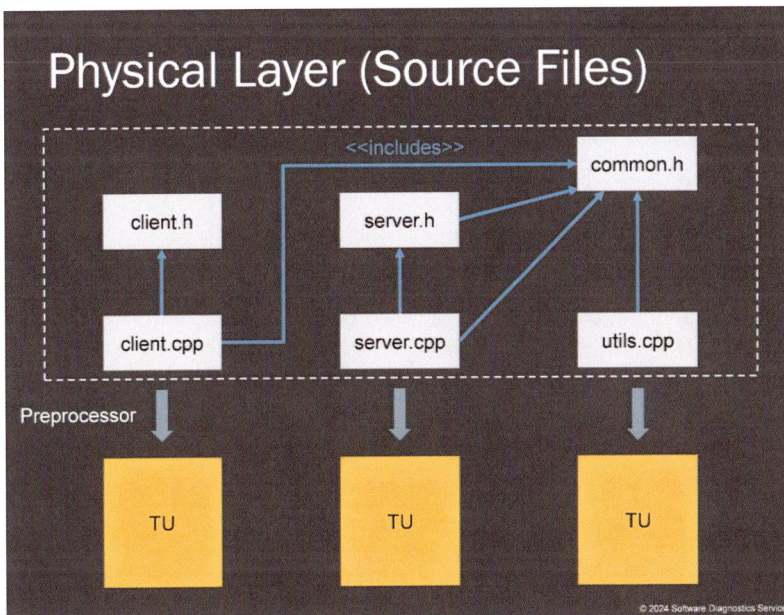

Although one physical source code file corresponds to one translation unit, it is passed through a preprocessor, which, among other things, looks for special directives to include other files, and those files may also contain directives to include other files. You can also see, as in the case of the *common.h* file, by transitivity of inclusion, that the same file may be included many times.

Inter-TU Sharing

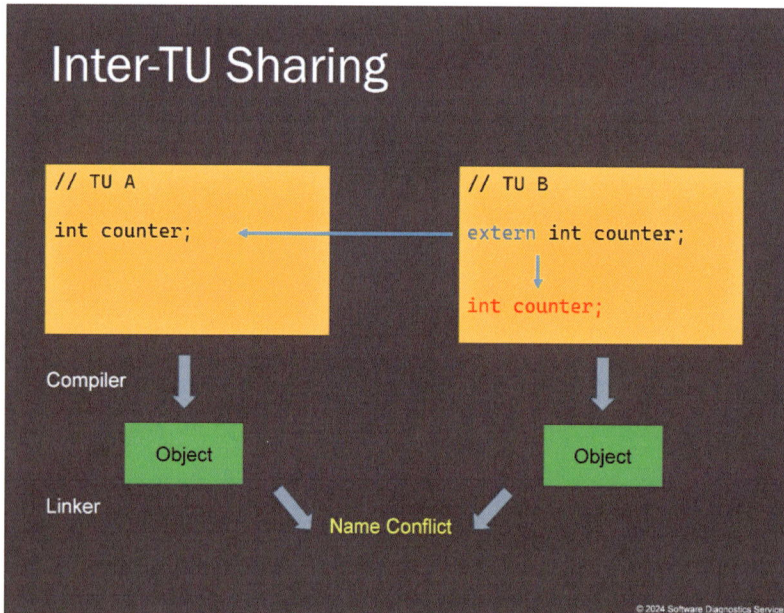

Variables in different translation units having the same name may conflict during the linkage phase.

Classic Static TU Isolation

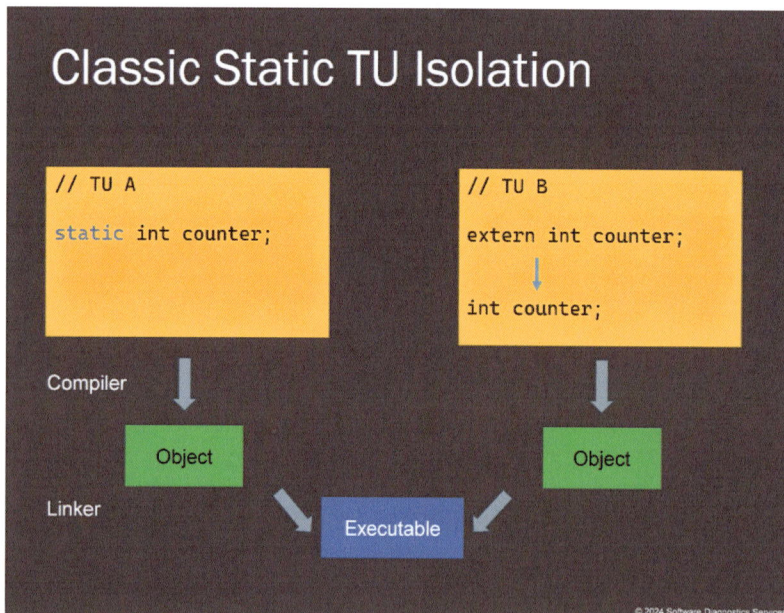

To avoid name conflicts during linkage, C and classic C++ suggest using the static specifier.

Namespace TU Isolation

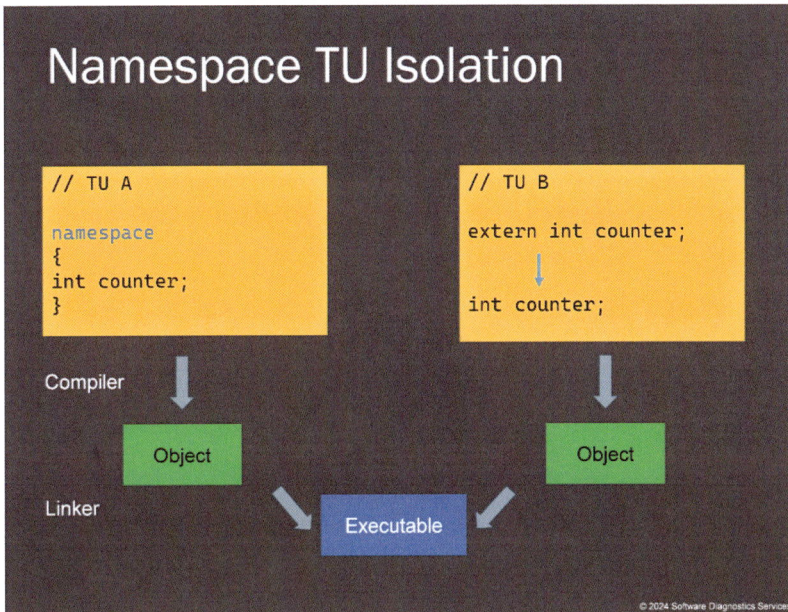

Modern C++ suggests using namespaces instead.

Declaration and Definition

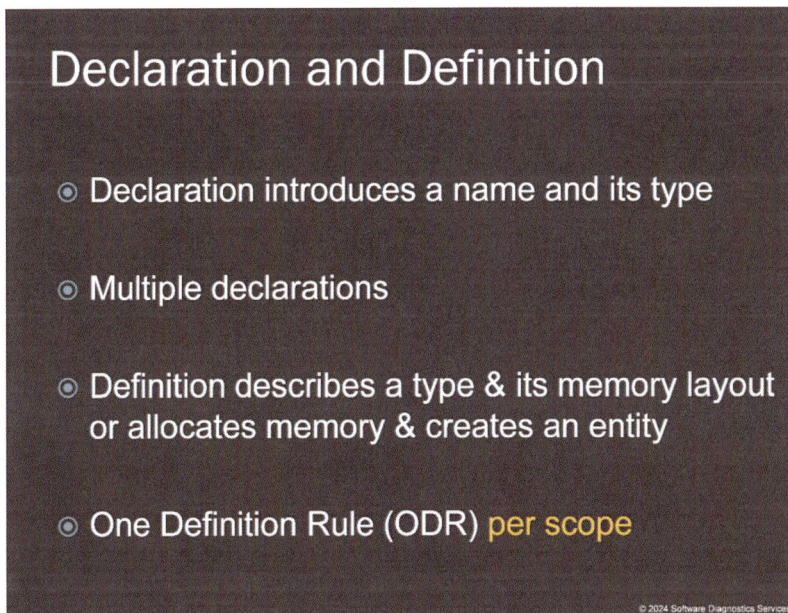

In C and C++, when reasoning about compilation, it is useful to consider the distinction between declaration and definition. The rule of thumb is that the latter usually describes the memory layout. Please also note that a definition is also a declaration.

TU Definition Conflicts

Multiple declarations of the same entity are allowed, but only one definition is allowed, the essence of ODR, One Definition Rule.

Classic C++

```cpp
#include "thirdparty.h"

// struct S {}; // error

std::cout << "--- TU Definition Conflicts ---" << std::endl;
{
    struct S {}; // OK, different scope

    S s;

    std::cout << "size of s: " << sizeof(s) << std::endl;

    {
        struct S { int _dummy;  }; // OK, different scope

        S s;

        std::cout << "size of s: " << sizeof(s) << std::endl;
    }
}
```

Output

```
--- TU Definition Conflicts ---
size of s: 1
size of s: 4
```

Fine-grained TU Scope Isolation

Named namespaces allow the fine-grained scope isolation.

Classic C++

```cpp
#include "thirdparty.h"

namespace mycode { struct S {}; }

std::cout << "--- Fine-grained TU Scope Isolation ---" << std::endl;
{
    mycode::S s;

    using namespace mycode;
    // S s2; // ambiguous
}
```

Conceptual Layer (Design)

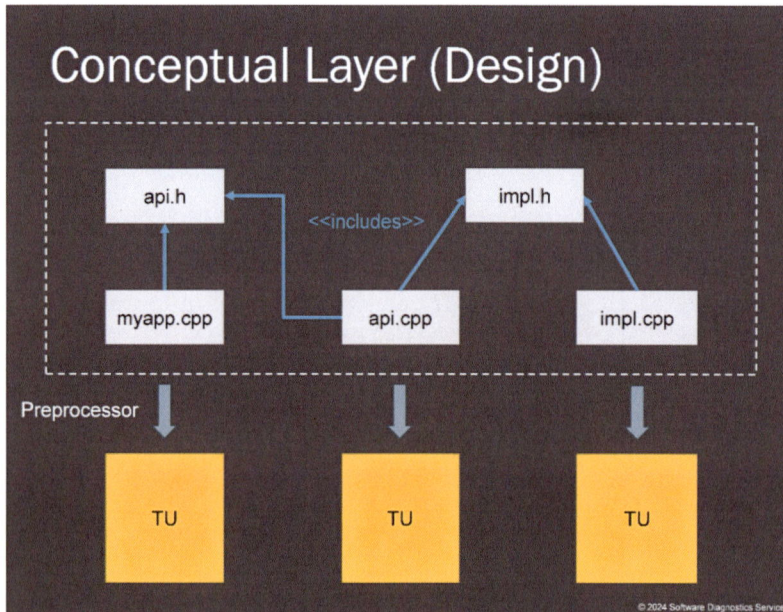

In the design layer, we may want to separate implementation details.

Incomplete Types

Such separation is achieved via incomplete types and the so-called **PImpl** (**P**ointer to **Impl**ementation) idiom.

Classic C++

```cpp
// source_code_organization_modern_cpp.cpp

#include "instrument.h"

std::cout << "--- Incomplete Types ---" << std::endl;
{
    struct MyStruct; // declaration

    MyStruct* pMyStruct; // (declaration and) definition

    Instrument instrument;

    instrument.getMeasurement();
}


// instrument.h

#pragma once

// PImpl (Pointer to Implementation) idiom

struct InstrumentImpl; // declaration

struct Instrument // (declaration and) definition
{
    Instrument();
    ~Instrument();

    int getMeasurement(); // declaration
private:
    InstrumentImpl* pImpl; // definition
};


// instrument.cpp

#include <iostream>
#include "instrument.h"
#include "instrumentImpl.h"

Instrument::Instrument() : pImpl(new InstrumentImpl) {}

Instrument::~Instrument()
{
        delete pImpl;
}

int Instrument::getMeasurement()
{
        std::cout << "Instrument::getMeasurement() called" << std::endl;
        return pImpl->getMeasurement();
}
```

```
// instrumentImpl.h

#pragma once

struct InstrumentImpl
{
        InstrumentImpl();
        int getMeasurement();

private:
        int value;
};
```

```
// instrumentImpl.cpp

#include <iostream>
#include "instrumentImpl.h"

InstrumentImpl::InstrumentImpl() : value(0) {}

int InstrumentImpl::getMeasurement()
{
        std::cout << "InstrumentImpl::getMeasurement() called" << std::endl;
        return value;
}
```

Output

```
--- Incomplete Types ---
Instrument::getMeasurement() called
InstrumentImpl::getMeasurement() called
```

References

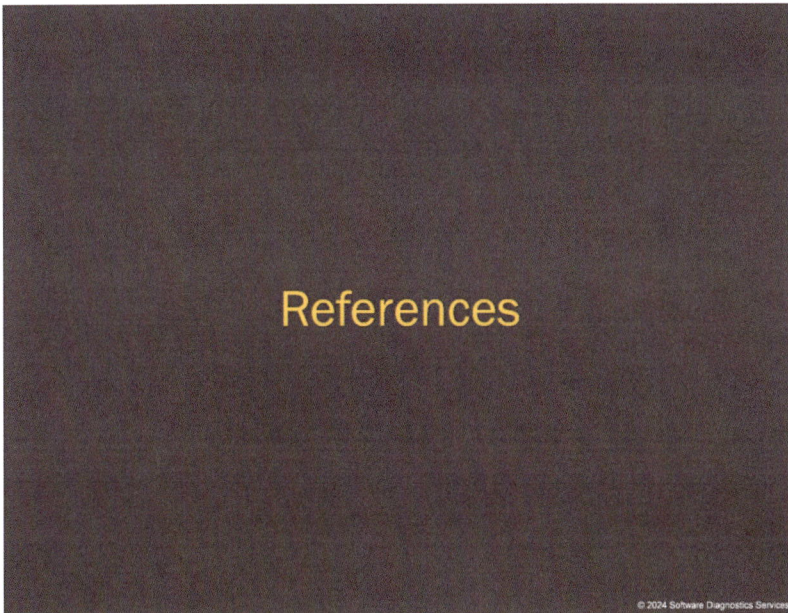

Now, a slide for C++ references. We plan to extend this section in the third edition.

The **references** project:

- `references_modern_cpp`   Modern C++

can be found in the archive[12]. In the following slide descriptions, we only show relevant code snippets and their output.

---

[12] https://www.patterndiagnostics.com/Training/ACPPLD/ACPPLD.tar.gz

Type& vs. Type*

From the memory perspective, references and pointers are the same things. The only difference is that you cannot have a dangling reference; it must be initialized.

Modern C++

```
std::println("--- Type& vs. Type* ---");
{
    int val{0};
    int& ref{val};
    int* ptr{&val};

    // int& & refref; // error
    // int&* pref; // error

    int i = ref;
    i = *ptr;

    std::println("value of ref as address: {} address of val: {}", &ref, &val);

    struct Struct
    {
        int field{0};
    } myStruct, * pStruct{&myStruct}, & rStruct{myStruct};

    rStruct.field;
    pStruct->field;
    (*pStruct).field;
}
```

Output (x64)

```
--- Type& vs. Type* ---
value of ref as address: 00007FFF9116A454 address of val: 00007FFF9116A454
```

<u>Output (A64)</u>

```
--- Type& vs. Type* ---
value of ref as address: 0000FFFFFAF03094 address of val: 0000FFFFFAF03094
```

Values

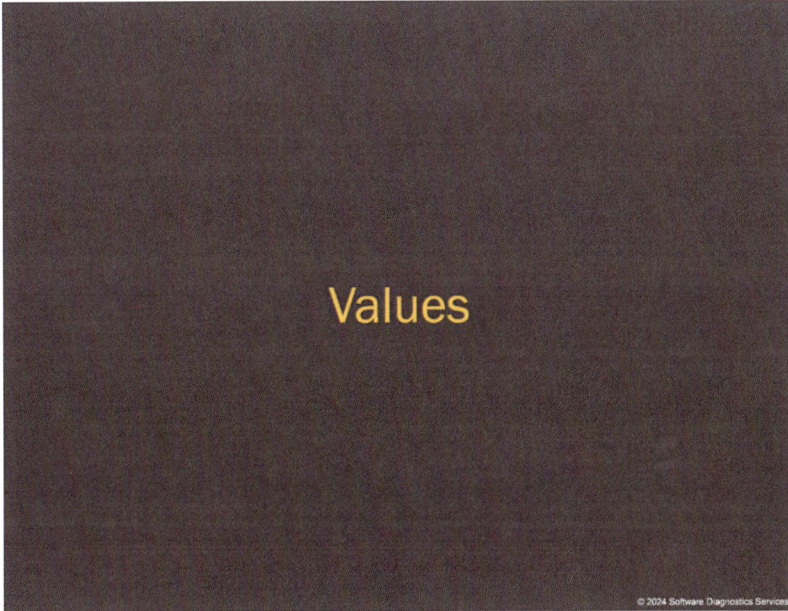

Let's now briefly discuss various categories of values. These are what is stored in memory. A pointer value is also a value that is interpreted as a memory address pointing to some other value elsewhere.

The **values** projects:

- `values_c`   C
- `values_c_cpp`   C++ as a better C
- `values_modern_cpp`   Modern C++

can be found in the archive[13]. In the following slide descriptions, we only show relevant code snippets and their output.

---

[13] https://www.patterndiagnostics.com/Training/ACPPLD/ACPPLD.tar.gz

Value Categories

When reading serious C++ documentation, you frequently see the so-called **lvalues** and **rvalues** mentioned. Crudely, you can think about them as **l**eft and **r**ight values in expressions, where the **r**ight value can be temporary, and the **l**eft value has to be backed up by some memory.

Classification

https://en.cppreference.com/w/cpp/language/value_category

C   C++ as a better C

```
int rvalue()
{
    return 0;
}

puts("--- Value Categories ---");
{
    int lvalue = rvalue(); lvalue = 1;
}
```

Constant Values

The values can also be constant, facilitating functional programming and code safety. Please note that there can be pointers and references to constant values, constant pointers to mutable variables, and both. The way to read such declarations is from right to left.

C   C++ as a better C

```
puts("--- Constant Values ---");
{
    const int cv = 1;
    int v = 0;

    printf("address of cv: %p address of v: %p \n", &cv, &v);

    const int* pc = NULL;
    pc = NULL;
    // *pc = 0; // error

    int* const cp = &v;
    // cp = NULL; // error
    *cp = 1;

    const int* const cpc = cp;
    // cpc = NULL; // error
    // *cpc = 0; // error
}
```

Output (x64)

```
--- Constant Values ---
address of cv: 0x7ffcd836f64c address of v: 0x7ffcd836f648
```

Output (A64)

```
--- Constant Values ---
address of cv: 0xffffcdc9005c address of v: 0xffffcdc90058
```

Modern C++

```cpp
std::println("--- Constant Values ---");
{
    int v{0};

    const int& rc{v};
    // rc = 1; // error

    int& r{v};
    r = 1;
}
```

Constant Expressions

There are different ways to define constants for later symbolic use. The C and classic C++ way is to use preprocessor (legacy) and `const`. The modern way is to use `constexpr`, which is more flexible.

Modern C++

```cpp
std::println("--- Constant Expressions ---");
{
    const int myConst = 1 + 1;

    constexpr int myConstExpr = 1 + 1;

    std::println("address of myConst: {} address of myConstExpr: {}", &myConst, &myConstExpr);
}
```
Output (x64)

```
--- Constant Expressions ---
address of myConst: 00007FFC66111058 address of myConstExpr: 00007FFC66111054
```

Output (A64)

```
--- Constant Expressions ---
address of myConst: 0000FFFFC5678C58 address of myConstExpr: 0000FFFFC5678C54
```

Functions

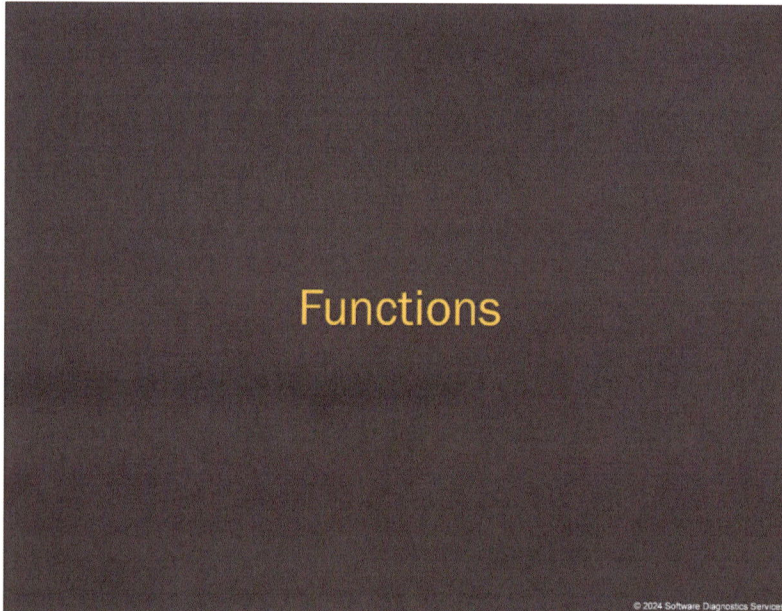

This section is the largest. We may split it up in the third edition once it grows more.

The **functions** projects:

- `functions_c`   C
- `functions_c_cpp`   C++ as a better C
- `functions_classic_cpp`   Classic C++
- `functions_modern_cpp`   Modern C++

can be found in the archive[14]. In the following slide descriptions, we only show relevant code snippets and their output.

---

[14] https://www.patterndiagnostics.com/Training/ACPPLD/ACPPLD.tar.gz

Macro Functions

Implementing the compilation phase functions during source code preprocessing to avoid runtime calculations is the oldest method starting from C. However, if not done carefully, these functions may produce incorrect results.

C   C++ as a better C

```
puts("--- Macro Functions ---");
{
#define SQUARE(x) x * x

    printf("value of SQUARE(2): %x value of SQUARE(2 + 1): %x \n",
        SQUARE(2), SQUARE(2 + 1));

    // assert(9 == SQUARE(2 + 1)); // fails

#undef SQUARE
#define SQUARE(x) (x) * (x)

    printf("value of SQUARE(2): %x value of SQUARE(2 + 1): %x \n",
        SQUARE(2), SQUARE(2 + 1));

    assert(9 == SQUARE(2 + 1));
}
```

Output

```
--- Macro Functions ---
value of SQUARE(2): 4 value of SQUARE(2 + 1): 5
value of SQUARE(2): 4 value of SQUARE(2 + 1): 9
```

constexpr Functions

constexpr functions are calculated during compilation if they are used in the constexpr context. In other contexts, the compiler may generate function bodies for runtime execution.

Modern C++

```cpp
std::println("--- constexpr Functions ---");
{
    // No function calls
    constexpr int result = SQUARE(2);
    constexpr int result2 = SQUARE(2 + 1);

    std::println("value of SQUARE(2): {} value of SQUARE(2+1): {}",
        result, result2);

    assert(9 == result2);

    // A function may be generated because we use it in a non-constexpr expression
    int result3 = SQUARE(3);
}
```

Output

```
--- constexpr Functions ---
value of SQUARE(2): 4 value of SQUARE(2+1): 9
```

Pointers to Functions

Functions are code bytes and, therefore, occupy some memory locations with their start addresses. It is possible to have pointers and references to functions:

```
int (*pf) (int) {foo};
pf = &foo;
int (&rf) (int) {*pf};
```

When having a pointer or reference to a function, it is possible to call the function with or without using the dereferencing syntax (*):

```
pf(10);
(*pf)(10);
rf(10)
```

C   C++ as a better C

```
int foo(int i)
{
    // ...
    return 0;
}

puts("--- Pointers to Functions ---");
{
    int (*pf) (int) = foo;
    pf = &foo;

    printf("address of foo: %p address of pf: %p value of pf: %p \n",
        foo, &pf, pf);

    pf(10);
    (*pf)(10);
}
```

Output (x64)

```
--- Pointers to Functions ---
address of foo: 0x401765 address of pf: 0x7fffa76e0e10 value of pf: 0x401765
```

```cpp
int foo(int i)
{
    // ...
    return 0;
}

std::cout << "--- Pointers to Functions ---" << std::endl;
{
    int (*pf) (int) = foo;
    pf = &foo;
    int(&rf) (int) = *pf;

    std::cout << "address of foo: " << foo << " address of pf: " << &pf <<
        " value of pf: " << pf << " value of rf: " << rf << std::endl;

    pf(10);
    (*pf)(10);
    rf(10);
}
```

Output (x64)

```
--- Pointers to Functions ---
address of foo: 0x404c96 address of pf: 0x7fff31cbc510 value of pf: 0x404c96 value of rf: 0x404c96
```

Function Pointer Types

Function pointer type declarations can be done using the classic `typedef` syntax or via the more modern `using` type alias.

```
puts("--- Function Pointer Types ---");
{
    typedef int (*PF)(int);

    PF func = foo;
    func(10);

}
```

Modern C++

```
std::println("--- Function Pointer Types ---");
{
    using PF = int (*)(int);

    PF func{foo};
    func(10);
}
```

Reading Declarations

Reading Declarations

◉ Left ← Right, []ᵣᵢ₉ₕₜ or ()ᵣᵢ₉ₕₜ → Right

◉ Examples:

```
const int* const* *arr[10];


int (*(*difficult)(int (*)(int), int))(int);
using DF = PF (*)(PF, int);
DF difficult2 {difficult};
```

© 2024 Software Diagnostics Services

It is worth knowing the rules of reading declarations since function pointer types can be quite complicated. The first example reads as an array of 10 elements, with each element a pointer to a pointer of constant pointers to constant integers. The next example is a pointer to a function that accepts a pointer to a function that accepts an integer and returns an integer, and accepts another integer, and returns a pointer to a function that accepts an integer and returns an integer. It can be simplified by using the common subtype PF. We can verify the compatibility of the two descriptions by initialization. GPT-4 is very good at deciphering such types.

```cpp
std::println("--- Reading Declarations ---");
{
    const int* const** arr[10]{};

    int (*(*difficult)(int (*)(int), int))(int){};

    using PF = int (*)(int);
    using DF = PF(*)(PF, int);
    DF difficult2{ difficult };
}
```

Structure Function Fields

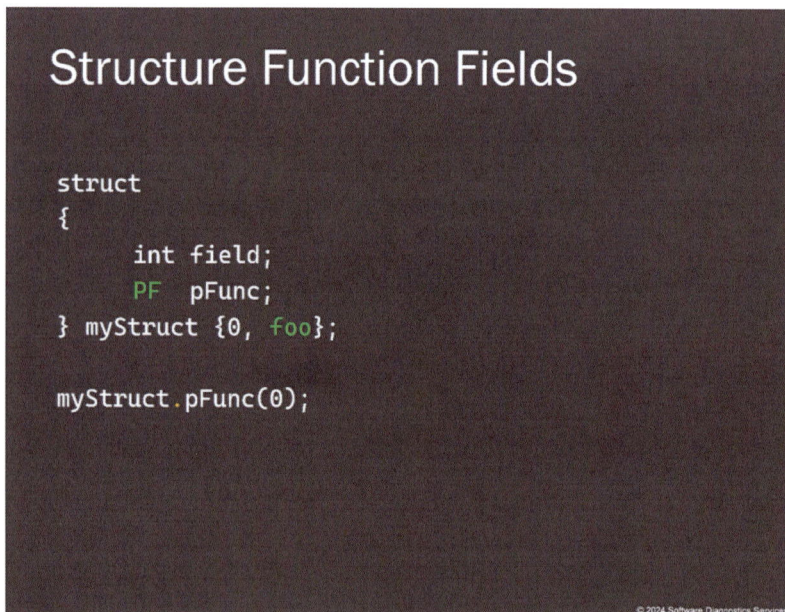

Structures may contain fields that are pointers to functions: the obvious way to implement OOP in C.

C   C++ as a better C

```cpp
puts("--- Structure Function Fields ---");
{
    typedef int (*PF)(int);

    struct
    {
        int field;
        PF   pFunc;
    } myStruct = { 0, foo };

    myStruct.pFunc(0);

    printf("address of foo: %p address of myStruct: %p \n"
        "address of myStruct.pFunc: %p value of myStruct.pFunc: %p \n",
        foo, &myStruct, &myStruct.pFunc, myStruct.pFunc);
```

```
}
```

Output (x64)

```
--- Structure Function Fields ---
address of foo: 0x401765 address of myStruct: 0x7fffa76e0e00
address of myStruct.pFunc: 0x7fffa76e0e08 value of myStruct.pFunc: 0x401765
```

Structure Methods

C++ introduced structure or class methods. They can be defined either inside the structure definition (next slide) or outside with the structure name qualification.

Classic C++

```cpp
typedef int (*PF)(int);

struct MyStruct
{
    int field;
    PF  pFunc;
    int method(int i);
} myStruct = { 0, foo };

int MyStruct::method(int i)
{
    return i;
}

std::cout << "--- Structure Methods ---" << std::endl;
{
    // std::cout interprets &MyStruct::method as a pointer to member instead (1)
    printf("address of myStruct: %p address of MyStruct::method: %p \n",
        &myStruct, &MyStruct::method);
```

```
    myStruct.pFunc(0);
    myStruct.method(0);
}
```

Output (x64)

```
--- Structure Methods ---
address of myStruct: 0x5d9130 address of MyStruct::method: 0x404ca4
```

Structure Methods (Inlined)

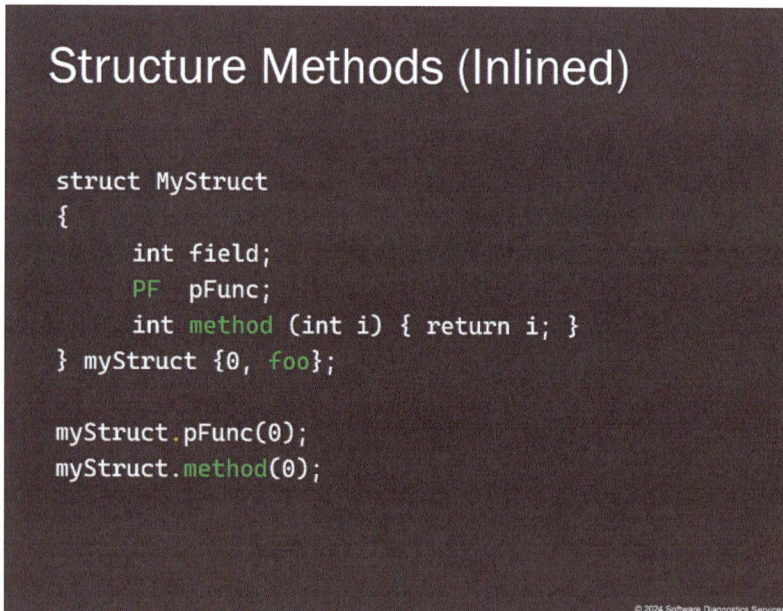

This is an alternative way to define short functions, although it exposes users to implementation details.

Classic C++

```
typedef int (*PF)(int);

std::cout << "--- Structure Methods (Inlined) ---" << std::endl;
{
    struct MyStruct
    {
        int field;
        PF  pFunc;
        int method(int i) { return i; }
    } myStruct = { 0, foo };

    // std::cout interprets &MyStruct::method as a pointer to member instead (1)
    printf("address of myStruct: %p address of MyStruct::method: %p \n",
        &myStruct, &MyStruct::method);

    myStruct.pFunc(0);
    myStruct.method(0);
}
```

```
--- Structure Methods (Inlined) ---
address of myStruct: 0x7fff31cbc500 address of MyStruct::method: 0x404e5c
```

Structure Methods (Inheritance)

In the case of inheritance, like with fields, the derived structure methods hide methods with the same name in the base type unless explicit base type name qualification is used. However, when we have a pointer to a base type, then the base type method is called even if the actual object belongs to a derived type:

Classic C++

```cpp
std::cout << "--- Structure Methods (Inheritance) ---" << std::endl;
{
    struct Base
    {
        int method(int i)
        {
            std::cout << "Base::method called" << std::endl;
            return i;
        }
    };

    struct Derived : Base
    {
        int method(int i)
        {
            std::cout << "Derived::method called" << std::endl;
            return ++i;
        }
    } myDerived;

    std::cout << "myDerived.method(0): ";
    myDerived.method(0);
```

```
    std::cout << "myDerived.Base::method(0): ";
    myDerived.Base::method(0);

    std::cout << "---" << std::endl;

    Base* pMyBase = &myDerived;
    std::cout << "pMyBase->method(0): ";
    pMyBase->method(0);
}
```

Output

```
--- Structure Methods (Inheritance) ---
myDerived.method(0): Derived::method called
myDerived.Base::method(0): Base::method called
---
pMyBase->method(0): Base::method called
```

Structure Virtual Methods

This previous slide problem is solved by introducing type-independent call virtual methods. In this case, the method of derived type is called when we have a pointer of a base type to it. The override specifier guarantees that we override the correct base method instead of introducing the new one by mistake.

Classic C++

```
std::cout << "--- Structure Virtual Methods ---" << std::endl;
{
    struct Base
    {
        int method(int i)
        {
            std::cout << "Base::method called" << std::endl;
            return i;
        }
```

```cpp
        virtual int vmethod(int i)
        {
            std::cout << "Base::vmethod called" << std::endl;
            return i;
        }
    };

    struct Derived : Base
    {
        int method(int i)
        {
            std::cout << "Derived::method called" << std::endl;
            return ++i;
        }

        virtual int vmethod(int i)
        {
            std::cout << "Derived::vmethod called" << std::endl;
            return ++i;
        }
    } myDerived;

    Base* pMyBase = &myDerived;
    std::cout << "pMyBase->method(0): ";
    pMyBase->method(0);
    std::cout << "pMyBase->vmethod(0): ";
    pMyBase->vmethod(0);
    std::cout << "pMyBase->Base::vmethod(0): ";
    pMyBase->Base::vmethod(0);
}
```

Output

```
--- Structure Virtual Methods ---
pMyBase->method(0): Base::method called
pMyBase->vmethod(0): Derived::vmethod called
pMyBase->Base::vmethod(0): Base::vmethod called
```

Modern C++

```cpp
std::println("--- Structure Virtual Methods ---");
{
    struct Base
    {
        int method(int i)
        {
            std::println("Base::method called");
            return i;
        }

        int method2(int i)
        {
            std::println("Base::method2 called");
            return i;
        }

        virtual int vmethod(int i)
        {
            std::println("Base::vmethod called");
            return i;
        }
```

```
    };

    struct Derived : Base
    {
        int method(int i)
        {
            std::println("Derived::method called");
            return ++i;
        }

        virtual int method2(int i) // override // error
        {
            std::println("Derived::method2 called");
            return i;
        }

        virtual int vmethod(int i) override // overrride is C++11
        {
            std::println("Derived::vmethod called");
            return ++i;
        }
    } myDerived;

    Base* pMyBase = &myDerived;
    std::print("pMyBase->method(0): ");
    pMyBase->method(0);
    std::print("pMyBase->vmethod(0): ");
    pMyBase->vmethod(0);
    std::print("pMyBase->method2(0): ");
    pMyBase->method2(0);
    std::print("pMyBase->Base::vmethod(0): ");
    pMyBase->Base::vmethod(0);
}
```

Output

```
--- Structure Virtual Methods ---
pMyBase->method(0): Base::method called
pMyBase->vmethod(0): Derived::vmethod called
pMyBase->method2(0): Base::method2 called
pMyBase->Base::vmethod(0): Base::vmethod called
```

Structure Pure Virtual Methods

If we want to make sure we never define objects of the base type and make sure we override all **pure** virtual methods in the derived type, we can make the virtual function pure by using `= 0`.

Classic C++

```cpp
std::cout << "--- Structure Pure Virtual Methods ---" << std::endl;
{
    struct Base
    {
        int method(int i)
        {
            std::cout << "Base::method called" << std::endl;
            return i;
        }

        virtual int vmethod(int i) = 0;
    };

    struct Derived : Base
    {
        int method(int i)
        {
            std::cout << "Derived::method called" << std::endl;
            return ++i;
        }

        virtual int vmethod(int i)
        {
            std::cout << "Derived::vmethod called" << std::endl;
            return ++i;
        }
    } myDerived;

    // Base base; // error
    Base* pMyBase = &myDerived;
    std::cout << "pMyBase->vmethod(0): ";
```

```
    pMyBase->vmethod(0);
}
```

```
std::println("--- Structure Pure Virtual Methods ---");
{
    struct Base
    {
        int method(int i)
        {
            std::println("Base::method called");
            return i;
        }

        virtual int vmethod(int i) = 0;
    };

    struct Derived : Base
    {
        int method(int i)
        {
            std::println("Derived::method called");
            return ++i;
        }

        virtual int vmethod(int i) override
        {
            std::println("Derived::vmethod called");
            return ++i;
        }
    } myDerived;

    // Base base; // error
    Base* pMyBase = &myDerived;
    std::print("pMyBase->vmethod(0): ");
    pMyBase->vmethod(0);
}
```

Output

```
--- Structure Pure Virtual Methods ---
pMyBase->vmethod(0): Derived::vmethod called
```

Structure as Interface

Pure virtual functions allow specifying abstract interfaces the derived types have to implement.

```cpp
std::cout << "--- Structure as Interface ---" << std::endl;
{
    struct Interface
    {
        virtual int vmethod1(int i) = 0;
        virtual int vmethod2(int i) = 0;
    };

    struct Implementer : Interface
    {
        virtual int vmethod1(int i)
        {
            std::cout << "Implementer::vmethod1 called" << std::endl;
            return ++i;
        }

        virtual int vmethod2(int i)
        {
            std::cout << "Implementer::vmethod2 called" << std::endl;
            return ++++i;
        }
    } myObject;

    Interface* pIface = &myObject;
    std::cout << "pIface->vmethod1(0): ";
    pIface->vmethod1(0);
}
```

Modern C++

```cpp
std::println("--- Structure as Interface ---");
{
    struct Interface
    {
        virtual int vmethod1(int i) = 0;
        virtual int vmethod2(int i) = 0;
    };

    struct Implementer : Interface
    {
        virtual int vmethod1(int i) override
        {
            std::println("Implementer::vmethod1 called");
            return ++i;
        }

        virtual int vmethod2(int i) override
        {
            std::println("Implementer::vmethod2 called");
            return ++++i;
        }
    } myObject;

    Interface* pIface = &myObject;
    std::print("pIface->vmethod1(0): ");
    pIface->vmethod1(0);
}
```

Output

```
--- Structure as Interface ---
pIface->vmethod1(0): Implementer::vmethod1 called
```

Function Structure

Functions may also encapsulate state. The best way to do it is via structures that implement function call operators.

Classic C++

```cpp
std::cout << "--- Function Structure ---" << std::endl;
{
    struct MyFunction
    {
        int field;

        int operator()()
        {
            return field;
        }
    } myFunction = { 1 };

    std::cout << "myFunction() return value: " << myFunction() << std::endl;
}
```

Modern C++

```cpp
std::println("--- Function Structure ---");
{
    struct MyFunction
    {
        int field{1};

        int operator()()
        {
            return field;
        }
    } myFunction;
```

```
    std::println("myFunction() return value: {}",
        myFunction());
}
```

Output

```
--- Function Structure ---
myFunction() return value: 1
```

Structure Constructors

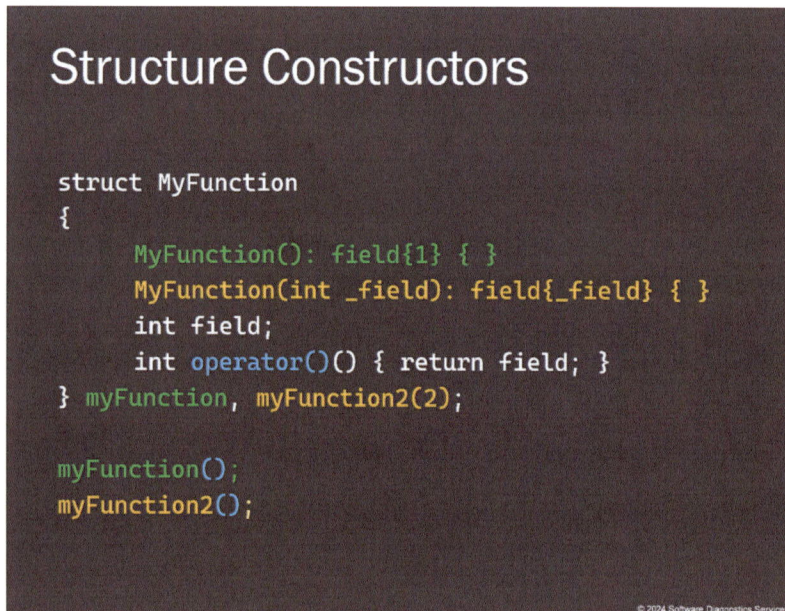

Now, we come to traditional OOP topics in classic C++. Constructors are methods with or without arguments for structure initialization with custom initialization logic inside, for example, acquiring required resources.

Classic C++

```
std::cout << "--- Structure Constructors ---" << std::endl;
{
    struct MyFunction
    {
        MyFunction() : field(1)
        {
            std::cout << "MyFunction::MyFunction() called" << std::endl;
        }

        MyFunction(int _field) : field(_field)
        {
            std::cout << "MyFunction::MyFunction(int _field) called" << std::endl;
        }

        int field;

        int operator()()
        {
```

```
            return field;
        }
    } myFunction, myFunction2(2);

    std::cout << "myFunction() return value: " << myFunction() << std::endl;
    std::cout << "myFunction2() return value: " << myFunction2() << std::endl;
}
```

<u>Output</u>

```
--- Structure Constructors ---
MyFunction::MyFunction() called
MyFunction::MyFunction(int _field) called
myFunction() return value: 1
myFunction2() return value: 2
```

Structure Converting Constructors

Constructors with one parameter are called converting constructors. If you don't want them to be called inadvertently during assignments, you can mark them explicit to be only called in their constructor form.

Classic C++

```
std::cout << "--- Structure Converting Constructors ---" << std::endl;
{
    struct MyFunction
    {
        MyFunction() : field(1)
        {
            std::cout << "MyFunction::MyFunction() called" << std::endl;
        }

        explicit MyFunction(int _field) : field(_field)
        {
            std::cout << "MyFunction::MyFunction(int _field) called" << std::endl;
        }
```

```cpp
        MyFunction(bool flag) : field(flag)
        {
            std::cout << "MyFunction::MyFunction(bool flag) called" << std::endl;
        }

        int field;

        int operator()()
        {
            return field;
        }
    };

    MyFunction myFunction = false;
    std::cout << "myFunction() return value: " << myFunction() << std::endl;

    MyFunction myFunction2 = 2; // truncation to bool warning
    std::cout << "myFunction2() return value: " << myFunction2() << std::endl;

    MyFunction myFunction3(3);
    std::cout << "myFunction3() return value: " << myFunction3() << std::endl;
}
```

Output

```
--- Structure Converting Constructors ---
MyFunction::MyFunction(bool flag) called
myFunction() return value: 0
MyFunction::MyFunction(bool flag) called
myFunction2() return value: 1
MyFunction::MyFunction(int _field) called
myFunction3() return value: 3
```

Structure Delegating Constructors

We can reduce error-prone duplicate initialization code in constructors by delegating such activity to other constuctors.

```cpp
std::println("--- Structure Delegating Constructors ---");
{
    struct MyFunction
    {
        MyFunction() : MyFunction(1)
        {
            std::println("MyFunction::MyFunction() called");
        }

        MyFunction(int _field) : MyFunction(_field, 0)
        {
            std::println("MyFunction::MyFunction(int _field) called");
        }

        MyFunction(int _field, int _field2) : field{_field}, field2{_field2}
        {
            std::println("MyFunction::MyFunction(int _field, int _field2) called");
        }

        int field;
        int field2;

        int operator()()
        {
            return field;
        }
    };

    MyFunction myFunction;
    std::println("myFunction() return value: {}",
        myFunction());

    MyFunction myFunction2(2);
    std::println("myFunction2() return value: {}",
        myFunction2());

    MyFunction myFunction3(3, 3);
    std::println("myFunction3() return value: {}",
        myFunction3());
}
```

Output

```
--- Structure Delegating Constructors ---
MyFunction::MyFunction(int _field, int _field2) called
MyFunction::MyFunction(int _field) called
MyFunction::MyFunction() called
myFunction() return value: 1
MyFunction::MyFunction(int _field, int _field2) called
MyFunction::MyFunction(int _field) called
myFunction2() return value: 2
MyFunction::MyFunction(int _field, int _field2) called
myFunction3() return value: 3
```

Structure Member Initialization

Structure fields are initialized in the order of their definition in the structure definition body, not in the order of their initialization in the constructor.

Classic C++

```cpp
std::cout << "--- Structure Member Initialization ---" << std::endl;
{
    struct MyFunction
    {
        MyFunction() : index(0), field(++index), field2(++index)
        {
            std::cout << "MyFunction::MyFunction() called" << std::endl;
        }

        int index;
        int field2;
        int field;

        int operator()()
        {
            return field;
        }
    } myFunction;

    std::cout << "myFunction() return value: " << myFunction() << std::endl;

    // assert(1 == myFunction()); // fails
}
```

Output

```
--- Structure Member Initialization ---
MyFunction::MyFunction() called
myFunction() return value: 2
```

Structure Copy Constructor

When we copy objects but need complex copying logic or nontrivial memory management copy constructor methods are quite handy. We pass the source object reference as const if we don't plan to modify it. In the presence of non-const source copy constructor, it is called instead of const-source copy constructor in the case of non-const source objects, as seen in the source code below.

Classic C++

```cpp
std::cout << "--- Structure Copy Constructor ---" << std::endl;
{
    struct MyFunction
    {
        MyFunction() : field(1) { }
        MyFunction(int _field) : field(_field) { }
        MyFunction(const MyFunction& src) : field(src.field)
        {
            std::cout << "MyFunction(const MyFunction& src) called" << std::endl;
        }
        MyFunction(MyFunction& src) : field(src.field)
        {
            std::cout << "MyFunction(MyFunction& src) called" << std::endl;
            ++src.field;
        }

        int field;

        int operator()()
        {
            return field;
        }
    } myFunction;

    MyFunction myFunction2(myFunction);
    MyFunction myFunction3 = myFunction;

    std::cout << "---" << std::endl;
```

```
    const MyFunction myFunction4;

    MyFunction myFunction5 = myFunction4;
}
```

Output

```
--- Structure Copy Constructor ---
MyFunction(MyFunction& src) called
MyFunction(MyFunction& src) called
---
MyFunction(const MyFunction& src) called
```

Copy vs. Move Semantics

The main difference between copy and move semantics is that moves reset sources to their default value, for example, to `nullptr` in case of pointer fields or default-initialized integer fields.

Structure Move Constructors

```
Structure Move Constructors

struct MyFunction
{
        MyFunction(): field{1} { }
        MyFunction(int _field): field{_field} { }
        MyFunction(const MyFunction& src):
                field{src.field} { }
        MyFunction(MyFunction&& src):
                field{src.field} { src.field = 1; }
        int field;
        int operator()() { field; }
} myFunction;

myFunction();
MyFunction myFunction2(std::move(myFunction));
MyFunction myFunction3 = std::move(myFunction2);

                                      © 2024 Software Diagnostics Services
```

We use move constructors when we don't want to copy the structure contents but move its values to another location. Such constructors reset source fields to their default values.

Modern C++

```cpp
std::println("--- Structure Move Constructors ---");
{
    struct MyFunction
    {
        MyFunction() : field{1} { }
        MyFunction(int _field) : field{_field} { }
        MyFunction(const MyFunction& src) : field{src.field} { }
        MyFunction(MyFunction&& src) noexcept : field{src.field}
        {
            std::println("MyFunction(MyFunction&& src) called");
            src.field = 1;
        }

        int field;

        void use() { ++field; }
        int operator()() { return field; }
    } myFunction;

    myFunction.use();
    std::println("myFunction() return value: {}",
        myFunction());

    MyFunction myFunction2(std::move(myFunction));
    std::println("myFunction() return value: {}",
        myFunction());
    std::println("myFunction2() return value: {}",
        myFunction2());

    MyFunction myFunction3 = std::move(myFunction2);
    std::println("myFunction2() return value: {}",
        myFunction2());
```

```
    std::println("myFunction3() return value: {}",
        myFunction3());
}
```

Output

```
--- Structure Move Constructors ---
myFunction() return value: 2
MyFunction(MyFunction&& src) called
myFunction() return value: 1
myFunction2() return value: 2
MyFunction(MyFunction&& src) called
myFunction2() return value: 1
myFunction3() return value: 2
```

Structure Copy Assignment

In the case of nontrivial assignments, we can implement an assignment operator. We, however, should be careful not to copy to itself (this), and we return the non-const reference to itself (*this) to allow chained copies.

Classic C++

```
std::cout << "--- Structure Copy Assignment ---" << std::endl;
{
    struct MyFunction
    {
        MyFunction() : field(1) { }
        MyFunction(int _field) : field(_field) { }
        MyFunction(const MyFunction& src) : field(src.field) { }
        MyFunction& operator=(const MyFunction& src)
        {
```

```cpp
            if (this != &src)
            {
                std::cout << "MyFunction& operator=(const MyFunction& src) called" << std::endl;
                field = src.field;
            }
            return *this;
        }

        int field;

        void use() { ++field; }
        int operator()() { return field; }
    } myFunction;

    myFunction.use();
    std::cout << "myFunction() return value: " << myFunction() << std::endl;

    MyFunction myFunction2;
    std::cout << "myFunction2() return value: " << myFunction2() << std::endl;

    myFunction2 = myFunction;
    std::cout << "myFunction2() return value: " << myFunction2() << std::endl;

    MyFunction myFunction3;

    myFunction3 = myFunction2 = myFunction;
}
```

Output

```
--- Structure Copy Assignment ---
myFunction() return value: 2
myFunction2() return value: 1
MyFunction& operator=(const MyFunction& src) called
myFunction2() return value: 2
MyFunction& operator=(const MyFunction& src) called
MyFunction& operator=(const MyFunction& src) called
```

Structure Move Assignment

If we want to move the structure contents instead of copying, we can implement the move assignment operator. However, we should be careful not to move to itself in the case of non-trivial semantics.

Modern C++

```cpp
std::println("--- Structure Move Assignment ---");
{
    struct MyFunction
    {
        MyFunction() : field{1} { }
        MyFunction(int _field) : field{_field} { }
        MyFunction(const MyFunction& src) : field{src.field} { }
        MyFunction(MyFunction&& src) noexcept : field{src.field}
        {
            std::println("MyFunction(MyFunction&& src) called");
            src.field = 1;
        }
        MyFunction& operator=(const MyFunction& src)
        {
            std::println("MyFunction& operator=(const MyFunction& src) called");
            if (this != &src)
            {
                field = src.field;
            }
            return *this;
        }
        MyFunction& operator=(MyFunction&& src) noexcept
        {
            if (this != &src)
            {
                std::println("MyFunction& operator=(MyFunction&& src) called");
                field = src.field;
                src.field = 1;
            }
            return *this;
```

```
        }

        int field;

        void use() { ++field; }
        int operator()() { return field; }
    } myFunction;

    myFunction.use();
    std::println("myFunction() return value: {}",
        myFunction());

    MyFunction myFunction2;
    myFunction2 = std::move(myFunction);
    std::println("myFunction() return value: {}",
        myFunction());
    std::println("myFunction2() return value: {}",
        myFunction2());

    MyFunction myFunction3;

    // Will have MyFunction& operator=(MyFunction&& src) called and
    // then MyFunction& operator=(const MyFunction& src) called:
    // myFunction3 = std::move(myFunction2) = std::move(myFunction);
    myFunction3 = std::move(myFunction2 = std::move(myFunction));
}
```

Output

```
--- Structure Move Assignment ---
myFunction() return value: 2
MyFunction& operator=(MyFunction&& src) called
myFunction() return value: 1
myFunction2() return value: 2
MyFunction& operator=(MyFunction&& src) called
MyFunction& operator=(MyFunction&& src) called
```

Structure Destructor

What if we want some complex logic, for example, releasing resources when the local object goes out of scope, or we delete it? Destructor is a method that is called automatically in such a case.

Classic C++

```cpp
std::cout << "--- Structure Destructor ---" << std::endl;
{
    struct MyFunction
    {
        MyFunction() : field(1) { }
        ~MyFunction()
        {
            std::cout << "~MyFunction() called" << std::endl;
        }
        MyFunction(int _field) : field(_field) { }
        MyFunction(const MyFunction& src) : field(src.field) { }
        MyFunction& operator=(const MyFunction& src)
        {
            if (this != &src)
            {
                std::cout << "MyFunction& operator=(const MyFunction& src) called" << std::endl;
                field = src.field;
            }
            return *this;
        }

        int field;

        void use() { ++field; }
        int operator()() { return field; }
    };

    {
        std::cout << "Before inner scope" << std::endl;
        {
            MyFunction myFunction;
```

```
        }
        std::cout << "After inner scope" << std::endl;
    }
}
```

<u>Output</u>

```
--- Structure Destructor ---
Before inner scope
~MyFunction() called
After inner scope
```

Structure Destructor Hierarchy

Conceptually, destructors are just like a normal method, so the wrong one may be called when we have a pointer of base type to an object of a derived type.

Classic C++

```
std::cout << "--- Structure Destructor Hierarchy ---" << std::endl;
{
    struct IFunction
    {
        ~IFunction()
        {
            std::cout << "IFunction::~IFunction() called" << std::endl;
        }
        virtual int operator()() = 0;
    };

    struct MyFunction : IFunction
    {
        ~MyFunction()
        {
```

```
        std::cout << "MyFunction::~MyFunction() called" << std::endl;
    }

    int field;

    int operator()() { return field; }
};

IFunction* pIFunction = new MyFunction;
pIFunction->operator()();
(*pIFunction)();
delete pIFunction; // ~IFunction()

MyFunction* pMyFunction = new MyFunction;
pMyFunction->operator()();
(*pMyFunction)();
delete pMyFunction; // ~MyFunction(), ~IFunction()
}
```

Output

```
--- Structure Destructor Hierarchy ---
IFunction::~IFunction() called
MyFunction::~MyFunction() called
IFunction::~IFunction() called
```

Structure Virtual Destructor

Structure Virtual Destructor

```
struct IFunction
{
    virtual ~IFunction() { }
    virtual int operator()() = 0;
};

struct MyFunction : IFunction
{
    ~MyFunction() override { /* close resources */ }
    int field;
    int operator()() override { return field; }
};

IFunction* pIFunction = new MyFunction;
pIFunction->operator()();
(*pIFunction)();
delete pIFunction; // ~MyFunction()
```

© 2024 Software Diagnostics Services

To make sure that the correct destructors are called, it is recommended to make them virtual too.

```cpp
std::cout << "--- Structure Virtual Destructor ---" << std::endl;
{
    struct IFunction
    {
        virtual ~IFunction()
        {
            std::cout << "IFunction::~IFunction() called" << std::endl;
        }
        virtual int operator()() = 0;
    };

    struct MyFunction : IFunction
    {
        ~MyFunction()
        {
            std::cout << "MyFunction::~MyFunction() called" << std::endl;
        }

        int field;

        int operator()() { return field; }
    };

    IFunction* pIFunction = new MyFunction;
    pIFunction->operator()();
    (*pIFunction)();
    delete pIFunction; // ~MyFunction()
}
```

Output

```
--- Structure Virtual Destructor ---
MyFunction::~MyFunction() called
IFunction::~IFunction() called
```

Structure Member Destruction

Structure members are destructed in the opposite order of their initialization.

Structure Member Destruction

```
struct MyFunctionContainer
{
    MyFunctionContainer() :
      myFunction1(1),
      myFunction2(2),
      myFunction3(3)
      { }

    MyFunction myFunction1; // destructed third
    MyFunction myFunction2; // destructed second
    MyFunction myFunction3; // destructed first
} myFunctionContainer;
```

© 2024 Software Diagnostics Services

Classic C++

```
std::cout << "--- Structure Member Destruction ---" << std::endl;
{
    struct MyFunction
    {
        MyFunction() : field(1) { }
        ~MyFunction()
        {
            std::cout << "~MyFunction() called. Value of field: " << field << std::endl;
        }
        MyFunction(int _field) : field(_field) { }
        MyFunction(const MyFunction& src) : field(src.field) { }
        MyFunction& operator=(const MyFunction& src)
        {
            if (this != &src)
            {
                std::cout << "MyFunction& operator=(const MyFunction& src) called" << std::endl;
                field = src.field;
            }
            return *this;
        }

        int field;

        void use() { ++field; }
        int operator()() { return field; }
    };

    struct MyFunctionContainer
    {
        MyFunctionContainer() : myFunction1(1), myFunction2(2), myFunction3(3) { }
```

```
        MyFunction myFunction1;
        MyFunction myFunction2;
        MyFunction myFunction3;
    } myFunctionContainer;
}
```

Output

```
--- Structure Destructor Hierarchy ---
~MyFunction() called. Value of field: 3
~MyFunction() called. Value of field: 2
~MyFunction() called. Value of field: 1
```

Destructor as a Method

Since a destructor is also a method, it is possible to call it directly in cases where we should not use standard delete methods, for example, when objects are allocated using placement `new`:

Classic C++

```cpp
std::cout << "--- Destructor as a Method ---" << std::endl;
{
    struct Resource
    {
        Resource() : m_hData(0x1234)
        {
            std::cout << "Resource() called" << std::endl;
        }
        ~Resource()
        {
            std::cout << "~Resource() called" << std::endl;
```

```
        }
    private:
        int m_hData;
    };

    char buf[sizeof(Resource)];
    Resource* pResource = new(buf) Resource();
    // ...
    pResource->~Resource();
}
```

Output

```
--- Destructor as a Method ---
Resource() called
~Resource() called
```

Structure Default Operations

If you define certain operations, you must define others as well. You can define their default implementation instead of writing the default code yourself.

Modern C++

```
std::println("--- Structure Default Operations ---");
{
    struct MyFunction
    {
        MyFunction(int _field) { }
        MyFunction(MyFunction&& src) noexcept : field{src.field}
        {
            std::println("MyFunction(MyFunction&& src) called");
            src.field = 1;
```

```
    }

    MyFunction() = default;
    MyFunction& operator=(const MyFunction& src) = default;
    ~MyFunction() = default;

    int field{1};

    void use() { ++field; }
    int operator()() { return field; }
};

MyFunction myFunction, myFunction2;
myFunction.use();
std::println("myFunction() return value: {}",
    myFunction());
myFunction2 = myFunction;
std::println("myFunction2() return value: {}",
    myFunction2());
}
```

Output

```
--- Structure Default Operations ---
myFunction() return value: 2
myFunction2() return value: 2
```

Structure Deleted Operations

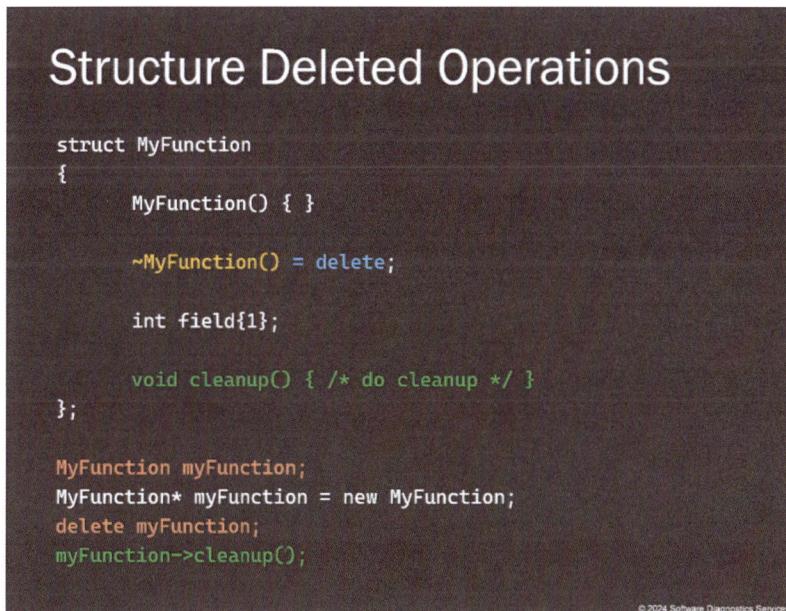

If you want to prevent behavior, for example, the ability to create objects on the stack, you can delete the destructor from the set of available operations.

```cpp
std::println("--- Structure Deleted Operations ---");
{
    struct MyFunction
    {
        MyFunction()
        {
            std::println("MyFunction() called");
        }

        ~MyFunction() = delete;

        int field{1};

        void cleanup()
        {
            std::println("cleanup() called");
        };
    };

    // MyFunction myFunction; // error

    MyFunction* myFunction = new MyFunction;

    // delete myFunction; // error

    myFunction->cleanup();
}
```

Output

```
--- Structure Deleted Operations ---
MyFunction() called
cleanup() called
```

Conversion Operators

Destinations for copy constructors and copy assignment operators are of the same type. What if we want to assign to a different structure type? We can define custom conversion operators (it is also possible to use a "conversion" constructor).

Classic C++

```cpp
std::cout << "--- Conversion Operators ---" << std::endl;
{
    struct A
    {
        A(unsigned int _u1, unsigned int _u2) :
            u1(_u1), u2(_u2) { }

        A(const A& src) : u1(src.u1), u2(src.u2)
        {
            std::cout << "A(const A& src) called" << std::endl;
        }

        unsigned int u1;
        unsigned int u2;
    };

    struct B
    {
        unsigned long ul;

        operator A()
        {
            std::cout << "operator A() called" << std::endl;

            return A
            (
                static_cast<unsigned int>(ul & 0xFFFFFFFF),
                static_cast<unsigned int>(ul >> 32)
            );
        }
    } b = { 0x0123456789abcdef };
```

```cpp
    std::cout << "value of b: " << std::hex << b.ul << std::endl;

    A a = b; // no copy constructor is called

    std::cout << "value of a: { " << std::hex << a.u1 << ", " << a.u2 << " }" << std::endl;
}
```

Output

```
--- Conversion Operators ---
value of b: 123456789abcdef
operator A() called
value of a: { 89abcdef, 1234567 }
```

Parameters by Value

When we pass parameters by values, any modifications inside functions are lost once we return. Passing basic types by value is efficient, but passing structures are not unless they are very simple: various functions may be called, for example, copy constructors and destructors unless optimized by a compiler. There is also a possibility of slicing when inheritance is used.

C

```c
void func(int i)
{
    printf("func: address of i: %p value of i: %x \n", &i, i);

    i = 0;
}

struct MyStruct
{
    int field;
};
```

```cpp
void func2(struct MyStruct ms)
{
    printf("func2: address of ms: %p value of ms.field: %x \n", &ms, ms.field);

    ms.field = 0;

    printf("func2: value of ms.field: %x \n", ms.field);
}

puts("--- Parameters by Value ---");
{
    func(1);

    struct MyStruct ms = { 1 };

    printf("main: address of ms: %p value of ms.field: %x \n", &ms, ms.field);

    func2(ms);

    printf("main: address of ms: %p value of ms.field: %x \n", &ms, ms.field);
}
```

C++ as a better C

```cpp
void func(int i)
{
    printf("func: address of i: %p value of i: %x \n", &i, i);

    i = 0;
}

struct MyStruct
{
    int field;
};

void func2(MyStruct ms)
{
    printf("func2: address of ms: %p value of ms.field: %x \n", &ms, ms.field);

    ms.field = 0;

    printf("func2: value of ms.field: %x \n", ms.field);
}

puts("--- Parameters by Value ---");
{
    func(1);

    MyStruct ms = { 1 }; // struct keyword can be omitted

    printf("main: address of ms: %p value of ms.field: %x \n", &ms, ms.field);

    func2(ms);

    printf("main: address of ms: %p value of ms.field: %x \n", &ms, ms.field);
}
```

<u>Output (x64)</u>

```
--- Parameters by Value ---
func: address of i: 0x7fffa76e0ddc value of i: 1
main: address of ms: 0x7fffa76e0dfc value of ms.field: 1
func2: address of ms: 0x7fffa76e0ddc value of ms.field: 1
func2: value of ms.field: 0
main: address of ms: 0x7fffa76e0dfc value of ms.field: 1
```

Parameters by Pointer/Reference

If we want efficiency for structures and also preserve changes to original values, we need to pass by reference. Again, this may be inefficient for basic types.

`C`

```c
struct MyStruct
{
    int field;
};

void func3(struct MyStruct* pms)
{
    printf("func3: address of pms: %p value of pms: %p value of pms->field: %x \n", &pms, pms, pms->field);

    pms->field = 0;

    printf("func3: value of pms->field: %x \n", pms->field);
}
```

```
puts("--- Parameters by Pointer ---");
{
    struct MyStruct ms = { 1 };

    printf("main: address of ms: %p value of ms.field: %x \n", &ms, ms.field);

    func3(&ms);

    printf("main: address of ms: %p value of ms.field: %x \n", &ms, ms.field);
}
```

C++ as a better C

```
struct MyStruct
{
    int field;
};

void func3(MyStruct* pms)
{
    printf("func3: address of pms: %p value of pms: %p value of pms->field: %x \n", &pms, pms, pms->field);

    pms->field = 0;

    printf("func3: value of pms->field: %x \n", pms->field);
}

puts("--- Parameters by Pointer ---");
{
    MyStruct ms = { 1 };

    printf("main: address of ms: %p value of ms.field: %x \n", &ms, ms.field);

    func3(&ms);

    printf("main: address of ms: %p value of ms.field: %x \n", &ms, ms.field);
}
```

Output (x64)

```
--- Parameters by Pointer ---
main: address of ms: 0x7fffa76e0df8 value of ms.field: 1
func3: address of pms: 0x7fffa76e0dd8 value of pms: 0x7fffa76e0df8 value of pms->field: 1
func3: value of pms->field: 0
main: address of ms: 0x7fffa76e0df8 value of ms.field: 0
```

Classic C++

```
void func4(int& ri)
{
    std::cout << "func4: address of ri: " << &ri << " value of ri: " << ri << std::endl;

    ri = 0;

    std::cout << "func4: value of ri: " << ri << std::endl;
}

std::cout << "--- Parameters by Reference ---" << std::endl;
{
    int i = 1;
```

```
    std::cout << "main: address of i: " << &i << " value of i: " << i << std::endl;

    func4(i);

    std::cout << "main: value of i: " << i << std::endl;
}
```

Output (x64)

```
--- Parameters by Reference ---
main: address of i: 0x7fff31cbc474 value of i: 1
func4: address of ri: 0x7fff31cbc474 value of ri: 1
func4: value of ri: 0
main: value of i: 0
```

Parameters by Ptr/Ref to Const

If we only want efficiency for structures, we need to pass by reference to const. In such a case, we also cannot modify the original values.

C

```
struct MyStruct
{
    int field;
};

void func5(const struct MyStruct* pms)
{
    printf("func5: address of pms: %p value of pms: %p value of pms->field: %x \n", &pms, pms, pms->field);

    // pms->field = 0; error
```

```
}

puts("--- Parameters by Ptr to const ---");
{
    struct MyStruct ms = { 1 };

    printf("main: address of ms: %p value of ms.field: %x \n", &ms, ms.field);

    func5(&ms);

    printf("main: address of ms: %p value of ms.field: %x \n", &ms, ms.field);
}
```

C++ as a better C

```
struct MyStruct
{
    int field;
};

void func5(const MyStruct* pms)
{
    printf("func5: address of pms: %p value of pms: %p value of pms->field: %x \n", &pms, pms, pms->field);

    // pms->field = 0; error
}

puts("--- Parameters by Ptr to const ---");
{
    MyStruct ms = { 1 };

    printf("main: address of ms: %p value of ms.field: %x \n", &ms, ms.field);

    func5(&ms);

    printf("main: address of ms: %p value of ms.field: %x \n", &ms, ms.field);
}
```

Output (x64)

```
--- Parameters by Ptr to const ---
main: address of ms: 0x7fffa76e0df4 value of ms.field: 1
func5: address of pms: 0x7fffa76e0dd8 value of pms: 0x7fffa76e0df4 value of pms->field: 1
main: address of ms: 0x7fffa76e0df4 value of ms.field: 1
```

Classic C++

```
void func6(const int& ri)
{
    std::cout << "func6: address of ri: " << &ri << " value of ri: " << ri << std::endl;

    // ri = 0; // error
}

std::cout << "--- Parameters by Ref to const ---" << std::endl;
{
    func6(1);
}
```

Output (x64)

```
--- Parameters by Ref to const ---
func6: address of ri: 0x7fff31cbc51c value of ri: 1
```

Parameters by Ref to Rvalue

Modern C++ added the possibility to explicitly pass references to temporary values. Since inside the function the values they refer to are backed by memory you can freely change the values inside the function.

Modern C++

```cpp
void func7(int&& ri)
{
    std::println("func7: address of ri: {:016X} value of ri: {}",
        reinterpret_cast<uintptr_t>(&ri), ri);

    ri = 0;

    std::println("func7: value of ri: {}", ri);
}

std::println("--- Parameters by Ref to Rvalue ---");
{
    func7(1);
}
```

Output (x64)

```
--- Parameters by Ref to Rvalue ---
func7: address of ri: 00007FFD1560103C value of ri: 1
func7: value of ri: 0
```

Possible Mistake

Possible Mistake

- ◉ Original value doesn't change …
- ◉ … but you want to make sure
- ◉ You used languages with implicit references
- ◉ You should use const& instead

```
void func(const MyStruct ms)        void func(const MyStruct& ms)
{ ms.field = 0; }                   { ms.field = 0; }

func(myStruct);                     func(myStruct);
```

© 2024 Software Diagnostics Services

Function Overloading

Function Overloading

- ◉ Different from overriding
- ◉ Name mangling in symbol files

```
◉ int funco (int i);
◉ int funco (int i, int j);
◉ int funco (long &rl);
```

© 2024 Software Diagnostics Services

Function overloading allows reusing the same function names for functions with different numbers and types of parameters.

Default Arguments

Default function arguments may help in avoiding the proliferation of overloaded functions.

Classic C++

```cpp
int funco(int i, int j = 0)
{
    std::cout << "value of i: " << i << " value of j: " << j << std::endl;

    return i + j;
}

std::cout << "--- Default Arguments ---" << std::endl;
{
    funco(1);
    funco(1, 2);
}
```

Output

```
--- Default Arguments ---
value of i: 1 value of j: 0
value of i: 1 value of j: 2
```

Variadic Functions

Variadic functions have a variable number of parameters. But they have undefined behavior when the number of the remaining parameters does not match the value for the number of arguments and their types are different.

C   C++ as a better C

```
puts("--- Variadic Functions ---");
{
    printf("product: %f \n", varfunc(3, 1.0, 2.0, 3.0));

    assert(6.0 == varfunc(3, 1.0, 2.0, 3.0));

    printf("product: %f \n", varfunc(5, 1.0, 2.0, 3.0, 4.0));

    // assert(24.0 == varfunc(5, 1.0, 2.0, 3.0, 4.0)); // fails

    printf("product: %f \n", varfunc(3, 1.0, 2.0, 3));

    // assert(6.0 == varfunc(3, 1.0, 2.0, 3)); // fails
}
```

Output (x64)

```
--- Variadic Functions ---
product: 6.000000
product: 144.000000
product: 0.000000
```

Immutable Objects

If you have `const` objects, you are only allowed to call methods that have the `const` specifier in their definition.

Classic C++

```cpp
std::cout << "--- Immutable Objects ---" << std::endl;
{
    struct MyStruct
    {
        MyStruct(int _field) : field(_field) { }
        int  get() const { return field; }
        void set(int newval) { field = newval; }
    private:
        int field;
    } myStruct(1);

    const MyStruct& myCStruct{ myStruct };

    myCStruct.get();

    // myCStruct.set(2); // error
}
```

Static Structure Functions

Static structure functions are only allowed to access static structure fields shared among objects.

Classic C++

```cpp
// multithreading issues are ignored here
struct MyStructS
{
    MyStructS(int _field) : field(_field) { ++count; }
    int  get() const { return field; }
    void set(int newval) { field = newval; }
    static auto get_count()
    {
        // field++; error
        return count;
    };
private:
    int field;
    static unsigned count;
};

unsigned MyStructS::count = 0;

std::cout << "--- Static Structure Functions ---" << std::endl;
{
    MyStructS myStruct1(1), myStruct2(2);

    std::cout << "count of objects: " << MyStructS::get_count() << std::endl;

    assert(myStruct1.get_count() == myStruct2.get_count());
}
```

Output

```
--- Static Structure Functions ---
count of objects: 2
```

Lambdas

> # Lambdas
>
> ◉ Interlude: necessary x64 and A64 disassembly
>
> ◉ Unnamed function objects
>
> ◉ A function parameter
>
> ◉ Optionally captures context
>
> ◉ A return value
>
> © 2024 Software Diagnostics Services

Before discussing lambdas introduced in C++11 and their internals, we take a brief tour around basic x64 and A64 disassembly.

x64 CPU Registers

> # x64 CPU Registers
>
> ◉ **RAX ⊃ EAX ⊃ AX ⊇ {AH, AL}** | RAX 64-bit | EAX 32-bit |
>
> ◉ ALU: **RAX, RDX**
>
> ◉ Counter: **RCX**
>
> ◉ Memory copy: **RSI** (src), **RDI** (dst)
>
> ◉ Stack: **RSP, RBP**
>
> ◉ Next instruction: **RIP**
>
> ◉ New: **R8 – R15**, **Rx(D|W|L)**
>
> © 2024 Software Diagnostics Services

There are familiar 32-bit CPU register names, such as **EAX,** that are extended to 64-bit names, such as **RAX**. Most of them are traditionally specialized, such as ALU, counter, and memory copy registers. Although, now they all can be used as general-purpose registers. There is, of course, a stack pointer, **RSP**, and, additionally, a frame pointer, **RBP**, that is used to address local variables and saved parameters. It can be used for backtrace reconstruction. In some compiler code generation implementtations, **RBP** is also used as a general-purpose register, with **RSP** taking the role of a frame pointer. An instruction pointer **RIP** is saved in the stack memory region with every function call, then restored on return from the called function. In addition, the x64 platform features another eight general-purpose registers, from **R8** to **R15**.

x64 Instructions and Registers

This slide shows a few examples of CPU instructions involving operations with registers, such as moving a value and doing arithmetic. The direction of operands is opposite to the Intel x64 disassembly flavor if you are accustomed to WinDbg on Windows. It is possible to use the Intel disassembly flavor in GDB, but we opted for the default AT&T flavor in line with our **Accelerated Linux Core Dump Analysis** and **Accelerated Linux Disassembly, Reconstruction, Reversing** books.

x64 Memory and Stack Addressing

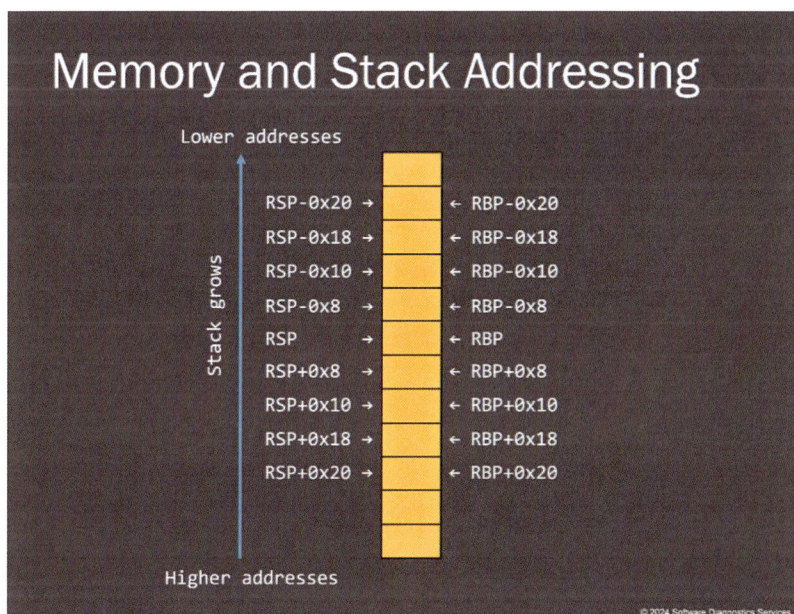

Before we look at operations with memory, let's look at a graphical representation of memory addressing. A thread stack is just any other memory region, so instead of **RSP** and **RBP,** any other register can be used. Please note that the stack grows towards lower addresses, so to access the previously pushed values, you need to use positive offsets from **RSP**.

x64 Memory Load Instructions

```
x64 Memory Load Instructions

⊙ Opcode Offset(SRC), DST

⊙ Opcode DST

⊙ Examples:

mov    0x10(%rsp), %rax      # value at address RSP+0x10 → RAX
mov    -0x10(%rbp), %rcx     # value at address RBP-0x10 → RCX
add    (%rax), %rdx          # RDX + value at address RAX → RDX
pop    %rdi                  # value at address RSP → RDI
                             # RSP + 8 → RSP
lea    0x20(%rbp), %r8       # address RBP+0x20 → R8

© 2024 Software Diagnostics Services
```

Constants are encoded in instructions, but if we need arbitrary values, we must get them from memory. Round brackets show memory access relative to an address stored in some register.

x64 Memory Store Instructions

```
x64 Memory Store Instructions

⊙ Opcode SRC, Offset(DST)

⊙ Opcode SRC|DST

⊙ Examples:

mov    %rcx, -0x20(%rbp)     # RCX → value at address RBP-0x20
addl   $1, (%rax)            # 1 + 32-bit value at address RAX →
                             #     32-bit value at address RAX
push   %rsi                  # RSP - 8 → RSP
                             # RSI → value at address RSP
inc    (%rcx)                # 1 + value at address RCX →
                             #     value at address RCX

© 2024 Software Diagnostics Services
```

Storing is similar to loading.

x64 Flow Instructions

x64 Flow Instructions

◉ Opcode DST

◉ Examples:

```
jmpq    0x10493fc1c        # 0x10493fc1c → RIP
                           # (goto 0x10493fc1c)

jmpq    *0x100(%rip)       # value at address RIP+0x100 → RIP

callq   0x10493ff74        # RSP − 8 → RSP
0x10493fc14:               # 0x10493fc14 → value at address RSP
                           # 0x10493ff74 → RIP
                           # (goto 0x10493ff74)
```

© 2024 Software Diagnostics Services

Goto (an unconditional jump) is implemented via the **JMP** instruction. Function calls are implemented via **CALL** instruction. For conditional branches, please look at the official Intel documentation.

x64 Function Parameters

x64 Function Parameters

◉ foo(…);

◉ Left to right via RDI, RSI, RDX, RCX, R8, R9, stack

© 2024 Software Diagnostics Services

On the x64 Linux platform, the first six C and C++ function parameters from left to right are moved to CPU registers, and the rest are passed via stack locations.

x64 Struct Function Parameters

x64 Struct Function Parameters

⊙ RDI

Implicit struct object memory address (&myStruct)

⊙ RSI, RDX, RCX, R8, R9, stack

Struct function parameters (MyStruct::foo(...);)

© 2024 Software Diagnostics Services

When an object struct nonstatic member function is called, the first parameter is implicit and, on the x64 Linux platform, is passed via **RDI**. It is an object address to help methods differentiate between objects of the same structure type and reference correct fields' memory. The rest of the parameters are passed as usual.

A64 CPU Registers

A64 CPU Registers

⊙ **X0 – X28, W0 – W28**

| X 64-bit | W 32-bit |

⊙ **X16 (XIP0), X17 (XIP1)**

⊙ Stack: **SP, X29 (FP)**

⊙ Next instruction: **PC**

⊙ Link register: **X30 (LR)**

⊙ Zero register: **XZR, WZR**

© 2024 Software Diagnostics Services

There are 31 general registers from **X0** and **X30**, with some delegated to specific tasks such as intra-procedure calls (**X16**, **XIP0**, and **X17**, **XIP1**), addressing stack frames (Frame Pointer, **FP**, **X29**) and return addresses, the so-called Link Register (**LR**, **X30**). When you call a function, the return address of a caller is saved in **LR**, not on the stack as in Intel/AMD x64. The return instruction in a callee uses the address in **LR** to assign it to **PC** and resume execution. But if a callee calls other functions, the current **LR** needs to be manually saved somewhere, usually on the stack. There's Stack Pointer, **SP**, of course. To get zero values, there's the so-called Zero Register, **XZR**. All **X** registers are 64-bit, and 32-bit lower parts are addressed via the **W** prefix. Next, we briefly look at some aspects related to our exercises.

A64 Instructions and Registers

This slide shows a few examples of CPU instructions that involve operations with registers, for example, moving a value and doing arithmetic. The direction of operands is the same as in the Intel x64 disassembly flavor if you are accustomed to WinDbg on Windows. It is equivalent to an assignment. **BLR** is a call of some function whose address is in the register. **BL** means Branch and Link.

A64 Memory and Stack Addressing

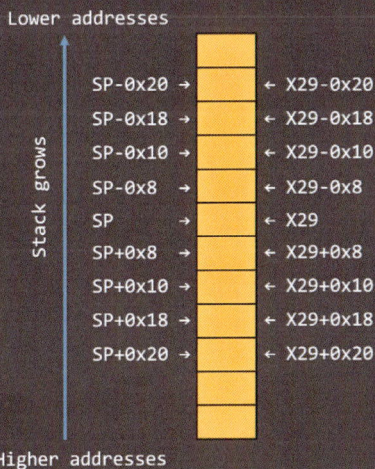

Before we look at operations with memory, let's look at a graphical representation of memory addressing. A thread stack is just any other memory region, so instead of **SP** and **X29** (**FP**), any other register can be used. Please note that the stack grows towards lower addresses, so to access the previously pushed values, you need to use positive offsets from **SP**.

A64 Memory Load Instructions

```
A64 Memory Load Instructions

⊙ Opcode DST, DST₂, [SRC, Offset]

⊙ Opcode DST, DST₂, [SRC], Offset // Postincrement

⊙ Examples:

ldr   x0, [sp]            // X0 ← value at address SP+0
ldr   x0, [x29, #-8]      // X0 ← value at address X29-0x8
ldp   x29, x30, [sp, #32] // X29 ← value at address SP+32 (0x20)
                          // X30 ← value at address SP+40 (0x28)
ldp   x29, x30, [sp], #16 // X29 ← value at address SP+0
                          // X30 ← value at address SP+8
                          // SP ← SP+16 (0x10)

                                    © 2024 Software Diagnostics Services
```

Constants are encoded in instructions, but if we need arbitrary values, we must get them from memory. Square brackets show memory access relative to an address stored in some register. There's also an option to adjust the value of the register after load, the so-called **Postincrement**, which can be negative.

A64 Memory Store Instructions

```
A64 Memory Store Instructions

⊙ Opcode SRC, SRC₂, [DST, Offset]

⊙ Opcode SRC, SRC₂, [DST, Offset]! // Preincrement

⊙ Examples:

str   x0, [sp, #16]       // x0 → value at address SP+16 (0x10)
str   x0, [x29, #-8]      // x0 → value at address X29-8
stp   x29, x30, [sp, #32] // x29 → value at address SP+32 (0x20)
                          // x30 → value at address SP+40 (0x28)
stp   x29, x30, [sp, #-16]! // SP ← SP-16 (-0x10)
                          // x29 → set value at address SP
                          // x30 → set value at address SP+8

                                    © 2024 Software Diagnostics Services
```

Storing operand order goes in the other direction compared to other instructions. There's a possibility to **Preincrement** the destination register before storing values.

A64 Flow Instructions

```
A64 Flow Instructions

⊙ Opcode DST, SRC

⊙ Examples:

adrp  x0, 0x420000      // x0 ← 0x420000

b     0x10493fc1c       // PC ← 0x10493fc1c
                        // (goto 0x10493fc1c)
br    x17               // PC ← the value of X17

0x10493fc14:            // PC == 0x10493fc14
bl    0x10493ff74       // LR ← PC+4 (0x10493fc18)
                        // PC ← 0x10493ff74
                        // (goto 0x10493ff74)

© 2024 Software Diagnostics Services
```

Because the size of every instruction is 4 bytes (32 bits), it is only possible to encode a part of a large 4GB address range, either as a relative offset to the current **PC** or via **ADRP** instruction. Goto (an unconditional branch) is implemented via the **B** instruction. Function calls are implemented via the **BL** (Branch and Link) instruction.

A64 Function Parameters

```
A64 Function Parameters

⊙ foo(…);

⊙ Left to right via X0 – X7, [SP], [SP+8], [SP+16], ...

© 2024 Software Diagnostics Services
```

On the ARM64 Linux platform, the first eight parameters are passed via registers from left to right and the rest – via the stack locations.

A64 Struct Function Parameters

- X0

  Implicit struct object memory address (&myStruct)

- X1 – X7, [SP], [SP+8], [SP+16], ...

  Struct function parameters (MyStruct::foo(...);)

When an object struct nonstatic member function is called, the first parameter is implicit and, on the ARM64 Linux platform, is passed via **X0**. It is an object address to help methods differentiate between objects of the same structure type and reference correct fields' memory. The rest of the parameters are passed as usual.

this

The address of the current object is contained in this pointer inside C++ source code. It can be used to refer to the current object fields and methods and can also be dereferenced.

Classic C++

```cpp
std::cout << "--- this ---" << std::endl;
{
    struct MyStruct
    {
        int a;
        int foo(/* myStruct* this, */ int i)
        {
            return a + i + this->a + (*this).a;
        }
        MyStruct* myAddress() { return this; }
    } myStruct;

    std::cout << "result of myStruct.myAddress(): " << myStruct.myAddress() <<
        " address of myStruct: " << &myStruct << std::endl;

    assert(myStruct.myAddress() == &myStruct);

    myStruct.foo(/* &myStruct, */ 1);
}
```

Output (x64)

```
--- this ---
result of myStruct.myAddress(): 0x7fff31cbc464 address of myStruct: 0x7fff31cbc464
```

Function Objects vs. Lambdas

Lambdas are internally implemented as function objects.

Modern C++

```
std::println("--- Function Objects vs. Lambdas ---");
{
    // struct $_0 // GCC <lambda(int)>
    // {
    //     auto operator()(int x) { return -x; }
    // } negate;

    // int negate(int)
    auto negate = [](int x) { return -x; };
    negate(10);

    [](int x) { return -x; }(10);
}
```

A64 Lambda Example

```
A64 Lambda Example

struct <lambda(int)> // Clang $_0
{
    auto operator()(int x) { return -x; }
} negate;

// int negate(int)
auto negate = [](int x) -> int { return -x; };
negate(10);

// GCC
add     x0, sp, #0x10
mov     w1, #0xa
bl      <<lambda(int)>::operator()(int) const>
```

The ARM64 GCC disassembly fragment for the previous lambda example.

Captures and Closures

```
Captures and Closures

{
    int b{0};

    auto negate1 = [](int x) { return b - x; };
    auto negate2 = [b](int x) { return b - x; };
    auto negate4 = [&b](int x) { return b - x; };
    auto negate5 = [=](int x) { return b - x; }; negate5(10);
    auto negate6 = [&](int x) { return b - x; }; negate6(10);
}

// [=] Clang                              // [&] Clang
struct $_0 {                              struct $_1 {
    int b;                                    int& rb;
    $_0(int _b) : b(_b) {}                    $_1(int& _rb) : rb(_rb) {}
    auto operator()(int x) { return b-x; }    auto operator()(int x) { return rb-x; }
} negate5;                                } negate6;

movl    $0x0,-0x4(%rbp)                   movl    $0x0,-0x4(%rbp)
...                                       ...
mov     -0x4(%rbp),%eax                   lea     -0x4(%rbp),%rcx
mov     %eax,-0x18(%rbp)                  mov     %rcx,-0x20(%rbp)
lea     -0x18(%rbp),%rdi                  lea     -0x20(%rbp),%rdi
mov     $0xa,%esi                         mov     $0xa,%esi
callq   <$_0::operator()(int) const>      callq   <$_1::operator()(int) const>
```

Inside lambda code, it is possible to use local objects from the outer scope either by copy or by reference. This mechanism is internally implemented by lambda function objects.

Modern C++

```cpp
std::println("--- Captures and Closures ---");
{
    int b{ 0 };

    // auto negate1 = [](int x) { return b - x; }; // error
    auto negate2 = [b](int x) { return b - x; };
    auto negate4 = [&b](int x) { return b - x; };
    auto negate5 = [=](int x) { return b - x; };
    auto negate6 = [&](int x) { return b - x; };
}
```

A64 Captures Examples

A64 Captures Example

```cpp
{
    int b{0};

    auto negate1 = [](int x) { return b - x; };
    auto negate2 = [b](int x) { return b - x; };
    auto negate4 = [&b](int x) { return b - x; };
    auto negate5 = [=](int x) { return b - x; }; negate5(10);
    auto negate6 = [&](int x) { return b - x; }; negate6(10);
}
```

```cpp
// [=] GCC
struct <lambda(int)> {
    int b;
    <lambda(int)>(int _b) : b(_b) {}
    auto operator()(int x) { return b-x; }
} negate5;

str     wzr, [sp, #36]
...
ldr     w0, [sp, #36]
str     w0, [sp, #32]
add     x0, sp, #0x20
mov     w1, #0xa
bl      <<lambda(int)>::operator()(int) const>
```

```cpp
// [&] GCC
struct <lambda(int)> {
    int& rb;
    <lambda(int)>(int& _rb) : rb(_rb) {}
    auto operator()(int x) { return rb-x; }
} negate6;

ldr     w0, [sp, #36]
str     w0, [sp, #24]
...
add     x0, sp, #0x24
str     x0, [sp, #48]
add     x0, sp, #0x30
mov     w1, #0xa
bl      <<lambda(int)>::operator()(int) const>
```

© 2024 Software Diagnostics Services

Lambdas as Parameters

Lambdas can be passed as function parameters. We can use `decltype` to specify their type. If a normal function pointer is expected, then a special invoker function is internally called that takes care of the call. If the lambda type parameter is expected, the lambda function object `operator()` is called.

`Modern C++`

```cpp
// --- Lambdas as Parameters ---

auto negate = [](int x) { return -x; };

int apply(int arg, int (*pf)(int)) {
    return pf(arg);
}

int apply2(int arg, decltype(negate) f) {
    return f(arg);
}

void fooP() {
    // Clang: apply(100, <$_0::operator int (*)(int)() const>(&$_0))
    apply(100, negate);

    apply2(102, negate);
}
```

A64 Lambda Parameter Example

In the second case of the lambda, we see an object copy. The size of the function object is one byte: the size of a struct without fields in C++.

Lambda Parameter Optimization

If you pass lambdas by reference, there is no function object copy.

In the disassembly, we see the function object address passed via RSI that later becomes an implicit RDI parameter for the `operator()`.

Modern C++

```cpp
// --- Lambda Parameter Optimization ---

auto negate = [](int x) { return -x; };

int apply3(int arg, const decltype(negate)& crf)
{
    return crf(arg);
}

void bar()
{
    apply3(103, negate);
}
```

A64 Optimization Example

A64 Optimization Example

```cpp
auto negate = [](int x) { return -x; };

int apply3(int arg, const decltype(negate)& crf)
{
    return crf(arg);
}

void bar()
{
    apply3(103, negate);
}
```

```asm
apply3:  // Clang
sub     sp, sp, #0x20
stp     x29, x30, [sp, #16]
add     x29, sp, #0x10
stur    w0, [x29, #-4]
str     x1, [sp]
ldr     x0, [sp]
ldur    w1, [x29, #-4]
bl      <$_0::operator()(int) const>
ldp     x29, x30, [sp, #16]
add     sp, sp, #0x20
ret
```

© 2024 Software Diagnostics Services

Lambdas as Unnamed Functions

However, the most common usage of lambdas is unnamed functions in a local context. In such a case, a temporary function object is created. However, no context capture is allowed if lambdas are passed where function pointers are expected.

Modern C++

```cpp
// --- Lambdas as Unnamed Functions ---

int apply(int arg, int (*pf)(int)) {
    return pf(arg);
}

void foo()
{
    int b{0};
    apply(100, [](int x) -> int { return -x - 4; });
    // apply(100, [=](int x) { return -x - b; }); // error
}
```

std::function Lambda Parameters

To allow passing lambdas to capture context, we can use std::function.

In disassembly, we see the function object constructor that captures the context.

Modern C++

```
// --- std::function Lambda Parameters ---

#include <functional>

int apply4(int arg, std::function<int(int)> f) {
    return f(arg);
}

void foo4() {
    int b{0};

    apply4(100, [=](int x) -> int { return -x - b; });
}
```

auto Lambda Parameters

To capture the context and allow more flexibility and efficiency, the modern way is to use auto.

In disassembly, we see all necessary functions are generated automatically.

Modern C++

```
// --- auto Lambda Parameters ---

int apply5(int arg, const auto& f) {
    return f(arg);
}

void foo5() {
    int b{0};

    apply5(100, [=](int x) -> int { return -x - b; });
}
```

Lambdas as Return Values

It is possible to return lambdas and thus mimic the so-called currying feature of functional programming.

Modern C++

```
// -- Lambdas as Return Values ---

auto getFunc(int par) {
    return [par](int x) { return -x - par; };
}

void foo6() {
    getFunc(200)(16);
}
```

254

Appendix

Output (A64, functions_c)

```
--- Macro Functions ---
value of SQUARE(2): 4 value of SQUARE(2 + 1): 5
value of SQUARE(2): 4 value of SQUARE(2 + 1): 9
--- Pointers to Functions ---
address of foo: 0x400814 address of pf: 0xffffc28c9e10 value of pf: 0x400814
--- Function Pointer Types ---
--- Structure Function Fields ---
address of foo: 0x400814 address of myStruct: 0xffffc28c9e00
address of myStruct.pFunc: 0xffffc28c9e08 value of myStruct.pFunc: 0x400814
--- Parameters by Value ---
func: address of i: 0xffffc28c9dcc value of i: 1
main: address of ms: 0xffffc28c9df8 value of ms.field: 1
func2: address of ms: 0xffffc28c9dc8 value of ms.field: 1
func2: value of ms.field: 0
main: address of ms: 0xffffc28c9df8 value of ms.field: 1
--- Parameters by Pointer ---
main: address of ms: 0xffffc28c9df0 value of ms.field: 1
func3: address of pms: 0xffffc28c9dc8 value of pms: 0xffffc28c9df0 value of pms->field: 1
func3: value of pms->field: 0
main: address of ms: 0xffffc28c9df0 value of ms.field: 0
--- Parameters by Ptr to const ---
main: address of ms: 0xffffc28c9de8 value of ms.field: 1
func5: address of pms: 0xffffc28c9dc8 value of pms: 0xffffc28c9de8 value of pms->field: 1
main: address of ms: 0xffffc28c9de8 value of ms.field: 1
--- Variadic Functions ---
product: 6.000000
product: -
1487517723922671261236157707546813625155327548762101854347749824161220732281141484713487947986968371477276
5749320521194365592726341272758467237829772473296179113318442603940168900423556325352362577315111510011008
859013456603754214195.000000
product: 0.000000
```

Output (A64, functions_classic_cpp)

```
--- Pointers to Functions ---
address of foo: 0x401d54 address of pf: 0xfffff4b43f90 value of pf: 0x401d54 value of rf: 0x401d54
--- Structure Methods ---
address of myStruct: 0x591048 address of MyStruct::method: 0x401d68
--- Structure Methods (Inlined) ---
address of myStruct: 0xfffff4b43f80 address of MyStruct::method: 0x401f20
--- Structure Methods (Inheritance) ---
myDerived.method(0): Derived::method called
myDerived.Base::method(0): Base::method called
---
pMyBase->method(0): Base::method called
--- Structure Virtual Methods ---
pMyBase->method(0): Base::method called
pMyBase->vmethod(0): Derived::vmethod called
pMyBase->Base::vmethod(0): Base::vmethod called
--- Structure Pure Virtual Methods ---
pMyBase->vmethod(0): Derived::vmethod called
--- Structure as Interface ---
pIface->vmethod1(0): Implementer::vmethod1 called
--- Function Structure ---
myFunction() return value: 1
--- Structure Constructors ---
MyFunction::MyFunction() called
```

```
MyFunction::MyFunction(int _field) called
myFunction() return value: 1
myFunction2() return value: 2
--- Structure Converting Constructors ---
MyFunction::MyFunction(bool flag) called
myFunction() return value: 0
MyFunction::MyFunction(bool flag) called
myFunction2() return value: 1
MyFunction::MyFunction(int _field) called
myFunction3() return value: 3
--- Structure Member Initialization ---
MyFunction::MyFunction() called
myFunction() return value: 2
--- Structure Copy Constructor ---
MyFunction(const MyFunction& src) called
MyFunction(const MyFunction& src) called
--- Structure Copy Assignment ---
myFunction() return value: 2
myFunction2() return value: 1
MyFunction& operator=(const MyFunction& src) called
myFunction2() return value: 2
MyFunction& operator=(const MyFunction& src) called
MyFunction& operator=(const MyFunction& src) called
--- Structure Destructor ---
Before inner scope
~MyFunction() called
After inner scope
--- Structure Destructor Hierarchy ---
IFunction::~IFunction() called
MyFunction::~MyFunction() called
IFunction::~IFunction() called
--- Structure Virtual Destructor ---
MyFunction::~MyFunction() called
IFunction::~IFunction() called
--- Structure Member Destruction ---
~MyFunction() called. Value of field: 3
~MyFunction() called. Value of field: 2
~MyFunction() called. Value of field: 1
--- Destructor as a Method ---
Resource() called
~Resource() called
--- Conversion Operators ---
value of b: 123456789abcdef
operator A() called
value of a: { 89abcdef, 1234567 }
--- Parameters by Reference ---
main: address of i: 0xfffff4b43ebc value of i: 1
func4: address of ri: 0xfffff4b43ebc value of ri: 1
func4: value of ri: 0
main: value of i: 0
--- Parameters by Ref to const ---
func6: address of ri: 0xfffff4b43f9c value of ri: 1
--- Default Arguments ---
value of i: 1 value of j: 0
value of i: 1 value of j: 2
--- Immutable Objects ---
--- Static Structure Functions ---
count of objects: 2
--- this ---
result of myStruct.myAddress(): 0xfffff4b43ea0 address of myStruct: 0xfffff4b43ea0
```

Output (A64, functions_modern_cpp)

```
--- constexpr Functions ---
value of SQUARE(2): 4 value of SQUARE(2+1): 9
--- Function Pointer Types ---
--- Reading Declarations ---
--- Structure Virtual Methods ---
pMyBase->method(0): Base::method called
pMyBase->vmethod(0): Derived::vmethod called
pMyBase->method2(0): Base::method2 called
pMyBase->Base::vmethod(0): Base::vmethod called
--- Structure Pure Virtual Methods ---
pMyBase->vmethod(0): Derived::vmethod called
--- Structure as Interface ---
pIface->vmethod1(0): Implementer::vmethod1 called
--- Function Structure ---
myFunction() return value: 1
--- Structure Delegating Constructors ---
MyFunction::MyFunction(int _field, int _field2) called
MyFunction::MyFunction(int _field) called
MyFunction::MyFunction() called
myFunction() return value: 1
MyFunction::MyFunction(int _field, int _field2) called
MyFunction::MyFunction(int _field) called
myFunction2() return value: 2
MyFunction::MyFunction(int _field, int _field2) called
myFunction3() return value: 3
--- Structure Move Constructors ---
myFunction() return value: 2
MyFunction(MyFunction&& src) called
myFunction() return value: 1
myFunction2() return value: 2
MyFunction(MyFunction&& src) called
myFunction2() return value: 1
myFunction3() return value: 2
--- Structure Move Assignment ---
myFunction() return value: 2
MyFunction& operator=(MyFunction&& src) called
myFunction() return value: 1
myFunction2() return value: 2
MyFunction& operator=(MyFunction&& src) called
MyFunction& operator=(const MyFunction& src) called
--- Structure Default Operations ---
myFunction() return value: 2
myFunction2() return value: 2
--- Structure Deleted Operations ---
MyFunction() called
cleanup() called
--- Parameters by Ref to Rvalue ---
func7: address of ri: 0000FFFFE1A63DFC value of ri: 1
func7: value of ri: 0
--- Function Objects vs. Lambdas ---
--- Captures and Closures ---
--- Lambda Parameter Optimization ---
--- Lambdas as Unnamed Functions ---
--- std::function Lambda Parameters ---
--- auto Lambda Parameters ---
--- Lambdas as Return Values ---
```

Virtual Function Call

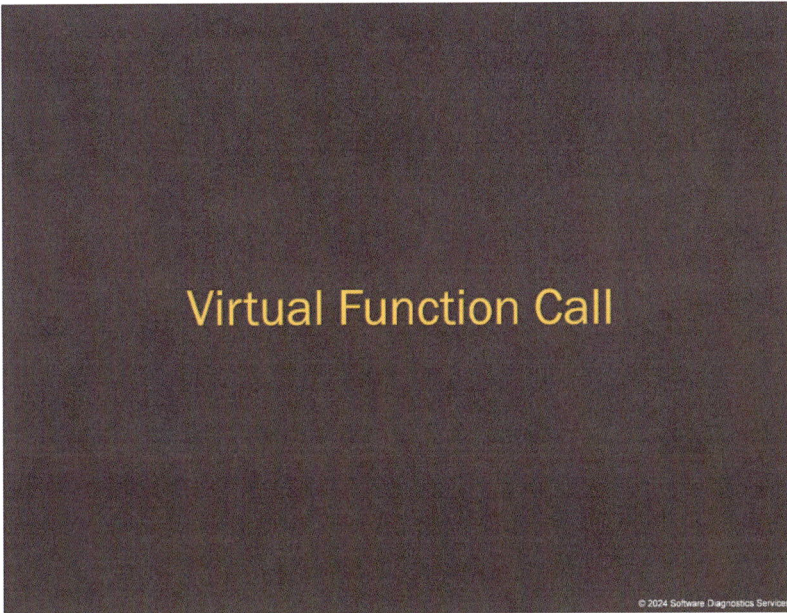

This section provides an overview of virtual function calls in C++.

The `virtual_function_call` project:

- `virtual_function_call_classic_cpp`   `Classic C++`

can be found in the archive[15]. In the following slide descriptions, we only show relevant code snippets and their output.

---

[15] https://www.patterndiagnostics.com/Training/ACPPLD/ACPPLD.tar.gz

VTBL Memory Layout

These virtual function calls are implemented uniformly by having a specific virtual function table (vtbl or vtable) for each structure where the addresses of the base structure methods are replaced with those of the derived structure methods, if any.

VPTR and Struct Memory Layout

Every object whose structure has virtual methods has an implicit virtual function table pointer (**_vptr**) as its first member containing an address of the corresponding structure virtual functions table. Therefore, each virtual function call from a base structure pointer is a type-independent call where the target function address is easily calculated based on the address of the virtual function table and virtual function offset.

Classic C++

```cpp
struct Base
{
        virtual void vmethod1() {}
        virtual void vmethod2() {}
} myBase;

struct Derived : Base
{
        int  field;
        void vmethod2() {}
} myDerived;

int main()
{
        Base* pMyBase = &myBase;
        pMyBase->vmethod2();

        pMyBase = &myDerived;
        pMyBase->vmethod2();

    return 0;
}
```

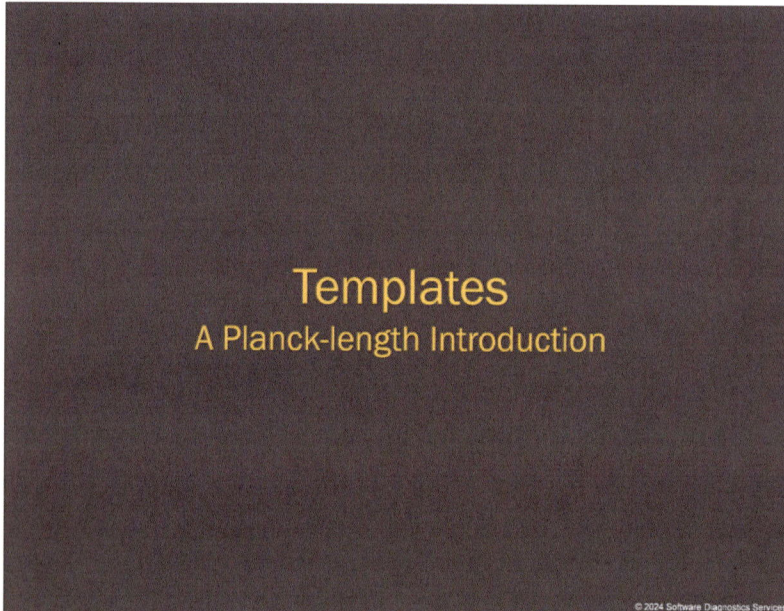

C++ templates and template meta-programming are a vast universe. We only cover a Planck-length distance in this introduction.

The **templates** project:

- **templates_modern_cpp**   Modern C++

can be found in the archive[16]. In the following slide descriptions, we only show relevant code snippets and their output.

Why Templates?

In the following slides, we briefly cover various "why" aspects.

Reusability

Templates allow us to write less code with higher abstractions, delegating implementation details to a compiler. The compiler checks that template arguments are compatible, for example, that they implement the required operations and methods.

Modern C++

```cpp
template<typename T>
T add(const T& op1, const T& op2)
{
    return op1 + op2;
}

std::println("--- Reusability ---");
{
    struct S
    {
        S(int _val) : val{ _val } {}
        S operator+(const S& s) const
        {
            return S(val + s.val);
        }
        int val;
    };

    // or:
    //
    // S operator+(const S& s1, const S& s2)
    // {
    //     return S(s1.val + s2.val);
    // }

    add<int>(1, 2);
    add<S>(S(1), S(2));
}
```

Types of Templates

The following code provides examples for struct, function, and (recent) variable template categories.

```cpp
template <typename T> struct TStruct { T data; };

struct FStruct
{
    template <typename T> T zero() { return T(0); }
};

template <typename T> T zero{0};

std::println("--- Types of Templates ---");
{
    TStruct<int> ts{0};

    FStruct fs;
    fs.zero<int>();

    auto z = zero<int>;
}
```

Types of Template Parameters

There are two categories of template parameters: type and non-type.

Non-type template parameters allow the generation of very compact code with a distinct purpose.

```cpp
template <int c> decltype(c) constant() { return c; }

std::println("--- Types of Template Parameters ---");
{
    constant<1>();
}
```

Type Safety

Compared to pointer casting, the general template code enforces type safety by checking the required operations and compatible types.

Modern C++

```cpp
template<typename T>
T add(const T& op1, const T& op2)
{
    return op1 + op2;

}

std::println("--- Type Safety ---");
{
    struct S
    {
        S(int _val) : val{_val} {}
        S operator+(const S& s) const
        {
            return S(val + s.val);
        }
        int val;
    };

    struct M
    {
        M(int _val) : val{_val} {}
        int val;
    };

    add(S(1), S(2));
    // add(M(1), M(2)); // error
}
```

Flexibility

It is also possible to specialize template definitions for specific types for performance and other reasons.

Modern C++

```cpp
template<typename T>
T add(const T& op1, const T& op2)
{
    return op1 + op2;
}

struct M
{
    M(int _val) : val{_val} {}
    int val;
};

template<>
M add<M>(const M& op1, const M& op2)
{
    return op1.val + op2.val;
}

template<>
decltype(13) constant<13>() { return 14; }

std::println("--- Flexibility ---");
{
    add(M(1), struct M(2));
}
```

Metafunctions

Metafunctions transform type: they take types as parameters and return types as output.

Modern C++

```cpp
template <typename T>
struct Pointer
{
    using type = T*;
};

std::println("--- Metafunctions ---");
{
    // see above

    Pointer<int>::type pInt{};    // int* pInt;
    Pointer<int*>::type ppInt{};  // int** ppInt;
    Pointer<M>::type pM{};        // M* pM;
}
```

Variadic Templates

Using variadic templates solves all problems with old-style variadic functions.

Modern C++

```cpp
template <typename ... Args>
auto varfunc(Args ... args)
{
    return (... * args);

};

std::println("--- Variadic Templates ---");
{
    // see above

    std::println("result: {}", varfunc(1.0, 2.0, 3.0));
    std::println("result: {}", varfunc(1.0, 2.0, 3.0, 4.0));
    std::println("result: {}", varfunc(1.0, 2.0, 3));

}
```

Output

```
--- Variadic Templates ---
result: 6
result: 24
result: 6
```

Iterators as Pointers

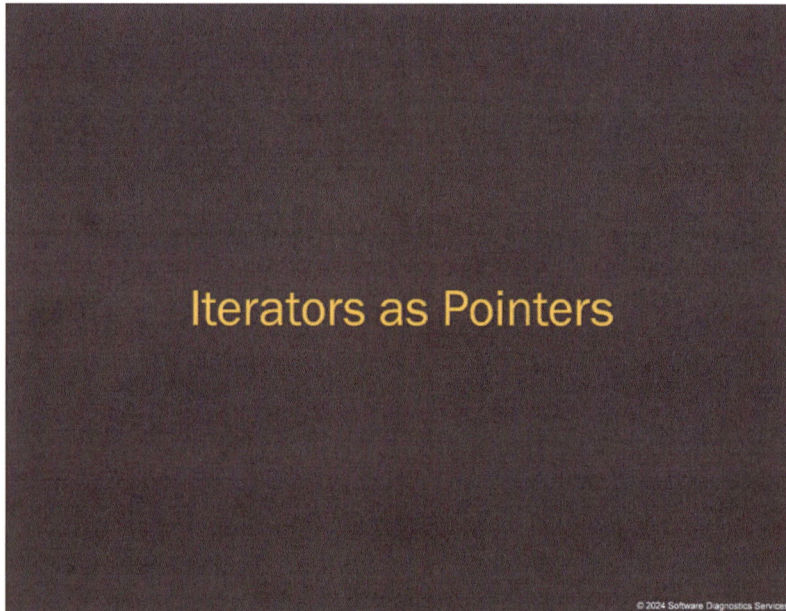

Now, we take a bird's eye view of standard library containers, iterators, and algorithms from a pointer perspective.

The `iterators_as_pointers` project:

- `iterators_as_pointers_modern_cpp`   Modern C++

can be found in the archive[17]. In the following slide descriptions, we only show relevant code snippets and their output.

---

[17] https://www.patterndiagnostics.com/Training/ACPPLD/ACPPLD.tar.gz

Containers

There are many container types in the standard C++ library (formerly called STL, Standard Template Library). In this course edition, we don't delve into their specifics. We hope the names intuitively suggest their semantics.

Iterators

An iterator is a pointer abstraction. You can move it (depending on container semantics) like a pointer increment/decrement, and you can dereference it like a pointer to get a value.

```cpp
std::println("--- Iterators ---");
{
        std::vector<int> v{1, 2, 3, 4, 5};
        std::vector<int>::iterator it = v.begin();

        while (it != v.end())
        {
                std::print("{} ", *it);
                ++it;
        }

        std::println("");

        int a[5]{1, 2, 3, 4, 5};
        int* pa = &a[0];

        while (pa != &a[5])
        {
                std::print("{} ", *pa);
                ++pa;
        }

        std::println("");
}
```

Output

```
--- Iterators ---
1 2 3 4 5
1 2 3 4 5
```

Constant Iterators

Like a pointer to constant values, there are constant iterators.

```cpp
std::println("--- Constant Iterators ---");
{
        std::vector<int> v{1, 2, 3, 4, 5};
        std::vector<int>::const_iterator cit = v.cbegin();

        while (cit != v.cend())
        {
                std::print("{} ", *cit);
                ++cit;
        }

        std::println("");

        int a[5]{1, 2, 3, 4, 5};
        const int* cpa = &a[0];

        while (cpa != &a[5])
        {
                std::print("{} ", *cpa);
                ++cpa;
        }

        std::println("");
}
```

Output

```
--- Constant Iterators ---
1 2 3 4 5
1 2 3 4 5
```

Pointers as Iterators

Pointers can also be considered as iterators.

```cpp
int arr[5]{1, 2, 3, 4, 5};
int* itarr = std::begin(arr);

// auto itarr = std::begin(arr);

while (itarr != std::end(arr))
{
        std::cout << *itarr;
        ++itarr;
}

const int* citarr = std::cbegin(arr);

while (citarr != std::cend(arr))
{
        std::cout << *citarr;
        ++citarr;
}
```

```cpp
std::println("--- Pointers as Iterators ---");
{
        int arr[5]{1, 2, 3, 4, 5};
        int* itarr = std::begin(arr);

        // auto itarr = std::begin(arr);

        while (itarr != std::end(arr))
        {
                std::print("{} ", *itarr);
                ++itarr;
        }

        std::println("");

        const int* citarr = std::cbegin(arr);

        while (citarr != std::cend(arr))
        {
                std::print("{} ", *citarr);
                ++citarr;
        }

        std::println("");
}
```

Output

```
--- Pointers as Iterators ---
1 2 3 4 5
1 2 3 4 5
```

Algorithms

```cpp
std::vector<int> vec{2, 1, 3, 5, 4};

std::sort(vec.begin(), vec.end());


int arr[5]{2, 1, 3, 5, 4};

std::sort(std::begin(arr), std::end(arr));
```

© 2024 Software Diagnostics Services

Both iterators and containers and pointers as iterators and arrays can be used with the C++ standard library algorithms.

Modern C++

```cpp
std::println("--- Algorithms ---");
{
        std::vector<int> vec{2, 1, 3, 5, 4};

        for (auto const& val : vec)
        {
                std::print("{} ", val);
        }
        std::println("");

        std::sort(vec.begin(), vec.end());

        std::for_each(vec.cbegin(), vec.cend(),
                [](auto const& val) { std::print("{} ", val); });
        std::println("");

        int arr[5]{20, 10, 30, 50, 40};

        for (auto const& val : arr)
        {
                std::print("{} ", val);
        }
        std::println("");

        std::sort(std::begin(arr), std::end(arr));

        std::for_each(std::cbegin(arr), std::cend(arr),
                [](auto const& val) { std::print("{} ", val); });
        std::println("");
}
```

Output

```
--- Algorithms ---
2 1 3 5 4
1 2 3 4 5
20 10 30 50 40
10 20 30 40 50
```

Memory Ownership

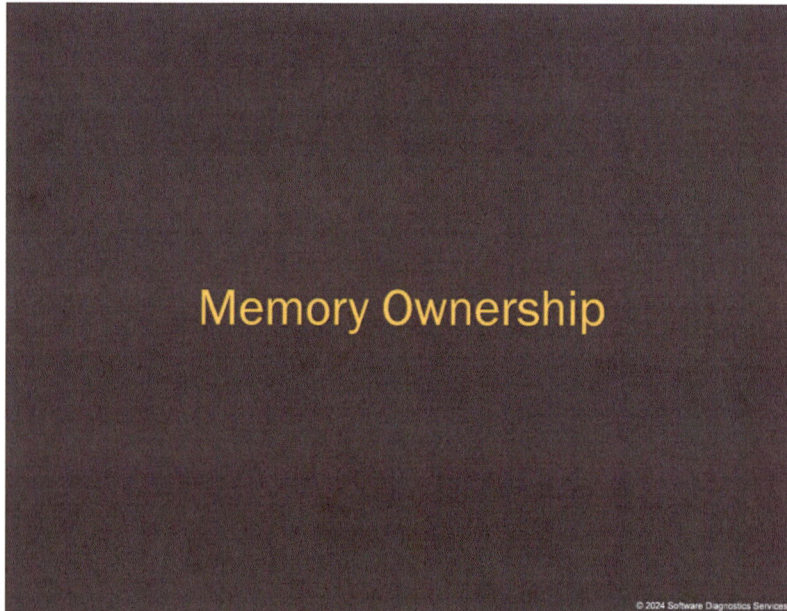

We now look at common memory ownership problems and see how they are resolved in modern C++.

Pointers as Owners

Pointers can be considered owners of dynamically allocated memory since they contain the address, and that memory can be accessed through them.

Problems with Pointer Owners

However, manual pointer usage is prone to multiple errors due to possible shared ownership, crashes due to possible multiple releases, and memory leaks due to dangling pointers and going out of scope.

Smart Pointers

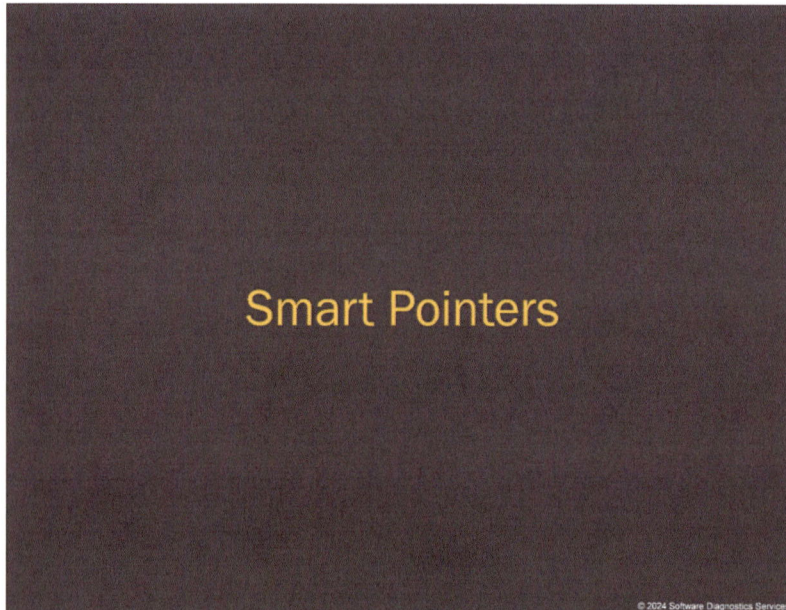

To solve memory ownership problems, modern C++ included several kinds of smart pointers in its standard library.

The **smart_pointers** project:

- `smart_pointers_modern_cpp`   `Modern C++`

can be found in the archive[18]. In the following slide descriptions, we only show relevant code snippets and their output.

---

[18] https://www.patterndiagnostics.com/Training/ACPPLD/ACPPLD.tar.gz

Basic Design

Basic Design

- A structure with operators mimicking pointer behavior such as dereferencing

- Encapsulates raw pointers

- Restricts undesirable behavior

- Contains reference count that tracks copies

- Provides a destructor to release memory if the reference count becomes 0

© 2024 Software Diagnostics Services

A smart pointer should include functionality similar to raw pointers for seamless use during the refactoring of legacy code and simultaneously eliminate most, if not all, problems with raw pointer usage.

Unique Pointers

Unique Pointers

```cpp
std::unique_ptr<int> fooU(std::unique_ptr<int> pIntPar)
{
    std::unique_ptr<int> pInt{pIntPar.release()};
    assert(pIntPar == nullptr);
    if (pInt)
        int n = *pInt; // *pInt.get();
    return pInt;
}

void barU()
{
    std::unique_ptr<int> pIntPar{new int(0)};
    std::unique_ptr<int> pIntRes{};
    assert(pIntRes == nullptr);
    pIntRes = fooU(std::move(pIntPar));
    assert(pIntPar == nullptr && pIntRes != nullptr);
}
```

© 2024 Software Diagnostics Services

For smart pointers without sharing functionality, the unique_ptr should be used. Copying must transfer ownership, making the source nullptr.

```cpp
std::unique_ptr<int> fooU(std::unique_ptr<int> pIntPar)
{
    std::unique_ptr<int> pInt{pIntPar.release()};
    assert(pIntPar == nullptr);

    if (pInt)
        int n = *pInt; // *pInt.get();

    return pInt;
}

void barU()
{
    std::unique_ptr<int> pIntPar{new int(0)};
    std::unique_ptr<int> pIntRes{};
    assert(pIntRes == nullptr);

    pIntRes = fooU(std::move(pIntPar));
    assert(pIntPar == nullptr && pIntRes != nullptr);
}

std::println("--- Unique Pointers ---");
{
    barU();

}
```

Descriptors as Unique Pointers

Descriptors as Unique Pointers

```cpp
// int fd = open(...);
// close(fd);

auto fdDeleter =
    [](auto pfd)
    {
        if (pfd && (*pfd != -1))
            ::close(*pfd);
    };

using FD = std::unique_ptr<int, decltype(fdDeleter)>;
```

© 2024 Software Diagnostics Services

File descriptors are good candidates for unique pointers, but they should be supplied with a custom deletion mechanism.

Modern C++

```cpp
std::println("--- File Descriptors as Unique Pointers ---");
{
    auto fdDeleter =
        [](auto pfd)
        {
            if (pfd && (*pfd != -1))
                ::close(*pfd);
        };

    using FD = std::unique_ptr<int, decltype(fdDeleter)>;
}
```

Shared Pointers

If we want to freely copy pointers around with all new copies pointing to the same memory, then our choice is shared_ptr.

Modern C++

```cpp
std::shared_ptr<int> fooS(std::shared_ptr<int> pIntPar)
{
    std::shared_ptr<int> pInt{pIntPar};

    std::println("fooS: pInt.use_count(): {} pIntPar.use_count(): {}",
        pInt.use_count(), pIntPar.use_count());
    assert(pIntPar != nullptr &&
        pInt.use_count() == 3 && pIntPar.use_count() == 3);

    if (pInt)
        int n = *pInt;

    return pInt;
}
```

```cpp
void barS()
{
    std::shared_ptr<int> pIntPar{new int(0)};
    std::shared_ptr<int> pIntRes{};

    std::println("barS: pIntRes.use_count(): {} pIntPar.use_count(): {}",
        pIntRes.use_count(), pIntPar.use_count());
    assert(pIntRes == nullptr &&
        pIntRes.use_count() == 0 && pIntPar.use_count() == 1);

    pIntRes = fooS(pIntPar);

    std::println("barS: pIntRes.use_count(): {} pIntPar.use_count(): {}",
        pIntRes.use_count(), pIntPar.use_count());
    assert(pIntPar != nullptr && pIntRes != nullptr &&
        pIntRes.use_count() == 2 && pIntPar.use_count() == 2);
}

std::println("--- Shared Pointers ---");
{
    barS();
}
```

Output

```
--- Shared Pointers ---
barS: pIntRes.use_count(): 0 pIntPar.use_count(): 1
fooS: pInt.use_count(): 3 pIntPar.use_count(): 3
barS: pIntRes.use_count(): 2 pIntPar.use_count(): 2
```

RAII

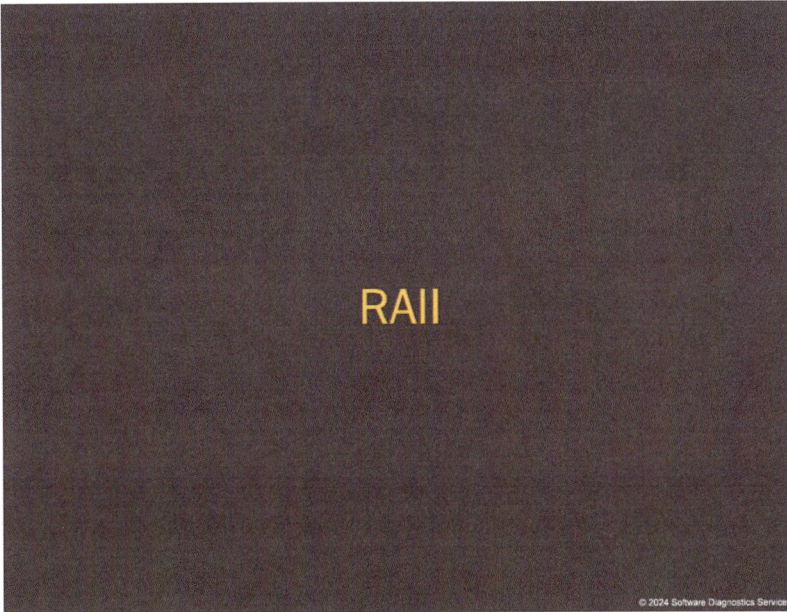

Finally, the **RAII** idiom is specifically about managing resources, including memory.

The `raii` project:

- `raii_modern_cpp`   Modern C++

can be found in the archive[19]. In the following slide descriptions, we only show relevant code snippets and their output.

---

[19] https://www.patterndiagnostics.com/Training/ACPPLD/ACPPLD.tar.gz

RAII Definition

RAII Definition

```
struct Resource
{
⊙ Resource Acquisition Is Initialization

    Resource()
    {
        // acquire resource, e.g., new
        // initialize resource, e.g., set memory values to 0
    }

⊙ Includes resource release

    ~Resource()
    {
        // release resource, e.g., delete
    }
};
```

© 2024 Software Diagnostics Services

An RAII structure encapsulates simultaneous "atomic" resource acquisition and initialization in its constructors and includes resource release logic in its destructor.

RAII Advantages

RAII Advantages

⊙ Resource safety

```
void foo { Resource r; }
```

⊙ Resource life-cycle predictability

⊙ Exception safety

```
try
{
    Resource r;
    throw -1;
}
catch (...)
{
}
```

© 2024 Software Diagnostics Services

There are several advantages to using the RAII idiom. When going out of scope, it automatically releases a resource due to a called destructor.

In the presence of exceptions, the destructor releases the acquired resource automatically. All these contribute to the predictable resource life cycle.

File Descriptor RAII

The code example of encapsulating file descriptors using the RAII idiom. We reuse the **FD** type from the previous *Descriptors as Unique Pointers* slide:

<mark>Modern C++</mark>

```cpp
auto fdDeleter =
    [](auto pfd)
    {
        if (pfd && (*pfd != -1))
            ::close(*pfd);
    };

using FD = std::unique_ptr<int, decltype(fdDeleter)>;

struct RAII_FD : FD
{
    RAII_FD(int _fd) : FD(&fd, fdDeleter), fd(_fd) {};
    void operator= (int _fd) { FD::reset(); fd = _fd;
                               FD::reset(&fd); }
    operator int() const { return fd; }
private:
    int fd;
};

int main()
{
    {
        RAII_FD fd = ::creat("test.txt", 0);

        if (fd == -1)
        {
            std::println("File has not been created successfully.");
            return -1;
        }
```

```
        std::println("File has been created successfully.");
        return 0;
    }
}
```

Output

```
File has been created successfully.
```

Threads and Synchronization

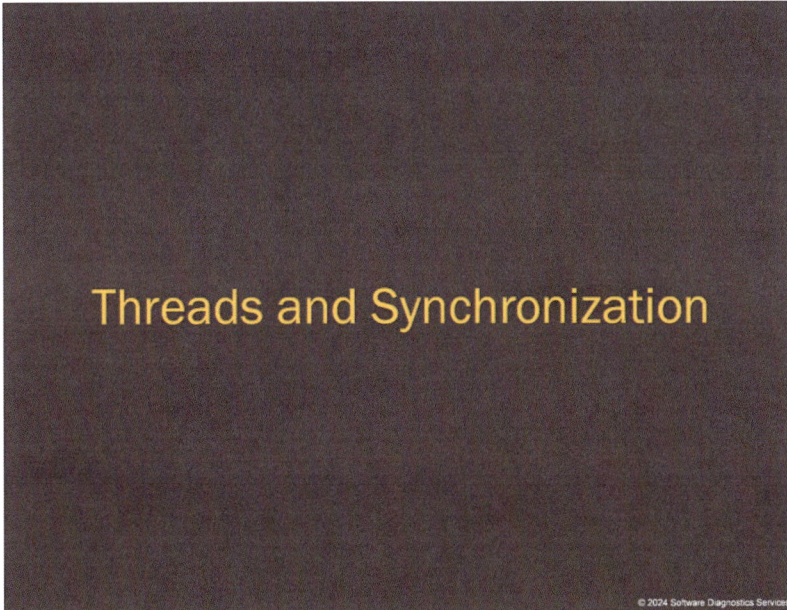

Our final section in this edition is about threads and synchronization in C++.

The `threads_synchronization` project:

- `threads_synchronization_modern_cpp`   Modern C++

can be found in the archive[20]. In the following slide descriptions, we only show relevant code snippets and their output.

_____

[20] https://www.patterndiagnostics.com/Training/ACPPLD/ACPPLD.tar.gz

Threads in C/C++

Traditional C/C++ threading using raw Linux API is limited. Passing any parameter type and casting it is error-prone.

Modern C++

```cpp
void *thread_proc (void *arg)
{
    sleep((unsigned long)arg);
    return 0;
}

std::println("--- Threads in C and Classic C++ ---");
{
    pthread_t tid;

    pthread_create (&tid, NULL, thread_proc, (void *)5);
}
```

Threads in C++ Proper

The proper C++ standard library thread allows the utilization of the power of modern C++ abstractions. Please also note the existence of jthread that combines both thread creation and join.

Modern C++

```cpp
void threadProcCpp(int param, std::string msg)
{
    ::sleep(param);
    std::cout <<
    "New Thread Created! " + msg << std::endl;
}

std::println("--- Threads in C++ Proper ---");
{
    std::jthread threadCpp(threadProcCpp, 6, "Hello");
}
```

Synchronization Problems

In the code example, the output from << operators from different threads is mixed and looks like garbage.

Modern C++

```cpp
long counter{0};

void threadProcCppProblem(std::string msg)
{
    int num{1000};

    while (num--)
    {
        std::cout << msg << ": " << ++counter << std::endl;
    }
}

std::println("--- Synchronization Problems ---");
{
    std::jthread thread1(threadProcCppProblem, "Hello1");
    std::jthread thread2(threadProcCppProblem, "Hello2");
}
```

Synchronization Solution

The following code example solves the data race problem by guarding access via scoped_lock that is implemented using mutex:

Modern C++

```cpp
std::atomic<long> counterAtomic{0};

std::mutex m;

void threadProcCppSolution(std::string msg)
{
    int num{1000};

    while (num--)
    {
        std::scoped_lock lock {m};
        std::cout << msg << ": " << ++counterAtomic << std::endl;
    }
}

std::println("--- Synchronization Solution ---");
{
    std::jthread thread1(threadProcCppSolution, "Hello1");
    std::jthread thread2(threadProcCppSolution, "Hello2");
}
```

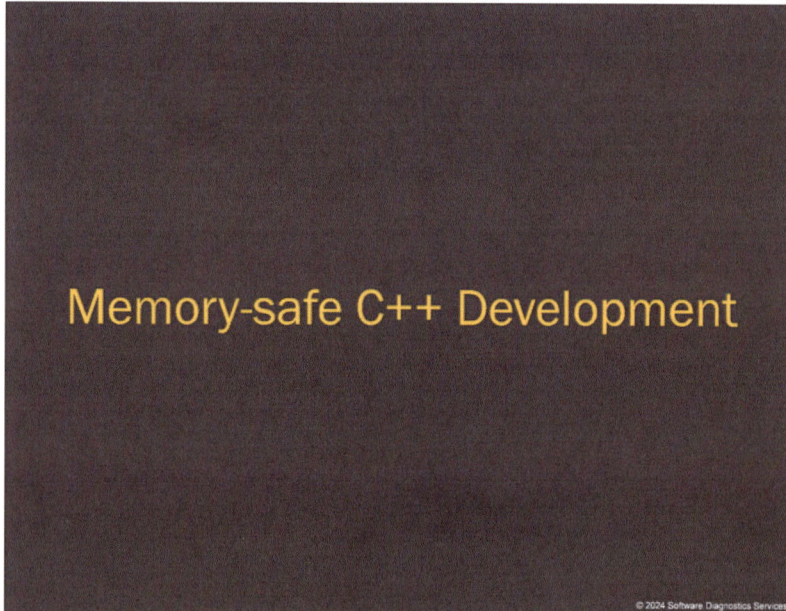

Here I share with you my own recommendation based on more than two decades of classic and modern C++ development experience.

URSS Principle

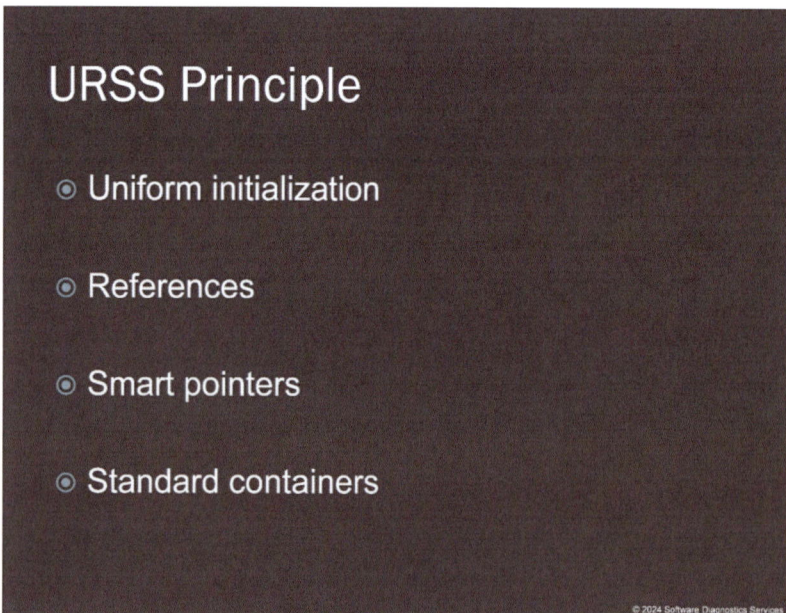

When writing in C++, I use two classic and two modern features that allow me to write memory-safe code that never has memory leaks or crashes. These are **U**niform initialization, **R**eferences, **S**mart pointers, and **S**tandard Containers (**URSS**). Although I also use standard library algorithms, I didn't include them in the set because they help eliminate another class of bugs – logic bugs.

Resources

© 2024 Software Diagnostics Services

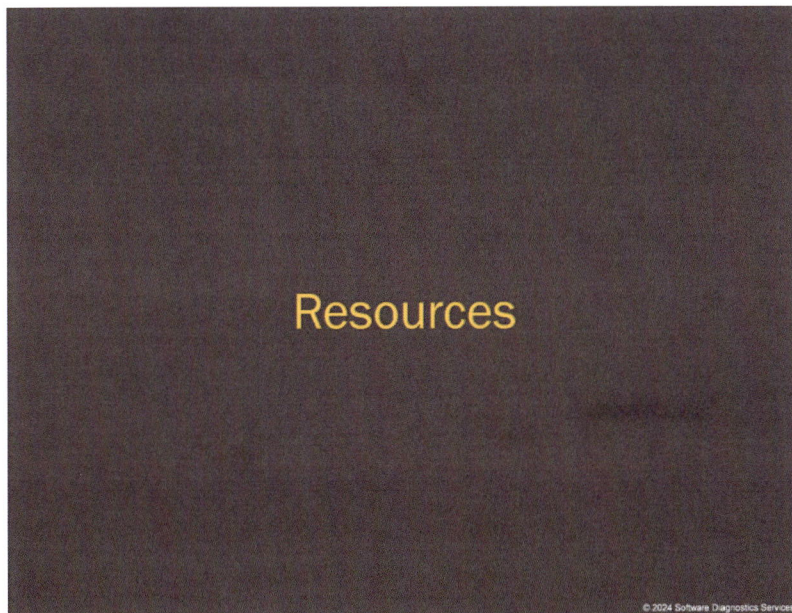

Now, I have a few slides about references and resources for further reading.

C and C++

C and C++

- My Road to Modern C++
- A Tour of C++, Third Edition
- Embracing Modern C++ Safely
- C++ Core Guidelines Explained
- C++ Template Metaprogramming in Practice
- cppreference

© 2024 Software Diagnostics Services

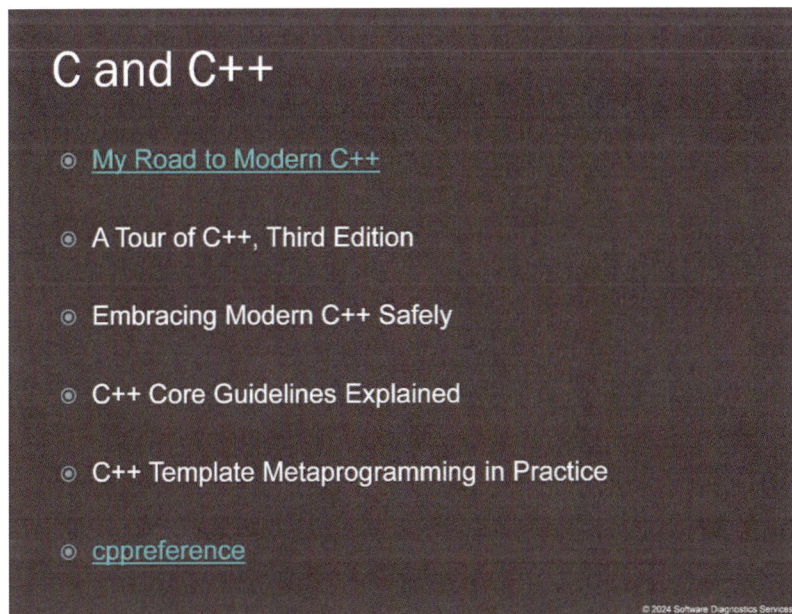

My reading list up to C++17:

My Road to Modern C++
https://www.linkedin.com/pulse/my-road-modern-c-dmitry-vostokov/

cppreference
https://en.cppreference.com/w/

Three recent books are also recommended:

- A Tour of C++, Third Edition
- Embracing Modern C++ Safely
- C++ Core Guidelines Explained
- C++ Template Metaprogramming in Practice

Training (Linux C and C++)

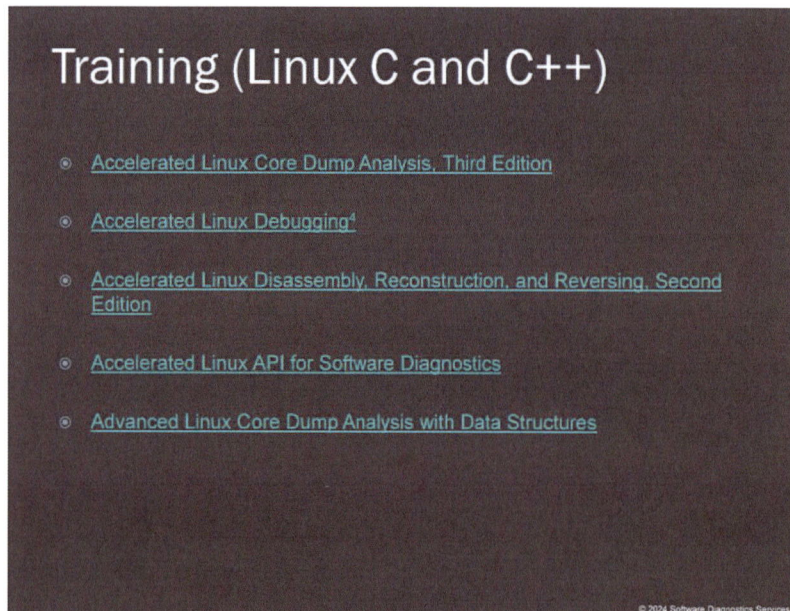

Additional training courses that use Linux C and C++:

Accelerated Linux Core Dump Analysis, Third Edition

https://www.patterndiagnostics.com/accelerated-linux-core-dump-analysis-book

Accelerated Linux Debugging[4]

https://www.patterndiagnostics.com/accelerated-linux-debugging-4d

Accelerated Linux Disassembly, Reconstruction, and Reversing, Second Edition

https://www.patterndiagnostics.com/accelerated-linux-disassembly-reconstruction-reversing-book

Accelerated Linux API for Software Diagnostics

https://www.patterndiagnostics.com/accelerated-linux-api-book

Advanced Linux Core Dump Analysis with Data Structures

https://www.patterndiagnostics.com/advanced-linux-core-dump-analysis

www.ingramcontent.com/pod-product-compliance
Lightning Source LLC
Chambersburg PA
CBRC091940210326
41598CB00013B/870